INSIDE
RTÉ

A Memoir

Betty Purcell

NEW ISLAND

Inside RTÉ
First published 2014
by New Island
2 Brookside
Dundrum Road
Dublin 14

www.newisland.ie

PRINT ISBN : 978-1-84840-320-8
EPUB ISBN : 978-1-84840-321-5
MOBI ISBN : 978-1-84840-322-2

British Library Cataloguing Data. A CIP catalogue record for this book
is available from the British Library

Front cover image © Derek Speirs. This, and all internal images, are not
for third-party use.

Typeset by JM InfoTech INDIA
Cover design by Mariel Deegan, New Island Books
Printed by ScandBook AB

To my mother,
who struggled hard,
but loved life.

*'Art is not a mirror to hold up to society,
but a hammer with which to shape it.'*

– Bertolt Brecht

Contents

Introduction

'It is not enough for journalists to see themselves as mere messengers without understanding the hidden agendas of the message and the myths that surround it.'

— John Pilger[1]

The tanks had rolled into Czechoslovakia, and the French students in belted coats threw stones at riot police. In Derry, Bernadette Devlin, in a miniskirt and white patent boots, talked from the back of a lorry about workers' rights. Nelson Mandela was breaking stones on Robben Island for challenging apartheid. It was 1969, and I was thirteen. I was hooked. I couldn't imagine anything more exciting than politics. It was going to change the world – I just needed to figure out where I fitted in.

Telling the story of society and its politics became an abiding passion. I listened to the voices and watched the flickering images. I wondered why some people were like me, while others took for granted their power and prestige. The suited barons and the imposing clerics used the airwaves to continue their dominance in society. Women were largely invisible, unless they were carrying cups of tea, or animatedly

---

1 John Pilger, *Hidden Agendas* (Vintage, 1998), p. 4.

discussing which powder washed whitest. The unfamiliar accents of the middle class seemed to dominate, and the views of working people were not important. The exception was when they were considering strike action, when the strident questions of interviewers would suddenly be trained on them. Humour often seemed to tell best what was going on.

Broadcasting exists in a space between the political establishment and the wider population. There are politicians who want to control it, and all are aware of its potential power, whether for or against them. The citizens who listen and watch desire the truth. Sometimes they get it. At other times they are confused by dissonant imagery, techniques of distraction and straightforward censorship. The journalists in the media should have the job of marshalling that distinction, and of trying to defend people's rights. Over the ten years between 1969 and 1979, I was involved in trying to change things politically, as a school student and as a university student, in the Labour Party and Socialist Labour Party, in smaller left-wing organisations like Movement for a Socialist Republic and People's Democracy, in the women's movement and the trade unions. I saw how difficult it was to get the anti-establishment message across, and wondered if I could work more effectively to improve things by becoming a journalist. It was then that I spotted an ad for a radio producer in RTÉ. I decided to apply.

Did I do the right thing? I'm still not sure. Certainly I've been lucky enough to contribute to programmes that helped to challenge those with power. On the other hand, I had to sign up to what John Pilger has so accurately described as 'the non-existent nirvana of neutrality.' He quoted the religious affairs correspondent of *The Times* describing this beatific state as 'the automatic habit of non-involvement in other people's crises.'[2] I certainly do not believe that journalists

---

2   John Pilger, *Heroes* (Jonathan Cape, 1986), Preface p. xiii.

and broadcasters should exist in this state of inert neutrality when they see at close hand what society is doing to its most vulnerable citizens. Media workers do have political views – how could they not? – and often they are strongly held. To me, this is not only understandable; it is essential. The only proviso is that when you have a strong belief, you must try to be fair to people with whom you disagree, allowing them to have their say and argue their position.

Impartiality and objectivity of the media can be obtained by ensuring that a range of different viewpoints are explored. The ideology of one group must not be allowed to become dominant. But make no mistake about it, a good journalist is not likely to approach their subject with a Zen-like sense of detachment; sometimes, a good journalist is an angry one. In many ways, it was my anger with the world in which I was brought up that led me to my subsequent career.

In RTÉ in the 1960s and 1970s, people with views of their own were already firmly ensconced inside the door. Todd Andrews, as second Chairman of the Authority, outlined his fear of radicals infiltrating the organisation:

> Some were idealists prepared to go to the scaffold to eliminate the injustices of society. Some were dissatisfied because their jobs did not give them the power and influence they felt capable of exercising on contemporary events.[3]

Perhaps it is a matter of vanity or ego, but many young people take up journalism in the hope of doing some good with their programmes, even if it is only to allow different voices to be heard.

---

3   John Horgan, *Broadcasting and Public Life* (Four Courts Press, 2004), pp. 213-214.

Writing of the early days of television drama in the 1960s, media academic Helena Sheehan noted that amongst those working in RTÉ:

> ... some in relatively influential positions, were a significant number of people of progressive and even radical views. Although their work never expressed the full force of their convictions, they nevertheless put up a formidable fight to secularise and to liberalise programme output.[4]

By the time I was appointed as a radio producer in 1979, there were many such figures in the station, most of them commendable. I hoped to join forces with them to forge a fairer and more open society. Broadcasting, for me, was a continuation of politics by other means, and was a route to effecting social change and exposing injustice. It was a career path about which I was, and remain, passionate.

The medium, however, was against us. Television and radio both exhibit a gravitational pull towards an ideological centre ground, whether consciously or not. What passed for that reasonable centre ground in the Ireland of the 1980s was dominated by the Church, and thus was anything but, and yet it was tacitly accepted. The way in which stories are told can form a powerful message in itself, to the extent that a broadcaster can have the superficial trappings of being objective, value-free and neutral, while in reality a very particular agenda is being pursued.

We are so often treated to the image of the 'objective' reporter, surrounded on both sides by extreme views, who finally delivers a consensus or middle view that seems, by comparison, a reasonable and fair summing up of the

---

4   John Bowman, *Window and Mirror: RTÉ Television 1961-2011* (Collins Press, 2011), p. 54.

situation. A programme that concluded that one party was entirely in the wrong would lay itself open to a charge of bias, however correct the view being defended. The insistence on balancing competing viewpoints, however, encourages the identification of conservatism with truth, the adoption of a safe centre ground being more or less guaranteed from the outset. It is not so much a matter of indoctrination as of incorporation, as Raymond Williams has argued. Viewers and listeners are encouraged, explicitly or otherwise, to buy into the consensus of 'being reasonable'.

Strathclyde media lecturer Gillian Skirrow also criticises this false notion of objectivity:

> In television, things are always seen from somewhere, and the work of television is to give a perspective, a view of the world that is framed, harmonious and encourages the viewer to see herself/himself in a central position. Ideas of presenting impartially or objectively for the viewer to judge can only reinforce the view of television itself; they have the effect of giving the viewer a sense of being above and outside the actions displayed, and of having a god-like relation to them.[5]

The poor suckers in front of the cameras and microphones trade punches, doing their best to convince the person at home on the couch, who, always at a safe distance from the mêlée, keeps score and then hands out judgement. In this sense, the language of television can itself be reactionary. The limited political and social participation of a viewer looking over events falls short of that of an activist who is involved within them, the former presenting a beguiling

---

5   Carl Gardner (ed.) *Media, Politics and Culture: A Socialist View* (The Macmillan Press, 1979), p. 30.

substitute for the latter, and without the inconvenience of leaving one's couch. Broadcasters could do more, and could be more, and I knew it.

If these were the ideas buzzing in my head in my early years in broadcasting, the reality was much more prosaic. The everyday business of the filling of slots and preparation of briefs became its own self-fulfilling activity. In reality, we had little time to change the world, for good or ill.

Ireland has a love–hate relationship with RTÉ. Whether they like or loathe it, Irish people listen and watch. They consider presenters to be like family. They gossip about them. They have strong views on their clothes. They care about their love lives. 'What is Gay Byrne really like?' is the most common question I was asked when I told people that I worked in RTÉ.

Crucially, though, citizens tend to trust what RTÉ tells them in its news, current affairs and factual programmes. This is one of the reasons that *Mission to Prey* was such a calamity. In a time of national difficulty, whether the crisis is Foot and Mouth disease, severe weather or political catastrophe, nearly 80 per cent of Irish citizens turn to RTÉ to find out what is happening. There is a reason for that.

RTÉ is a public service broadcaster, in a similar tradition to the BBC. Public service broadcasters have as their remit the modus operandi promulgated by John Reith: to educate, entertain and inform, without fear or favour. It has been sixty years since Seán Lemass tried to constrain RTÉ by describing it as 'an instrument of public policy'. RTÉ staff, and many in management, have spent the intervening decades attempting to disprove that thesis. They have fought against government control, commercial pressure and audience conservatism, with varying degrees of success. They have maintained their audience share in the face of a multiplicity of better-funded competitors from abroad. With the important exception of the political censorship of Section 31, they have opposed most attempts to stifle programmes and institute pro-government bias.

The dual-funding model, by which RTÉ is funded both through advertising and licence fee, has led to many battles over the years where ministers have tried to curtail RTÉ's ability to sell advertising, while refusing to index-link the licence fee to ensure financial stability. There were attempts to use that licence fee as a lever for the censorship of broadcasters, which were opposed by unions and management alike. While there has been a certain amount of ratings-chasing in television (driven by the need to maintain advertising, where the licence fee has become a shrinking percentage of RTÉ's income), the overall balance between quality and popular programmes has been maintained.

The cultural context is also important. RTÉ became a symbol of Ireland's independence, and could only totter towards distancing itself from the edicts of archbishops. Politicians remained suspicious of the broadcaster. Newspapers regarded the station as a rival that had a popular advantage in the pursuit of advertising. Artists and intellectuals often saw RTÉ as too 'dumbed down'. Commercial interests thought of the medium as a way of selling goods, but mistrusted many of the programme-makers.

Within the besieged fortress of RTÉ worked a group of staff who were a mixture of the hard-working, bright, devious, arrogant, frustrated, elated and the depressed. They were creative and demanding, and spent days rushing to meet deadlines, but often without time to contribute to the larger picture. This has become a more common complaint in recent years, where programmes are endlessly rolled out, with little pause for piloting and developing ideas and talent. To staff who care about the output, it can sometimes feel that they are part of a haphazard machine, and yet they continue to strive for the best.

The issue that dominates the agenda for both staff and management is the financial crisis of RTÉ. At a time when people are being asked to pay new taxes for property and water, while their take-home income is eroded by pay cuts and universal charges, there may be little sympathy for RTÉ's problems, but they are acute. When Noel Curran agreed to take the job of Director General in October 2010, RTÉ's deficit was €5m. When he walked through the door a mere three months later to commence work, that deficit had risen to €30m. He has had to deal with that crisis, while preventing the staff from becoming demoralised. He is hopeful of breaking even by the end of 2014, but the licence fee is at full stretch for those who pay it, and television advertising continues to fall in the recession.

The way forward for RTÉ, in the context of a multiplicity of choice for the audience, has got to be its programmes. Specifically, they have to be high-quality and varied. Most importantly, however, they must form a central part of the national conversation, addressing concerns, critical and pertinent. RTÉ cannot compete with the budgets of the BBC in nature programming, but it can offer the specific artistic vision of Gerrit van Gelderen. Its political programmes will not be as outspoken as Vincent Browne can be, but it can deliver real change with a *States of Fear* or a *Leas Cross* programme. Among an array of music programmes, it can foster specialists who reflect our own traditions, like Peter Browne and Ellen Cranitch. In all these spheres, it is hard-working staff who deliver the results. Senior management needs to be aware that all the cuts in staff numbers and wages are having a crushing effect on morale. Only the hope of better times to come can maintain the critical and creative flow that is so vital.

This book is a personal account of my thirty-three years working in programmes in RTÉ, first as a radio producer, and later as a producer-director and series producer in television. By its nature, the account is partial rather than comprehensive. My varied life in broadcasting saw conflicts and controversies, alongside highlights and moments of substance, which are worthy of sharing. Occasionally, RTÉ covered itself in glory; at other times not. As an individual, I sometimes rose to the challenge; at other times not.

This is my insider's story of what it was like to be *Inside RTÉ*. It is an attempt to give an honest account of what was a tumultuous period in Irish radio and television.

1

Grand Canal Street Roots

'A free press can, of course, be good or bad, but most certainly without freedom the press will never be anything but bad.'

— Albert Camus[1]

St Joseph's Orphanage in Tivoli Road, Dun Laoghaire, was a grey Victorian stone building with grounds and a chapel. It was run by a French order of nuns, and later became a set of Health Board offices.

It was 1958, and I have one very clear memory of this time. I was two and a half when I awoke on my first night there, put my feet on the cold stone floor, and went in search of my older sister, Mary. Earlier that day, our mother had brought us there, 'for a while', until she could organise her life, just after separating from my father. I was put in the downstairs dormitory with the under-fives. I know now there were about forty children in the dormitory, but to me it seemed like hundreds. Mary, I was sure, was in the room upstairs, with children of her age-group. She was three years older than me. If I could find her, I would be all right. I

---

1   Albert Camus, *Resistance, Rebellion and Death* (Vintage Books, 1974).

padded down the length of the dormitory and slipped out onto the landing, then quickly up the grey stairs. I picked my way along the row of sleeping girls until eventually, and almost miraculously, there was Mary. I told her I couldn't sleep, and she let me slip into bed beside her. It was just what I needed. I went back to sleep and rested peacefully.

The next day, I woke up to pandemonium. It seems it was the practice to dress and feed the smaller children first. When the nuns came to wake me, they found my bed empty. A search of the grounds had ensued, and the gardaí were about to be called, when I emerged, unharmed and rubbing my eyes, from the upstairs dormitory. There was a lot of shouting followed by huge relief from the nuns on duty that morning.

Later that day I was escorted to the office of Miss Murray, the orphanage principal. (Although she and the other staff were nuns, they were known by the title of Miss, and dressed in ordinary clothes, which was distinctly progressive in the pre-Vatican II era.) On the way to the principal's office I was told that it was rare for a child to be brought there, but my misdemeanour was so grave that only the headmistress could handle it. I shuddered as I was brought into the large and gloomy room lined with dark wood, but I was lucky. Miss Murray was kind. She put me sitting up on her knee, and explained quietly and seriously that I had caused huge alarm and worry with my 'disappearance' that morning. She understood that I had wanted to be with my sister, and that I was very little and frightened. But, she explained, I could have fallen on the stairs in the dark. I could have got lost in the building. She herself would be in great trouble if that had happened. I had to promise that I would never climb out of my dormitory bed and go wandering again. I could feel that the situation was extremely grave, and I gave my word earnestly.

Looking back on this small incident in my life, I am aware of the implications that my rambling might have had for the school. But I remember the almost adult conversation that Miss Murray had with me that day. She handled the incident brilliantly, and from then on I always kept to my bed at night. My former colleague, Mary Raftery, who did such groundbreaking work on religious institutions and the abuse of children in care, told me, many years later, that St Joseph's was among the best of Dublin's orphanages at the time. My mother had innocently thought of placing us in Goldenbridge, but had been warned off by her younger sister, my aunt Anna. Anna spent her evenings at the time doing voluntary work with the homeless for Catholic Social Services organisations. She had heard disturbing things about Goldenbridge, and, after enquiries, suggested St Joseph's as an alternative.

It all started with what would now be a not unusual family situation. My parents had separated, and my mother needed some time to readjust. She and my father were both in the drapery trade, working as shop assistants in the early 1950s. They had managed, through their joint savings and with help from both families, to buy a house in Booterstown in County Dublin. My mother was very happy there, but problems emerged in the relationship. My father was a gambler, and was unable to hold on to money. He frequently came home on a Friday with nothing to show for his week's work, having lost his wages in the bookie's. Strain was showing in the marriage, and with three children to be supported, my mother was worried. He blamed her family for voicing their concerns and, as he saw it, 'interfering'. They decided to go to London for a time, to see if they could work things out between them. We children – my brother Tony aged eight, sister Mary aged five and myself aged two and a half – were left with our maternal grandparents in Merrion for two months.

Things did not improve in England. My father was now drinking as well as gambling. My mother got a letter from her friend and neighbour in Booterstown, Mrs Gillick, to say that she had seen that our house was up for sale. She rushed home to Ireland, but the house had been sold 'over her head' by my father's mother. Her mother-in-law believed that Mam would be forced to stay in London with no home to return to here. Instead, the house sale ended any attempts to save the marriage. Mam was devastated and alone. This was the context of her decision to place Mary and me in St Joseph's Orphanage. My brother was kept at home and sent to the Christian Brothers in Westland Row. My mother found a two-roomed flat in Lower Mount Street at this time, and proceeded to get work in Clerys in O'Connell Street. Eventually, she organised a half-house to take us home to, in Grand Canal Street in Ringsend. This took two and a half years for her to accomplish. In the meantime we were in the care of the nuns, where she was confident that we would be well fed and schooled.

In the event, she was right. The nuns did their best. We were often cold, but I do not remember ever being hungry. The stone walls and floors were not easy to heat, and we moved quickly in the mornings. Downstairs was a bit better. We learned to grow things in the orphanage's garden. The first flowers I managed to grow were tiny white alyssums. I remember the excitement of seeing them peep their heads above the ground, and of knowing that they were the result of my planting and watering. Miss Doyle, a severe-looking nun with glasses, was in charge of the garden. She enthused about my flowers as if they were small miracles. I played the baby Jesus in the Christmas play, despite having measles. Some of the nuns were very strict, but they were never cruel. My mother came to visit every Sunday, which I loved. For my sister, it was a mixed blessing. The girls in Mary's age-group, being older and more aware of being orphans, took out their upset on her, and would beat her up for the sweets Mam brought. Mary begged Mam not to bring us anything more.

On Sundays, we had special tea. This was the day when prospective adoptive parents came to visit. We would be down in the big dining room, and they would stand at the top of the stairs and point to children to whom they had taken a liking. We were, of course, ruled out for adoption, which led to tension with the other girls. It was an unholy beauty contest, and I watched as the pretty little blonde girls found homes, while the less presentable children were repeatedly disappointed.

We finally left St Joseph's in 1961, after two and a half years, and returned to the comfort of a loving home in Grand Canal Street. Mam employed a local woman, Mrs O'Rourke, to be there when we came in from the Holy Faith School in Haddington Road, and she gave us cheese or jam sandwiches and supervised our homework. My mother was fortunate to have found a decent employer in Mrs Guiney of Clerys. She received a letter of recommendation from a Fianna Fáil Dáil deputy, through her old friend and Booterstown neighbour Mrs Gillick, and began work in the knitwear department. The wages were not high, but Mam had special permission to come in at 9.15 each morning, which allowed her time to get us to school. She cycled down to O'Connell Street, and came home every lunchtime to cook us a proper meal. I remember stews and steaks at one o'clock in the day, while listening to the daily soap, *The Kennedys of Castlerosse*, on the radio. At six o'clock she would be home for the night, washing clothes and cooking dinners in the small scullery off the kitchen, and then she would sit down and promptly fall asleep.

We had no television, on my mother's insistence, and were encouraged to read or play the piano in the evening. If Mam managed to stay awake, she would recite to us passages from *The Merchant of Venice*, in particular the Borrowing Scene, and Portia's speech. I remember going to sleep with the lines of 'The quality of mercy is not strained' turning over in my head. Her other favourites, at Christmas, when she would indulge in a glass or two of sherry with her three sisters, were from Robert Service: *The Cremation of Sam McGee* and *The Shooting of Dan McGrew*. She would always precede these recitations by saying, 'This is a man's piece really, but I'll give it a try.' Although we rarely went to the theatre as children, every Christmas my mother would bring us, with my cousins, to whatever Gilbert and Sullivan operetta was on. She loved *The Mikado* and *The Gondoliers*. Her favourite operatic song was 'Take a Pair of Sparkling Eyes', which my father had sung to her on bended knee when he proposed to her back in 1947.

My mother was highly theatrical, and if her circumstances had been different she would have loved to have been on the stage. As it was, she turned the stories of her life in Clerys into small vignettes, to which we would listen, spellbound. She was in charge of the Aran jumpers counter, and would tell the American customers elaborate stories of how the cabling on the sweaters each had a distinctive family motif so that when fishermen would drown, they could be identified by their jumpers. She would also go into detailed descriptions as to where leprechauns could best be found (early in the morning in long, damp grass), which seemed to make the Americans very happy. She loved her work, and it gave her a stage on which to perform.

As a small child, I was always amazed that when we went to visit Santa in Clerys (the real Santa was always in Clerys, other shops just had his helpers!), my mother seemed to be on friendly terms with him. One year I remember seeing her leaning over and handing Santa a Baby Powers whiskey. 'You must be freezing sitting there', she said. Santa smiled his appreciation.

Religion was a central part of her life. Every night before we went to bed, we would all have to kneel down to say the family rosary, with the 'trimmings' at the end: extra prayers for special intentions. The final prayer was always a Hail Mary for 'the conversion of Russia and the defeat of Communism'.

This was odd, since my mother was always politically radical, but it was a tradition handed down from her own parents. (They had been big Fine Gael supporters in Offaly in the 1930s, when the Blueshirts were touring the country shouting fascist slogans.) Tony would manage to read his *Beano* or *Dandy* comics during the rosary, giving a cough each time he needed to turn a page. Mam never noticed.

I was impressed by religious people I had met, who seemed kindly and good. But I was spooked by a picture that hung over the kitchen table that declared, in ancient script: 'Christ is the Head of This House, the unseen guest at every meal, and the silent listener to every conversation.' I would repeat the lines over and over in my head.

Although my mother had a small income, she refused to allow it to limit us, always managing to pay for school trips and for piano lessons. We benefited hugely from her optimistic view of the world. She was also very active in the ITGWU trade union in Clerys, and the shop steward, Christy Walsh, would ask her opinion before contemplating a strike ballot. She always had her ear to the ground.

One day, Mam was queuing at the sweet counter in Clerys to get our Easter eggs, when she heard a Poor Clare nun trying to buy thirty Easter eggs for an orphanage of which she was in charge. The nun hadn't enough money. Mam intervened and said to the assistant, 'Wrap up the eggs, and I'll pay for them.' From that day on, she organised an annual Easter egg appeal among Clerys staff, and the delivery men brought boxes of Easter eggs to various orphanages around Dublin.

Growing up in the full gaze of our mother's love and dedication, we were pretty much thriving. Our flat in Grand Canal Street was in one of those big draughty Victorian houses, with a substantial hall and sizeable rooms. Our rented half consisted of three main rooms. There was a front room, where visitors were brought, and it contained the piano.

This was also where Tony slept. Mary and I shared the back bedroom with Mam, and then down three little stairs were the toilet and kitchen. It was always cold in the flat, except in the evening when an oil heater and a fire in the grate kept the kitchen toasty warm. We had our lunches made, and tea and jam in the afternoon from Mrs O'Rourke.

The house, which was owned by the International Meat Company across the street, also had an upstairs flat, which was let to their night watchman and his family. When our flat needed to be painted, three painters would arrive over from the meat company, and would contrive to stay for months on end. Mam would leave them cigarettes, and they would teach us card games and regale us with funny stories in the afternoon when Mrs O'Rourke had gone. One painter, Joe, was a gentle giant of a man. He used to do the ironing for my mother, in thanks for the cigarettes, and leave the ironed clothes in a neat pile on the kitchen table on a Friday.

When we first moved into Grand Canal Street, we did not have a bathroom. Saturday night was bath night, and my mother would spend an hour heating saucepans and kettles of water to fill the tin bath in front of the fire. I was the first to have a bath, followed by Mary, and last of all Tony. Then he pulled the bath out the back and the water sloshed down the shore. We were now clean and ready for Mass on Sunday. When we finally got a bathroom put in, it always seemed to me to be a cold and damp room, after the luxury of being first into the fireside bath, but I am sure it must have been a great relief for my mother to have hot running water and a proper water outlet.

Saturday night was also the night when we wrote to our father, who was still living in London. Each of us would sit down and write a page, with our news of the week. Mam felt it was important for us to maintain contact with him, and never encouraged us to be bitter about his absence. When we received his replies, including newspaper clippings of the comic strip 'Andy Capp', who seemed to spend his life in the pub or the bookie's, we would count the number of kisses on the end of each letter. Tony often got one or two extra.

On Sunday afternoons we would go to the house in Booterstown, which was shared by two of my mother's sisters, Tess and Anna. They served delicious Sunday lunches of either roast beef or lamb, followed by apple tart and thick cream. My aunt Tess was a talented cook. I remember those Sunday meals being accompanied by spirited debates about politics and religion: the abandonment of Michael Collins in the Treaty negotiations; the status of limbo in theology; should the Church sell its property and art to help the poor; would the Soviet Union remain Communist? The conversations rang around my ears until I was old enough to participate and shout as loud as anyone else!

Our summer holidays consisted of two weeks in a caravan by the seaside, in either Portmarnock or Skerries. Mam prepared for these trips ten miles up the road as for an expedition. She would pack jam, tea and cornflakes, as though there were no shops at the seaside, and we would each have large bags to take care of. At the end of week one, her annual expectation of sun invariably gave way to reality, and Tony was sent home to Grand Canal Street to 'collect the wellingtons'. Each subsequent year brought the hope that they would not be needed this time.

In the main, things were developing in a good way, although our poor circumstances always meant that we were in danger as a family. Tony, who was spirited and bright, was consistently beaten by some of the Christian Brothers in Westland Row. The main culprit was a Brother Long, who was notorious among the boys as a bully and a sadist. My mother went to the school to complain many times. She was told that Tony tended to be a bit wild, but that things would improve. They never did. I always suspected that Tony was particularly vulnerable in not having a dad at home to speak up for him. Many of the other fathers paid angry visits to the school, and their sons were treated less cruelly as a result. Some years later, when Mam, Mary and I were sitting on the beach on holiday in Skerries, three Christian Brothers walked by, also on their holidays. One broke away from the others to come over and say to my mother: 'It was terrible what happened to Tony. He was beaten mercilessly, and we knew the Brother concerned was a complete thug. He has now been taken out of teaching and forcibly retired.' To my mother, this honest revelation, while welcome, made only a small difference. It confirmed her worst suspicions, and demonstrated that all Tony had alleged had been true, but it was too late for him. He refused to go back to school after his Inter Cert, even though an uncle of ours offered to pay for him to go to Belvedere to be taught by the softer Jesuits. Although Tony made a life for himself, and is a huge reader of books of biography and modern history, his ambition was thwarted by his school experience, and he never completed his education.

When I was about eight (Mary was eleven), a busybody neighbour tried to deliver us into the control of Social Services. Mary and I were home sick from school. Mrs O'Rourke, who normally only came in the afternoon, was with us in the morning, but had left at half past twelve to make dinner for her husband, Phil. Mam would be home as usual at one o'clock. We were in our pyjamas, when, at about a quarter to one, there was a knock at the door. A man announced that he was from the Sacred Heart Home in Drumcondra, and that they had had a complaint that children were on their own, sick, in number 39, and therefore had been neglected. Mary showed him into our front room, and said that our mother would be home in minutes and that the housekeeper had just left. When Mam arrived on her bike, she was confronted with the arbitrary power of officialdom. The social worker announced that he was taking us immediately into care, and that the courts would decide afterwards whether she was a fit mother.

Luckily enough, my mother came from a capable and educated background. She immediately went to a nearby phone box and rang a solicitor, who stayed the hand of Social Services. Mrs O'Rourke offered to sign a statement that she had been with us until half past twelve; she would stand up in court and say so if necessary, she told my mother. She remembered that the midday Angelus bell had rung out when she was making tea and toast to bring up to us in bed. Mam was fortunate to have a person as strong as Mrs O'Rourke to offer evidence on her behalf. I recall so clearly that lunchtime seeing my able mother, in floods of tears, being comforted by Mary, still wearing her pyjamas. It seemed a shocking thing to me, to see her so reduced. The fear of official intervention is a real and present danger for families without means, who are struggling to do their best in difficult circumstances. My mother had remarkable resilience, and came back from attacks such as this with renewed strength and determination to see us through to a fulfilled adult life.

The sixth of nine children in the Killian family, her own background was a remarkably stable one. Her people had for generations been teachers in County Offaly. Her great-grandfather had been a hedge schoolmaster in the early 1820s, when the Stanley Education Bill proposed to provide widespread primary education in Ireland. He was teaching Latin to a number of children in a field when the local landowner, Lord Trimbleston, came by. Impressed by what he witnessed, the landowner promised to build a school for the children, and this was how Trimbleston National School in Rhode, Offaly was established. The next four generations of Killians taught in that school, and my mother's parents were both national teachers.

In 1920, the year before my mother was born, but with five other children already in the family, the Black and Tans called by the schoolhouse in Rhode. They put my grandfather up on the back of their truck, and told my grandmother, 'If he's a good boy, we'll bring him back, and if not, we'll put a bullet in his head.' She waited until nine o'clock that night, when he was finally returned unharmed. He had been driven around and shown holes in the road, which had been cratered by the IRA, and which made it difficult for the Army trucks to get by. My grandfather was told to organise a group of men to fill in the holes. He never did. He waited in trepidation for the same Black and Tans to return to take their revenge on him, but, fortunately, they never came back.

When my mother died in October 2011, at the age of ninety, she left us a legacy of the memories, songs and stories of generations of her midland family. Her father had worked for the election of Oliver J. Flanagan as a Fine Gael TD. He had helped him to devise a proposal to break Ireland's link with sterling in 1940. Oliver J. became a synonym for conservative Catholic Ireland when he famously declared in the late 1960s that there had been no sex in Ireland before television! In Laois/Offaly he was known as a dedicated Dáil deputy, his son Charles following him into politics. Charles Flanagan demonstrated the generational change with his own, more liberal, views on sexual ethics.

I grew up with a range of influences, but I was very much a product of the working-class environment in which I was reared. Money was always tight. I lived with the sense of jeopardy that went with the early days in St Joseph's. I was enamoured of the character and warmth of the people who lived around us, and of the importance of community to them. I was also convinced of the possibility that education would deliver me a better life, and that beauty and poetry were as essential to the human spirit as bread. From the age of thirteen I was also determined to play a part in the movement for social change that was sweeping the world, from American Civil Rights to the Paris student revolt. The

Labour Party seemed to be a part of that movement for change, with its slogan 'The Seventies will be Socialist'. In 1971, aged fifteen, I joined the Pearse Street branch of the Labour Party.

I went on my first demonstration in January 1970. The South African rugby team was playing Ireland. The Springboks had no black players, and were a powerful symbol of apartheid South Africa. The Anti-Apartheid Movement organised a demonstration at Lansdowne Road, where we tried to discourage Irish supporters from attending the game. Afterwards, we sat on the road as people were leaving the ground shouting 'Shame! Shame! You're to blame.' I recently found the first silkscreen poster I ever made. On a white background, it states simply in red: 'Stop the Springboks' Rugby Tour'. I made it with Wladek Gaj in the basement of a building in Merrion Row, and we glued them up in the vicinity of Lansdowne Road.

The weekly meetings were held in an old sports hall opposite Pearse House flats. The only source of heat was a pot-bellied stove, around which a dozen or so of us huddled. John Byrne, the branch chairman, had been in the Labour Party for nearly forty years, going to meetings, putting up posters, calling to the flat complexes and helping people with their housing problems. Others were less socially committed. One member announced to me early on that he was there in the hope of getting a council house. He was also attending meetings of Fianna Fáil, to cover all bases.

I had spent my early teenage years reading works by James Connolly and Karl Marx. At school, in 1971, I became involved in founding the Irish School Students' Union, with Patrick Farrelly, who became a lifelong friend, and later a colleague in RTÉ Radio. When Bernadette Devlin was elected as a Westminster MP in 1969, I was allowed to go up to the local pub regularly to stand and watch her on the nine o'clock news (we had no television at home). I was entranced by her. In this, I was not alone. The chatter in the pub would immediately hush when Bernadette spoke, and I would watch and report back to my mother what she had said.

Noel Browne was the Labour TD for Dublin South-East. He was a diffident and intense figure, but with a fierce determination and integrity. We were all aware that he was the man who had eradicated tuberculosis, which had killed my mother's youngest sister, Betty, at the age of nineteen. He had also taken on the Catholic Church with his Mother and Child Scheme. When I was fifteen, I began to work with him in his constituency clinic every Tuesday night. He was extremely kind to everyone who came in. My job was to take the notes, which he would later act upon. The stories I heard at that clinic made a deep impression on me. One night a woman spoke about the poor level of accommodation that she, her husband and three children had to endure. The previous night, the baby had been bitten by a rat as she slept in a cot under the kitchen table. She showed us the child's injury. Noel Browne had the case dealt with as a housing emergency, and the constituent had an offer of a house within a very short space of time.

When British Paratroopers shot thirteen civil rights protesters dead in Derry in January 1972, I led a group of school students from my own class to the British Embassy in Merrion Square to join the protest. The following morning I was called in by Sister Anna, the school's vice-principal. She told me that she was not concerned about the fact that I was clearly on the road to hell. What worried her was the possibility that I would drag others there with me. I was quite shaken by this altercation. It seemed such a harsh thing to say, and I did not see myself as an evil person. I would have to toughen up.

I made two decisions around this time. I was an incredibly shy teenager. Being timid was a real impediment, which I knew would prevent me from making an impact in life. So I made a conscious decision to pretend to be extrovert. To this day, the real me is painfully shy, although I have been acting the part of being an outgoing person for so long that only my closest friends recognise that it's a performance. The second thing I resolved was that I would always try to speak the truth as I saw it in any situation, even if that was the unpopular view in the room. That was a viewpoint that I have maintained in broadcasting, whether in deciding on a programme's content, contesting State censorship, confronting management on a particular issue, or being candid at meetings of the RTÉ Authority. In the end, the truth will usually come out anyway, so being devious or two-faced is only a slow way to a similar resolution.

I was still marked by a certain hesitancy, which came from my difficult family background. I always felt slightly on the defensive in ordinary social interactions. Although there was jubilation when I got a good Leaving Certificate, it immediately caused difficulties. My mother was keen that I should go to university, but it was going to be difficult for us financially. The student grant would cover the fees, and provide a minimal living allowance (£300 a year then, in two instalments). I got a waitressing job, which helped me to become more financially independent.

I remember clearly my first day in University College Dublin. I was overawed by the numbers of students, their articulate confidence, and their sense of belonging. The arts block was vast and modern, with concourses where students who seemed to already know one another were having a sociable time. I thought 'I'll never fit in here', and would have run out of the door in fright had it not been for Patrick, who was now my boyfriend. He was funny and caustic in his assessment of the other students, and he steadied my nerve and said that we would soon meet like-minded people in the university. Till then, we just had to get through each day, one at a time. I have the greatest understanding of people who are beset by panic attacks, because that moment of losing self-belief can be so overwhelming. Stepping into such a large, competitive arena as UCD is a terrifying experience for many working-class students, and this point was underlined to me in a later conversation with Tony Gregory TD, who had a similar moment of doubt at the start of his college life.

I moved further to the left as I began to settle into UCD, studying Politics, Economics and History. Over the next number of years I was at various times a member of the Young Socialists, then the Revolutionary Marxist Group, the Socialist Labour Party and People's Democracy. In college, I became a founder member of the Socialist Society and UCD Women's Group. We spent all our time organising meetings and putting up posters in the student canteen. When Liam Cosgrave as Taoiseach came to the campus in 1975, we had a hostile protest around student fee increases, which culminated in a Special Branch car being overturned. They were not quiet times. We were fortunate not to be arrested.

Women in Irish society at the time were generally oppressed, second-class citizens. I was a committed feminist, having seen my own mother's struggle for justice, and the lack of basic rights, such as contraception, infuriated me. In Dublin, one of the more important initiatives I was involved with in the mid-1970s was the establishment of a Women's Movement around a charter of demands, including equal pay, legal contraception, divorce, and the right to a freely expressed sexuality. The Women's Movement became known as Irish Women United, and I served on its editorial board, with feminist and socialist stalwarts such as Anne Speed, Anne Conway, Nell McCafferty, Marie McMahon, Marie Redmond, Sally Shovelin and Anne O'Brien. The charter idea was Anne Speed's; it was an innovative way to unite women of very different backgrounds and inclinations, under an agreed agenda. There were radical feminists, socialist feminists, liberal feminists and women who were just curious and willing to be involved. We petitioned up and down Ballymun flats on the issue of domestic violence. We occupied the offices of the Federated Union of Employers on Fitzwilliam Place when they refused to implement equal pay. We had meetings with Mary Robinson in her office in Merrion Square as she drafted her Private Member's Bill on family planning. I had the honour of supporting Fine Gael TD Nuala Fennell in meetings of Action Information Motivation (AIM) when she was working to get special protection for the family home in marital disputes. By the mid-1980s these issues had become mainstream, but at the time they were controversial and radical. When the Family Home Protection Bill became law in 1976, I was satisfied to know that no woman would ever again have the family home sold over her head, as had happened to my own mother.

One of the many protests we organised was at the Forty Foot bathing place in Sandycove, which was traditionally for men only. It was a beautiful part of the coast, made famous in the opening scene of James Joyce's *Ulysses*, yet it had a prominent sign: 'Gentlemen's Bathing Place'. Women and children were confined to the tiny harbour area around the corner, while the misogynists of Sandycove strutted naked in their Grecian paradise. In 1978, a bunch of us took our togs and towels and went there, headed by the inimitable Elaine McWilliams, a woman of sharp tongue and great strength. Unfortunately, what I didn't realise was that the water was quite wild around the Forty Foot, and beset by large rocks. I was a mediocre swimmer. As we all dived in to make our protest, I realised that I was in trouble: I was about to drown in a very choppy sea. Humiliatingly, I had to be rescued by Elaine, who was a much more powerful swimmer than me. My punishment was complete as I was offered sympathy and condescension by the 'gentlemen' of the Sandycove Bathers Association.

In college, my political activities intensified. I was involved in many campaigns, both inside and outside UCD.

I was editor of a student newspaper, *Student Voice*, and a women's magazine called *Bread and Roses*. The rival student newspaper, *Student*, was edited by Fintan O'Toole. In one edition, *Student* ran a cartoon depicting the editorial board of *Student Voice* having its meeting on the back seat of the number 10 bus! I attended lectures very rarely until my final year, but I was fortunate that I had friends who took good notes. While I would be putting up posters on some issue around the campus, a pal would pass by and offer me notes from that week's lectures. The classes were large enough that my absence was not noted. Continuous assessment would not have suited my lacklustre attention to study.

In my second year I ran for President of the Students' Union, against the conservative candidate, Adrian Hardiman. Although I received the largest number of first-preference votes, later counts saw Hardiman elected. I went on to be elected Vice-President. At one stage, my election campaign workers put a huge poster for me across Belfield Bridge, to catch students as they got off one of the buses that drove into the campus. It was unfortunate that my mother decided to pay a visit to UCD that day, where she was met by a twelve-foot poster screaming: 'Contraception on Campus, Vote Betty Purcell'.

An episode from my childhood was about to revisit my independent college self. Back in 1966, when he was sixteen, my brother had run away to England to try to find my father. He knew from his letters that he lived in Harlesden in north London and drank in a pub called The Green Man. Tony found his way there, and asked the barman whether he knew a Dennis Purcell. The barman looked at his watch. 'He'll be here in half an hour', he told him. My brother's leaving caused my mother to have a nervous breakdown, and she ended up in Saint Patrick's hospital, where she was given electric shock treatment. The bizarre reasoning of the psychiatrists of the time was that Mam was in trauma over Tony's departure, and that the shock treatment would dull that pain. In reality, of course, she was correct to be deeply upset at a sixteen-year-old running away. She should have been given the support to go and find him. Although I was only ten at the time, she grabbed my arm when I was in visiting her and asked me to intervene to stop the electric shock treatment because it frightened her so much. I spoke to my aunt Anna, who was looking after Mary and me at the time, and she managed to prevent the treatment continuing.

Now, nine years later, and in my second year in college, I announced that I was moving in with my boyfriend Patrick. Mam fought me hard on this, believing that living together, 'in sin', would condemn me to eternal damnation. We fought for days. Her whole body shook with grief, and her face swelled up like a marrow. I was distraught, but would not give in. I went to see Father Donal O'Mahony, a Capuchin monk, and later founder of Threshold, whom I knew from his work with the homeless. He came to visit my mother, and she explained her heartbreak to him. She told him that I would be condemned to hell for this continuing sin. He took her hand and asked her if she really believed that the God that both of them loved would be so upset to witness the love of two young people that he would damn them for eternity – however mistaken we were on the point of living together. Within hours, the swelling reduced in my mother's face, and although she still found my decision hard to condone, she was able to find a form of acceptance. Father O'Mahony was one of those inspirational Christians who was also gifted with an immense human kindness. I lived with Patrick for the next seven years, and we often talked about the generous response of that deeply religious man to a challenging dilemma.

During my student period I had the experience of debating with Garret FitzGerald, then Minister for Foreign Affairs, and the writer Sean O'Faolain on Cathal O'Shannon's television programme *The Way We Were*. I berated the state of Irish society and its lack of progress on poverty and other social issues. I was extremely argumentative, and even belligerent, towards Garret FitzGerald, pointing to his government's failure to ameliorate the position of disadvantaged members of society. The record of that Fine Gael–Labour coalition government was one of social inequity, and also political repression, as evidenced by the activities of the Garda Heavy Gang. Afterwards, in RTÉ's hospitality suite, I was anxious to dash off to work. Garret was immediately on his feet, offering to give me a lift in his State car, wherever I needed to go. I was going to work for the evening in Gaj's restaurant on Lower Baggot Street, owned by Margaret Gaj; it was a haunt of every radical and revolutionary in Dublin at the time. The two Special Branch men who were Garret's drivers were taken aback to be asked to call by Gaj's restaurant to drop me off. It was typical of Garret's personal kindness. I was to meet him many times subsequently when I worked in current affairs in RTÉ.

There was a consistency to all my activities in the years before I joined RTÉ. I was left-wing, radical, and feminist. Many other former students were on a similar path, people such as Joe Little, Mary Raftery, Fintan O'Toole, Julian Vignoles and Alex White. When I signed up to work at the national broadcaster, I was very concerned about losing my political freedom. I believed that I would gain an important platform to raise issues that could hasten a fairer society, but I would no longer be free to organise or support a protest about an issue that concerned me. Under the Broadcasting Act, RTÉ staff were excluded from engaging politically in either campaigning or in party politics. I decided to give it a try for a while. Surprisingly, I stuck it out for thirty-three years.

I joined RTÉ in as a radio producer in May 1979. In 1983, I met actor and playwright Donal O'Kelly at, of all things, a Good Friday party. This was an era when pubs were closed, and music was quiet on that day in Ireland. We talked for hours at the party, and afterwards at my house played Micheal MacLiammoir's record *I Must Be Talking to My Friends* and Seán Ó Riada's *Mise Eire* until the early hours. We found we had a lot in common, and spent our time intensively together from that moment on. We decided to move in together only two weeks after we met. We married three years later in Nicaragua.

It was 1986, and I had taken a year's leave of absence from RTÉ to do some solidarity work. Donal and I had gone out initially to pick coffee in support of the left-wing Sandinista government, against whom a war was being waged by US-backed rebels, the Contras. I later worked as a stringer – a correspondent retained on a part-time basis to report on events in Nicaragua – for National Public Radio in the United States. We shared a house in Managua with some insightful international journalists who were there covering the war. While I was in Nicaragua, I travelled with a London colleague, Pushpinder Khaneka, to the north of the country, which was bearing the brunt of the war. I witnessed the aftermath of the bombing of villages in northern Nicaragua by the Contra fighters, and watched as the tiny white coffins of three local children were laid to rest in Estelí in 1986. It was a heartbreaking sight, to see these poor families huddle in grief around the tiny bodies of their offspring. Their only crime had been to vote for a government that promised a fairer society.

The experience of working in Nicaragua has stayed with me to this day. Oxfam published a booklet in the 1980s called *Nicaragua, the Threat of a Good Example*, and that to me is the key truth of what occurred there. Here was a poor country that took power in its own hands, ousted the big landowners, and divided the land up for the people who worked it. They had advanced health care and free education provision for the whole community. They had open prisons and restorative justice more advanced than the Scandinavian model. Democracy was not just a vote every five years; it was constant meetings, which would be visited by government ministers and the president, where difficulties could be freely debated. At weekends people visited the volcanic lake, Xiloá. A former playground for the rich, it had been converted to a people's park. Ordinary Nicaraguans were able to go there and swim, dance and play music in the time of the Sandinista government. Above all, I remember the laughter and chat as Nicaraguans took time at the roadside for a drink of mandarina, guava or tamarindo juice. They were convinced that the road ahead was to a better life for their children. But despite the optimism and progress, the constant bombardment by US weapons led to demoralisation and recurring grief.

The housekeeper who looked after us in Managua, Jacoba, had lost her eighteen-year-old son to the Contras, and worried constantly about her second son, who was deployed in the north of the country in the fighting. We sat and talked about the sacrifice being demanded of families like hers, and she wept quietly. I wrote a book about what I witnessed in that period in Nicaragua, *Light After Darkness: An Experience of Nicaragua.*[2] The time I spent there gave me an insight into what can be visited upon an impoverished people who want to design an egalitarian political system for their community. The Contra war was depicted in the United States as a form of global politics, defending American interests in the region, but to me it was a clear war crime against the Nicaraguan people.

Donal and I were together for seventeen years, and we were lucky enough to have two amazing daughters, Katie and Clara. No matter how difficult or stressful life sometimes became in programmes in RTÉ, they provided a consistent

---

2   Betty Purcell, *Light after Darkness: An Experience of Nicaragua* (Attic Press, 1988).

optimism in my life; they kept me in touch with what mattered, and gave reason to the political and later environmental debates we were having on radio and television. Happily, our daughters grew into confident, cheerful, conscientious adults, with an unswerving instinct for justice and fair play.

2

Women Today

'Go to where the silence is, and say something.'

— Amy Goodman[1]

It was a bright May morning when I climbed the steps of the RTÉ Radio Centre as a member of staff for the first time. An abundance of trees – cherry blossoms, hawthorns and oaks – give a pleasant setting to the unremarkable building that was to become my daily home for the next eleven years. I was pretty excited. I had a good feeling about radio, and I was proved to be right. Many of my colleagues there would become friends for life, and we were planning on making programmes that would change the country!

I reported to the office of Michael Littleton, Head of Features and Current Affairs. Michael was grey-haired and severe, but with a sense of humour I would get to know over the coming years. He had been a brilliant current affairs

---

1   Quoted in the *Washington Post*, 10 March 2003.

broadcaster himself, but now, using the guile and calculation that twice made him an Irish chess champion, he was busy second-guessing senior management and developing programme strategies. At my interview he had pushed across the table a picture of me speaking at a meeting on contraception in Liberty Hall. He asked me how I would feel about having my freedom to speak out publicly curtailed. He made me think that I had no hope of being appointed, but when the results were announced, I was in, along with other opinionated student activists such as Patrick Farrelly, Ronan O'Donoghue, Julian Vignoles and Ian Wilson.

Michael spoke about my first assignment. It was to work with fellow producer Clare Duignan to develop a new strand of programming for women, which would be broadcast on radio at two o'clock each weekday. There was no further stipulation, but Michael said that he knew from my interview and CV that this was a subject I understood, and to which I was committed. His parting words were: 'Do the best programme you can, and I will back you up.' Little did I realise how important that support would become.

Clare was politically conservative, hard-working and ambitious. Cleverly, Michael Littleton had placed her in the position of series producer, knowing that she would be fair-minded and would look after the interests of the organisation. But his real genius was to surround her with people who would take risks and be audacious in the subjects they were prepared to tackle. The key person was Marian Finucane, who had been working as a continuity announcer, and who was now to join us from the presentation area. Marian had a mischievous sense of humour, a warm sympathy with ordinary women, and a passion for change. She could talk to people in an intimate way, and get them to reveal much of what was troubling them. She had earned a reputation as a reporter on *Day by Day*, where she had done groundbreaking interviews with prostitutes, and had made a documentary with a woman travelling to England for an abortion. This programme went on to win the prestigious Prix Italia radio prize. She was determined that the new women's programme would make an impact.

Marian joined me, Patrick Farrelly and Hilary Orpen in what became the more radical element within the programme. Patrick was coming from a temporary contract as researcher on the new *Day by Day* programme, where he had made a significant impression. Memorable programmes included one on the occupation by unemployed people of the expensive Mirabeau restaurant, and another on bank robbers, broadcast on a bank holiday Monday. Hilary had been a founding member of the Women's Liberation Movement in the suburb of Sutton, where she lived. She brought huge energy and commitment to her role as a reporter, believing that social and legal change were essential to improve women's lives. I was from a similar place, with the additional compulsion to give a platform to working-class women, whose voices were rarely heard on radio at that time. We realised that this was a big opportunity to have a daily slot on the national airwaves for women's voices to be heard, and to take on all the patriarchal ideas that were still dominant in 1979. We were joined by Micheal Holmes as researcher. Micheal was not the campaigning type, but he had a fascination with good stories, and with the use of technology and gadgets to help find ways of illustrating people's lives.

We set to work, getting to know one another and beating out the philosophy of the new strand. The first thing we needed was a title. We debated it for days, recognising that it would become a barometer for the programme's stance. We would be on air at two o'clock, and so there were suggestions along the lines of *Women at 2* or *Women by 2*. *Women's Lives* and *The Woman's Programme* were also popular. It was Patrick who came up with the name of *Women Today*, and immediately it seemed the obvious choice. It was modern, fresh and challenging, and would alert both the listeners and the institutions of State and Church to the fact that we were moving the women's agenda forward with determination. The conservative Catholic opposition began to watch us closely, and complaints, orchestrated or not, began from day one.

The next major issue to decide on was the content of the opening programme. It is hard to fathom now, but it was still a matter of debate in 1979 whether women should work outside the home. It was only six years since the marriage bar had been lifted for women in the public sector. This regressive regulation had insisted that women should resign their position in the public service upon marriage. Years later, in television, I was still meeting ambitious and active women who had been forced to leave work when they married, and were returned on temporary, casual contracts with few rights, and no prospect of promotion. I proposed, as our first subject, a debate between Sylvia Meehan, who was head of the newly established Employment Equality Agency, and Dr Cyril Daly, whom I had known from my time in the *Irish Medical Times*. Cyril was an extreme conservative in his views, but he was articulate and stroppy, and well capable of dispute.

The programme was launched on 31 May 1979 with a strongly argued debate about women working outside the home, which was close to many women's hearts. The phones began to ring, and they didn't stop over the following years. The people who liked what we were doing tended to phone. Those who rejected what we stood for tended to write rather than approaching us directly.

On my first day in the studio, I walked in carrying my research files, notebooks and tapes, and encountered one of the older radio sound operators. I held out my hand to shake his, and was met by, 'I have to say that I don't believe in lady producers, and never have.' I replied that this was unfortunate, but we now had a job to get on with. I was a bit shaken. Over the years, I worked with that man on many occasions, and we overcame our early difficulties. On the day he retired, I sought him out to wish him well, and he replied that he had changed his mind on the issue of women in authority. He had found me, and other women producers, fair and capable over the years. He admitted that he might have been too tough on me. Prejudices rarely survive daily contact with their objects. As more women are in positions of authority, and people experience new ways of working, attitudes change. The reality of women in positions of authority in the workforce changes attitudes towards women; seldom the other way around. When women can be criticised exactly as their male peers are, and the judgement, gender-blind, is on their actual performance, then the glass ceiling will show some serious cracks.

Women Today gained a reputation for being a campaigning programme, fearless in embracing subjects that had been taboo over the years. Looking back at files on the topics we included, they were certainly varied. In 1979/80 the subjects we covered included: mothers and sons, sexual harassment at work, keeping a maiden name after marriage, gifted children, contraception, menstrual difficulties, romance, the Girl Guides, vanity, women in trade unions, pornography, women teachers and promotions, pre-marital courses, romantic relationships, contract cleaners, medical self-examination, men's talk/women's talk, housework, registry office weddings, maternity hospitals, sports 'widows', lesbian mothers, disability, marriage breakdown, women in farming, women prisoners and widowhood. This demonstrates the broad spectrum of issues covered, but the reputation of the programme centred on the subjects of a sexual nature, which were merely part of the mix.

We also interviewed many significant and famous female figures, such as Siobhán McKenna, Sally Mugabe, Bernadette McAliskey, Shirley Williams, Indira Gandhi and Erin Pizzey.

The programme offered an analysis of Margaret Thatcher on her accession to power, which was both hard-hitting and funny. During the early 1980s Nell McCafferty did a regular radio column for us, which later transferred to *The Women's Programme* on television.

During my time in the early Women's Movement there had always been a tension between those of us who wanted to campaign on issues (mainly socialist feminists) and women who placed the emphasis on consciousness-raising (largely radical feminists). Consciousness-raising involved sharing experiences of women's lives in a relaxed setting of trust. I had learnt to respect the importance of women sharing their most intimate stories, and developing a mutual confidence based on the similarity of many of these experiences. Hilary Orpen and I were instrumental in pushing this model of shared intimacy on *Women Today,* and of course radio was the perfect vehicle for calm, one-to-one conversation, which touched on hugely important and personal subjects.

On 19 September 1979, we broadcast one of several programmes about women who were experiencing sexual difficulties. A doctor and a psychotherapist were on hand to answer questions. Some listeners found it too difficult to go on air themselves, and asked Marian to read out their problems. It was groundbreaking broadcasting, like shining a light into a dark crevice of human suffering.

A woman asked the doctor in the studio to discuss sexual fantasies during intercourse, saying that she felt guilty about this technique, which her family doctor had advised her to adopt.

A Limerick woman poignantly asked where she could go for help in achieving orgasm. She had been married for twenty-five years and had never felt any pleasure in sexual intercourse. She felt that she could not discuss this with her husband, and wondered whether, if she attended a doctor, her husband would be pressured to attend.

A County Tipperary listener told us that she lived in a country town where, if someone sneezed at eight in the morning, everybody knew about it by noon. She had sexual problems, but could not imagine talking to her doctor or priest about it, since she would be greeted by intense embarrassment. She said that she had driven to a doctor in Waterford just to get a cervical smear test carried out.

Jennifer Lavelle of AIM (Action, Information, Motivation, a reforming Women's Movement founded by Nuala Fennell) in Dundalk wrote in to say that many women called to their women's centre to talk about sexual problems. She felt that such difficulties led to tension and even alienation in a marriage. She sensed that ignorance of sexuality by both women and men appeared to be the main stumbling block to a happy and fulfilled relationship.

Another listener rang to say that, following a serious operation three months earlier, she was finding sexual intercourse extremely painful, and wondered whether this would ease with time.

This is just a sample of a huge postbag *Women Today* received on the subject of women's sexual difficulties, but there were many people who objected to the subject being treated on prime time radio. A group of women wrote to the *Evening Press*: 'Most people learn about sexuality naturally and accept it without thinking about problems or without thinking about it too much. It is the morbid over-emphasis on sex, of which this programme is an example, which causes and aggravates the problem.'

A listener in Sligo wrote directly and personally to Marian Finucane:

I wish to protest in the strongest possible way about your recent programme. Take care you do not become an instrument of the devil, who is so busy these times! It's very sad to see a lady of your capabilities putting your talent to such use, when you have the ways and means to lift us up from the slush which this country has sunk to. Remember your day too will come, when you will have to answer to the Lord! How did you use the talents he bestowed on you? Don't meet him with empty arms.

The letter concluded with 'God Bless'.

All these letters and many more are in the files of *Women Today*, and reflect the controversy such discussion programmes caused. It is worth bearing in mind that this debate happened just one year after the intense argument inspired by *The Spike*, a controversial television drama. A member of the Catholic campaigning organisation, the League of Decency, J. B. Murray, had been so incensed by the series that he had a heart attack while ringing a newspaper to complain. The Director General of the time, Oliver Maloney, stopped the programme after Episode Five, which showed a fleeting glimpse of a nude woman modelling for a human figure art class. The recriminations were widespread and harsh. It turned out that the Department of Posts and Telegraphs had passed to RTÉ many letters of complaint about the series. The Taoiseach Jack Lynch, at that year's Jacob's Awards, took the opportunity to agree with the Director General's axing of the series. Noel Browne quizzed the responsible minister in the Dáil, Padraig Faulkner, stating that this was a new form of censorship to be added to the existing political censorship.

Within RTÉ, the ramifications were profound. The series producer and Head of Drama were moved out of drama. The Controller of Television, Muiris Mac Conghail, expressed disagreement in writing with the action of the Director General, and the Authority at its meeting in January 1978 expressed serious dissatisfaction with Mac Conghail over this. The meeting noted that Muiris Mac Conghail's judgement was 'idiosyncratic in editorial matters'. He defended his statement by arguing that the 'withdrawal of the series was likely to lead to strong reaction from staff and particularly from key producers in the programmes division.' He was anxious to 'defuse such reaction and to minimise any adverse consequences.' The Authority viewed this statement as 'an error of judgement, and were concerned that legitimate questions could be raised about Mac Conghail's loyalty to and support for decisions of the Director General.' As quoted in the minutes of the Authority, Muiris had to insist that there was 'no question of his loyalty to the DG, and if he had made a mistake he regretted it.' In the final move in this debacle, Muiris Mac Conghail was moved from being Controller of Programmes to a position as Head of Features. In March 1983, he returned as Controller of Programmes.

The institutional fear of the opinion of the Catholic Church formed the background to *Women Today* stepping onto the broadcasting stage. A new Director General, George Waters, had taken over from Oliver Maloney at the end of 1978, and he knew that resisting conservative religious pressures could derail executive careers. From the start of *Women Today* in May 1979, and over the next number of years, there was constant pressure at editorial board (the most senior editorial managers in RTÉ) and Authority (the government-appointed Board) levels to rein in the programme's controversial aspects. To the credit of the management in the Radio Centre, Michael Littleton in particular, this did not percolate down to the programme team. We were allowed to continue making the best programmes we could, while being only mildly aware of the drumbeat of criticism directed at *Women Today* regularly at Authority meetings. The Director of Radio at the time was Michael Carroll, who was rumoured in the Radio Centre himself to be a member of the Knights of Columbanus. Next down the chain of control, the Controller of Radio One was former documentary producer Kieran Sheedy. They, along with Michael Littleton, had the task of defending the programme at the two main forums of discussion: the editorial board, and at the monthly meetings of the Authority.

From early 1980 the Authority, which had the job of representing the public interest, and being RTÉ's main contact with the government, regularly discussed *Women Today,* with members 'expressing concern about the content and timing of the items discussed.'[2] In October 1980, a request from me to interview former IRA member Rose Dugdale on the programme was refused, even though we had a letter from her solicitor stating that she was not a member of Sinn Féin, and therefore not covered by Section 31. Dugdale was a notorious revolutionary from an upper-class English background who was involved in stealing paintings from Alfred Beit, the South African diamonds millionaire. She had just been released from prison after serving seven years for her part in that art robbery. As reported, the Director General said that he understood why a producer might wish to pursue such an interview, but noted that 'this would inevitably draw attention to the revolutionary tendencies of the lady. This could not be justified under the Act.' The fact that drawing attention to someone's 'revolutionary tendencies' was not covered by Section 31 was beside the point. RTÉ was augmenting the censorship by helpfully adding its own categories of people to be banned. The interview request had to be shelved, 'for the time being'.[3]

On 13 July 1981, Fred O'Donovan was appointed as chairman of the RTÉ Authority, and a more interventionist monitoring of programmes began to take place. In November 1981, Authority member and former GAA president Con Ó Murchú stated his position that programmes, *Women Today* in particular, were becoming 'obsessed with sex and obscenity', and the lengths to which recent programmes had

2   Authority minutes, April 1980.
3   Ibid.

gone had been disgraceful. ITGWU executive member Sheila Conroy countered that RTÉ should be proud of *Women Today*, and that RTÉ had been admired internationally because of the openness of its programming. The Director General added that the proportion of time spent on such topics was 'statistically quite small'.

An examination of the minutes of the editorial board of RTÉ from 1980 to 1982 also shows an undercurrent of pressure from conservative Ireland. The programmes on women's sexual problems caused a huge public reaction, of course, but, more surprisingly, the Director General referred to the subject of the menopause as one that 'seemed to have been treated excessively'.[4] A programme pointing to the unreliability of the Billings method as a form of family planning led to criticism by senior management, while the Head of Information pointed to many complaints that the programme series was 'unbalanced'.

In January 1982 the Controller of Radio, Kieran Sheedy, highlighted an article in the *Sunday Press* by the conservative columnist Desmond Fennell. He felt that it was worth reading as an indication of the 'failures of the programme'.[5] I debated with Fennell about the points he had raised, on John Bowman and Peter Feeney's new television media programme. I was amused that Fennell, a nationalist, pointed approvingly to the altogether calmer and collected subjects covered on *Women's Hour* on BBC radio. We should emulate that quieter range of domestic topics rather than shouting from the rooftops, he said. It seemed a strangely contradictory position for lifelong anti-colonialist Fennell, and I told him so.

In November 1981 there seems to have been a spirited discussion at editorial board level, which was attended by Head of Features and Current Affairs, Michael Littleton.

---

4   Editorial board minutes, 6 November 1981.
5   Editorial board minutes, 8 January 1982.

Kieran Sheedy 'drew attention to the subjects dealt with on *Women Today* which sometimes caused concern to the editorial board.'[6] Michael Littleton responded that the overall balance of the programme was closely monitored, and was achieved. In a move that demonstrates the pressure he was under, Littleton had placed the programme under the guidance of Father Pat McInerney, a staff member in the features department. I remember him sitting in on our meetings, listening but saying very little for a few months, before moving on to other, more demanding, duties. At the editorial board meeting, Kieran Sheedy had argued that it was 'quite difficult to find upholders of conservative positions who could speak articulately.' The DG said that he had given an assurance to the Authority that balance would be maintained on the programme. He himself felt that programmes like *Women Today* had been responsible for a succession of other programmes containing unacceptable levels of bad language, immoral behaviour and controversial content.

In fairness to the senior management in radio, they were confronted by a major campaign of letter writing and pressure from councillors and Dáil deputies. The difficulty was expressed by the Controller of Radio One:

> The dilemma for RTÉ is in necessarily covering sensitive subjects which might be offensive to some older members of the audience. While RTÉ had sympathy, it could not be deflected from its obligation to reflect the changes occurring in society in its coverage.[7]

On 25 March 1982, the Head of Information, who often had the job of meeting face to face with unhappy viewers and

---

6   Editorial board minutes, 13 November 1981.
7   Editorial board minutes, 8 January 1982.

listeners, reported that a pressure campaign was being waged against RTÉ from Church quarters because of *Women Today*. He complained that Bishop Brendan Comiskey had been to the forefront of these meetings, 'at one of which he had been harried and abused'.[8] He felt that RTÉ should be ready to receive representations about particular programmes, but that 'it should be slow to accede to demands for suppression'.

Mary Kennedy of the Irish Family League complained about *Women Today*'s coverage of the divorce issue in 1982, and asked for a programme to represent the opposite viewpoint. Her complaint was not upheld by the Broadcasting Complaints Commission.

In May 1983, a letter was sent to senior management objecting to the description, by *Women Today* and other programmes, of the upcoming Amendment as 'the proposed Amendment in relation to abortion'. The letter argued that this depiction was a reflection of the NUJ's pro-abortion policy, and it insisted on the title of the Pro-Life versus anti-amendment nomenclature. The Director of News, having consulted with the political staff, ruled that there should be no change in the description of the two sides.

During 1982, 1983 and 1984, Authority discussions regularly began with concerns about topics covered by the programme, and concluded that RTÉ should 'endeavour to maintain the highest standards of public morality and decency'. No directives or management-inspired changes in personnel occurred. We continued to build the reputation of the programme as fearless and modern, with only the occasional tremor filtering down to programme-team level. The *Women Today* experience is a good example of the management doing its utmost to protect programmes from recurring criticism, while allowing programme-makers to continue doing their work, largely untroubled.

---

8   Editorial board minutes, 25 March 1982.

Women Today was an amazing place for me to work as my first experience in RTÉ. The team was close, helped by the fact that our time slot meant that we were required to eat lunch together every day. I remember spirited discussions with Marian, Clare, Hilary, Patrick, and later Doireann Ní Bhriain, on topics as diverse as interior design, contract catering, cars, management strategies, immigrant labour, child-rearing, health issues, family carers and Northern Ireland. Over bad sandwiches and cups of tea, we developed a team spirit that was essential in facing the weekly onslaught from organised forces in the wider society. Even now, thirty-five years later, there is an easy shorthand in talking to those colleagues of the early 1980s. The closeness, galvanised in the struggle to change women's position and lives, stays with us. We remain that very simple thing, old friends, and can fall back into conversation easily and without a struggle.

In the late 1980s, Marian Finucane and John Clarke's lovely daughter Sinéad contracted leukaemia, and had a drawn-out battle for survival. We knew her as a six-year-old when she had come into the office and 'helped' on the programme by carrying in the listeners' comments to the studio. At home in Marian's house, Sinéad and her brother Jack were the light of their parents' eyes, and in fact they had moved to the country to give the children the freedom of a rural childhood, with horses and diverse other animals, and fields in which to roam. The news of Sinéad's illness was devastating, but Marian was determined to continue working. In some ways, she confided one day, it was the only thing keeping her sane. The programme we were then working on was *Women Today*'s replacement, *Liveline*. As Sinéad became more ill, and her condition clearly life-threatening, Marian's routine became one of visiting the hospital in the morning, then coming in before lunchtime and going straight to the studio. She could not face the office and the concerned questions of her colleagues. Working with her involved bringing down the research and briefs for the day's programme, and being careful not to ask about Sinéad before transmission. When the programme was over, she would talk and cry, and explain what was happening in her daughter's treatment. Through the work of the hospice movement, Marian and John were able to bring Sinéad home from hospital for the last six weeks of her life, where she reverted to more normal life pursuits despite her illness.

I can explain the historic success of *Women Today* in two ways. Firstly, the programme consciously mirrored the subject matter of the very active and vocal Women's Movement. It gave a platform to women who had been isolated in their homes, and to others who had been put upon in their workplaces. It popularised the technique of using the voices of real people on the phone to talk about subjects that were hitherto taboo or hushed. The second factor in its success was Marian Finucane's singular ability to make the most intimate conversations happen over the airwaves. Her particular skill was to make radio presentation seem easy and casual, and listeners were happy to share their lives with her in a deep and personal way.

Women Today also broadcast extremely telling reports on aspects of Irish life. One such was on the subject of men-only pubs, which were still common in that period. Hilary Orpen, Patrick Farrelly and I headed out to visit some of these establishments, carrying our audio recording equipment. Patrick would first go into the pub and order three pints of lager. When he was served, we would come in to join him, leading to outraged exchanges with bar staff and, commonly, the patrons. When this happened in The Black Sheep in Coolock, some locals banged their fists on the bar counter shouting, 'Jeremy Thorpe, Jeremy Thorpe!' Thorpe was the leader of the Liberal Party in Britain at the time, and had just come out as a gay man. The implication clearly was that Patrick must be homosexual to want to have a drink with two women. Strange logic indeed. In another instance, a customer explained on tape to Hilary that he was happy to leave his wife at home, while he frequented the bar most evenings. 'I like golf', he said. 'That doesn't mean I want to take my golf bags with me everywhere!'

Arriving at Fagans bar in Drumcondra (later to become well-known as Bertie Ahern's favourite watering hole when he was Taoiseach), we were fortunate to come upon the owner. He outlined in colourful language why women were not welcome in his bar. Men needed a place to get away from the constant dreary nagging at home. We were clearly recording the conversation, and when Hilary explained that we were from *Women Today,* and preparing an item for broadcast, the pub's owner said, 'Youse aren't from RTÉ; youse are a pair of hoors!' It was radio gold, and was greeted with hilarity when we broadcast the piece two days later.

On another occasion we accompanied a group of women from the Women's Movement who were campaigning against particular pubs that would not serve women pints. One such pub was the handsome Neary's of Chatham Street. Fifteen women entered the bar in small groups and ordered gin and tonics, and vodka and oranges. After these were served and mixed, they added, '… and fifteen pints of lager.' The barman politely pointed out that he was not allowed to serve pints to females. But he had a dilemma, because the women refused to pay for the 'shorts' until they were served the pints. A phone call to the manager or owner ensued, and the pints were allowed to be served 'on this one occasion'. A victory was recorded, and within a year the pint ban in Neary's was lifted. These small achievements added up to a larger picture of helping women achieve equality in the social sphere, and of countering the idea that there were spaces that were inaapropriate for women to inhabit.

In October 1981, when Garret FitzGerald was Taoiseach, I wrote and asked him if he would come in and face a panel of women who wanted to quiz him about issues concerning their lives under his administration. The 1980s were a difficult time for people economically, and this would be the broad thrust of our programme. Garret was immediately agreeable to the idea, and told me to set up a date with the government press office. I contacted the Government Information Service reluctantly, certain that every element of the programme would be dissected and rehearsed, but Garret was as good as his word. He came in and faced an angry group of women, without any notes or civil servants, and with no idea of who the women were. He had the intellectual confidence that he would be able to answer any questions he was asked.

I had a number of categories of issues in my mind. Anne Speed, a trade unionist from Cabra, represented working women; Margaret McCloskey, a teacher from south Dublin, wanted to talk about issues in education; Jacinta Deignan was young and unemployed; Breda Kelly was a Dublin housewife and mother of four children; and Betty Fahy represented farming women. None held back. We had an hour-long programme that day, and we ranged over each of the subjects in great detail. Things took a personal turn when Jacinta Deignan asked the Taoiseach whether he could live on the pittance she received in social assistance. Garret replied that he could not, but that budgets were tight and restrained, and the government could not provide adequately for everyone in the State. The real issue, he felt, was to create jobs again, so that people would not have to depend on State handouts.

Breda Kelly was quick to add her piece:

> From where I sit, it seems that the only people who are benefitting in this society are the politicians. It's all very well to sit there and give me all these percentages, but I don't really understand them. All I understand is that you expect me to feed a family of six on £130 a week.

The phones leapt as people at home rang in about their own concerns.

The programme was a highlight of the year for us. We had a huge listenership, and it was clear that this was an organic moment with no vetting of subjects. Garret seemed a bit frayed as he came out of studio with Hilary Orpen, who presented the programme, but there was a part of him that loved the cut and thrust of debate. Despite the fact that he did not emerge unscathed, he told me that he found the experience stimulating. Significantly, there was no complaint to senior management about how things went. That was not his style.

I worked on *Women Today* as producer from 1979 to 1981, when a dispute arose about a report I had made on a protest at Armagh prison. (This is detailed in Chapter 3, under section 31, where it more appropriately belongs.) I was moved sideways in the features and current affairs department for a year, before Michael Littleton was able to bring me back, first to *Day by Day*, and then to *Women Today* as series producer in 1983. He argued that I had gained a maturity in the time out, and was therefore rehabilitated. Michael was always moving the chess pieces in ways that were in our best interests. I do not underestimate the difficulties he had to endure. I spent another three years in *Women Today*, and we made many memorable programmes on subjects such as family law, juvenile crime, women and religion, domestic violence and illegitimacy.

The biggest response we got to a series, after the deluge of post and phone calls in 1979 for our programmes on women's sexual problems, was in 1983 on the subject of adoption. In early September of that year, we announced that we would be having a number of experts in on the following day's programme, and, unexpectedly, an avalanche of calls and letters ensued. It transpired that we had pulled back a curtain to reveal a huge number of stories of heartbreak and loss, involving both mothers and their children who had been given up for adoption. Padraig O'Morain, former social affairs correspondent of *The Irish Times*, has written of the period from the 1950s to late 1970s: 'it is fair to say that when a girl became pregnant outside marriage, she lost control of her life.' Women were placed under irresistible pressure to hand over babies for adoption, both in Ireland and abroad.

A picture of the period emerges from the 2013 Interdepartmental McAleese report on the Magdalene laundries. Thousands of women were seized from their families and society, and were placed behind high walls where they were forced to endure a harsh work regime, without receiving any recompense. When they tried to escape, they were arrested and brought back to the convent. It was, as the Irish Human Rights Commission has stated, a form of servitude and enforced labour, in breach of international covenants and directives to which Ireland had already signed up. Apart from the objective hardship of their situation, there was a further cruelty involved. Denied the possibility of making friends in the laundries, each of these women had to face alone the emotional turmoil of childbirth, followed by enforced adoption. Many had been placed there by their own families, who had disowned them because of their pregnancy. They were brought into oak-clad rooms only to sign the papers allowing for the adoption of their baby. Where an adoption abroad was involved, they had to nurse their child for a year or more before it could be legally taken away. They spoke about dressing their baby on the morning the child was adopted, of trying to watch as their loved one was driven away. Sometimes the adopted children got the chance of a better life away from the stigma of their birth. Left behind were the scarred mothers, distraught, pilloried and abandoned, their self-esteem destroyed.

These were the voices we began to hear on our phone lines. The programme was so inundated with calls that the producers and researchers joined the call-takers in the room beside the studio to note the women's stories. I remember myself being moved to tears while taking down the comments of women who were calling in.

Not all the callers had been through the extreme end of the Magdalene laundry system. Many had 'gone abroad' or to Dublin to work during their pregnancies, and were delivered in Mother and Baby homes before returning to a version of their former lives. Yet even those who went on with education, who later married and had other children, remembered their first-born, and the intense disapproval that forced them to part with their first baby.

On the other side of this picture was the number of women and men, now adult, who were desperately trying to contact their birth mothers through the expert advice we had available on the programme. Their stories were poignant in a very different way. Many of them had agonised for years about their early 'rejection'. They wondered if they had been unlovable; if their mothers ever thought about them again; whether they had brothers and sisters. We listened and read. We managed to connect some of the mothers and children, and some even spoke together on *Women Today*. This was public service broadcasting in the best sense. We were really glad to be involved, but the strange thing was that we had not anticipated it. We had discussed whether the subject would sustain a whole programme. In the event, the adoption theme went on for several weeks.

In 1984, we ran a hugely popular competition: 'The *Women Today* Man of the Year'. There was only a little irony in the title, given the programme's feminist profile. I was on the judging panel, and was very moved by the number and range of issues represented in the nominations. In the end, our Man of the Year was an elderly doctor from County Mayo, who frequently treated less well-off patients for free. We received many examples of his kindness and care to patients in his practice. When he came to Dublin to receive his award, he was determined to make a night of it. Reporter Hilary Orpen and I were cajoled into accompanying him to a Dublin nightclub before we finally dropped him back to his hotel after two in the morning!

It is no coincidence that *Women Today* was eventually replaced by *Liveline*, presented first by Marian Finucane and later by Joe Duffy. One of the legacies of *Women Today* was an opening of the airwaves to the stories of unknown people. As had happened with the adoption story, we as a team were often led by the volume and intensity of the phone comments. It is hard to believe that as we entered the 1980s, family planning and divorce were still illegal, women were domiciled in their husband's place of residence, domestic violence was commonplace, and equal pay was a distant prospect. All these issues exercised the programme on a frequent basis. So did less political, but equally revealing issues – of women's health and work, of family and friendships, of losing children to emigration, of widowhood and grief. We even did a programme about the popular ad for Harp lager that featured 'Sally O'Brien, and the way she might look at you'! Each of the stories added a little understanding to a world until now closed and silent.

An insight into the times we lived through is echoed in a discussion that took place at the editorial board of RTÉ in 1983. The subject was the forthcoming transmission of a Royal Variety Show from the BBC, which featured singer and feminist Dory Previn. RTÉ took the precaution of asking two priests to look, in advance, at the programme, and to implement some changes on foot of their advice. It was decided to edit out a humorous song called 'Did Jesus have a baby sister?' which included the line, 'did they give her a chance?' The editorial board feared that the song 'might have given offence to a substantial part of the audience.' It is noteworthy that this was the year that the Pro-Life

Amendment Campaign managed to engineer change in the Irish Constitution to accord equal status to the foetus as to the mother carrying it. I can only look back and feel some sympathy for RTÉ management as it tried to tread the path of modernisation, while avoiding alienating the vocal, conservative section of the listenership. In the case of *Women Today*, they managed to do that with a minimum amount of interference, allowing us as programme-makers to build a programme profile that was modern, audacious and relevant for a period of seven years. The issues were not resolved as *Women Today* gave way to *Liveline* in 1986, but women had developed the confidence to air their grievances in that mixed-gender forum.

3

Section 31:
'A thick cloud over everything'

'To limit the press is to insult a nation; to prohibit the reading of certain books is to declare the inhabitants to be either fools or slaves.'

— Claude Adrien Helvétius[1]

'The censor is no longer at his desk ... he is in my head', the Czech writer Zdenek Urbánek told John Pilger in 1986.[2] My memory of working under Section 31, which banned Sinn Féin and other organisations from the airwaves during the period of the Troubles, was precisely this insidious reality: censorship invaded the heads of broadcasters. RTÉ's guidelines, issued by management to staff – the practical effect of which was even wider than the strict application of the Act, in that it banned all members as well as spokespersons – caused a climate of paranoia. The political effects of

---

1   Claude Adrien Helvétius, *A Treatise on Man, his Intellectual Faculties and his Education* (Thoemmes, 1999), Vol. 1 Sec. 4.
2   John Pilger, *Heroes* (Jonathan Cape, 1986), p. 14.

the exclusion of Sinn Féin, in particular, delayed by many years the process of dialogue that would eventually lead to the peace process in Northern Ireland. In a wider context, Section 31 led to marginalisation and fear in the coverage of working-class communities and their problems. At the most ludicrous level, it led to the inability of RTÉ News to cover fires and industrial disputes, because of an unnecessarily strict interpretation of the Section. It besmirched the good name of journalism and its practitioners in RTÉ, since most preferred their well-paid jobs and promotions to consistently challenging what Section 31 was doing to their craft. The esteemed political commentator Mary Holland wrote in *The Irish Times* in April 1978: 'Self-censorship had been raised to the level of an art. Caution lay like a thick cloud over everything.'[3]

In 1991, I took a case to the European Commission on Human Rights to challenge the Irish government and Section 31.[4] It was the culmination of many years of attempting by different means, with other union colleagues, to fight the censorship and to allow the people of Ireland to make up their own minds about the fraught issue of Northern Ireland. The court, by a majority, found against us, but the case certainly helped to highlight the issue. When Michael D. Higgins, as Minister for Arts, Culture and the Gaeltacht, bravely moved to repeal Section 31 in January 1994, he referred to the European case and his desire to free journalists to pursue the truth without fear.

To this day, the need for investigation, explanation and open debate is fundamental. In my early years in RTÉ

---

3   Mary Holland, quoted in Bill Roston, *The Media in Northern Ireland: Covering the Troubles* (Macmillan Academic and Professional Ltd., 1991), p. 55.

4   *Purcell v Ireland* [1991] ECmHR 77 (Application No. 15404/89), 16 April 1991.

I experienced the climate of fear to which Mary Holland referred. Section 31 was like a monkey on our back; it made broadcasters cautious, listeners and viewers cynical, and successive governments aggressive in their relationship with RTÉ. The fear engendered in 1972, when the RTÉ Authority was sacked after Kevin O'Kelly had reported an interview with then IRA chief of staff Seán Mac Stíofáin, never left the organisation. In fact, it deepened. RTÉ staggered through the 1970s and 1980s, barely making sense of what was going on in Northern Ireland. Internally, those with an axe to grind (specifically the Workers' Party, which was effectively the political rival of Provisional Sinn Féin), did their best to support the censorship, and to pillory those opposed to it.

When RTÉ (radio and television) was established as a public broadcaster under the Broadcasting Act of 1960, it was charged with presenting news and current affairs 'in an objective and impartial manner and without any expression of the Authority's own views.' It was to be 'fair to all interests concerned' in the reporting of stories, and was subject to the same legal rules concerning libel and official secrets as applied to the press. In addition, Section 31 allowed the minister responsible for RTÉ to prevent 'the broadcasting of a particular matter or any matter of a particular class [which] would be likely to promote crime or would tend to undermine the Authority of the State.'

Before it was ever invoked, Section 31 represented an ugly attempt at a stranglehold over the national broadcaster. In the US, the First Amendment insisted on the fundamental right of a free press, limited only by such laws as concern libel, defamation and copyright. In Ireland, by contrast, the State was concerned to control and censor the press. The explicitly stated aim of this censorship was to preserve the authority of the state – a phrase that would prove to be open to very wide interpretation. Should the truth about any matter whatsoever prove to be injurious to the authority of the state, then this legislation imposed a duty upon the broadcaster to protect the former at all costs. In the tumultuous years that were to follow, and with regard to the Northern Ireland conflict, successive governments would attempt to wield this power against the interests of the public's right to know.

On 1 October 1971, the responsible minister, Fianna Fáil's Gerry Collins, issued the first ever Ministerial Order under the statute, an all-encompassing directive that he then refused to explain or clarify. The campaign for Civil Rights in Northern Ireland had been met with violent opposition from the majority Unionist community. Nationalists had been burned out of their homes. A context was created that led to a new growth of the IRA there. RTÉ was directed to ban broadcasts adjudged to be supportive of the aims and activities of any organisation 'which engages in, promotes, encourages or advocates the attaining of any political objective by violent means.'[5] That night, on a *Seven Days* programme presented by John O'Donoghue, the RTÉ Authority, in a statement, appeared to demur. Its statutory obligation obliged it to 'present current affairs impartially', and it would be failing in that duty if it ignored the interests of any significant player, legal or illegal. Only a year later, that Authority, which had the temerity to question the directive on behalf of its viewers, had been sacked on account of the Mac Stíofáin interview. A Section 31 mentality took full possession of the rooms and corridors of RTÉ's news and current affairs.

In October 1976, Conor Cruise O'Brien was part of a coalition government headed by Liam Cosgrave, which placed a large emphasis on law and order. It was the period of the 'heavy gang' operating within the Garda Síochána in the

---

5   Taoiseach Jack Lynch issued the first directive under Section 31 of
     the Broadcasting Act on 1 October 1971.

Republic. Cruise O'Brien, although a member of the Labour Party, shared Cosgrave's instincts. As Minister for Posts and Telegraphs, he issued a further directive to RTÉ that specified the organisations whose members were banned from broadcasting; they included Provisional but not Official Sinn Féin, the Provisional and Official IRA, and all organisations proscribed in Northern Ireland. (As an interesting aside, Northern Ireland as a political entity was not recognised by the government of the Republic at that time; yet the British administration in Northern Ireland was given the power to decide who could and could not be interviewed on RTÉ's airwaves.) Cruise O'Brien prided himself on his strong anti-republican views. In 1975 he invited a group of Ireland's foremost political journalists to dinner in a top hotel. When the meal was over, he proposed a toast: 'To our democratic institutions, and the restrictions on the freedom of the press which may become necessary to preserve them.'[6] He later went on to attack many of the journalists present, and to call them 'Provo Stooges' – a tactic that would be later used by the Workers' Party to instil fear among broadcasters.

Conor Cruise O'Brien became the foremost advocate for the restrictions imposed by Section 31. On 18 March 1979, as editor-in-chief of *The Observer* newspaper, he addressed the British Independent Broadcasting Authority, just two months before I joined RTÉ.[7] He described seeing an RTÉ programme on violence in Northern Ireland in the mid-1970s when he was minister, which he believed concentrated too heavily on violence perpetrated by the British Army and did not show any IRA violence:

> I viewed the programme in the presence of the then Chairman of the Authority and the then Director

---

6   Rolston, *The Media and Northern Ireland: Covering the Troubles*, p. 55.
7   *The Irish Times*, 19 March 1979.

General. At the end of it I enquired whether the IRA
had been in actual physical occupation of the station
when the programme was made and when it was
broadcast. It transpired that this was not the case. But
the IRA propagandists had contrived ... to penetrate
the station and attain a spiritual occupation sufficient
to secure the making and transmission of such a
programme ... I directed the Authority to refrain
from broadcasting interviews with spokesmen for
the IRA (both wings) and for Provisional Sinn Féin
... I could have left that decision to the Authority
itself ... In the circumstances I have described, I
thought it safer to act myself.[8]

One can only imagine the feeling of fear felt by the
Authority's Chairman, and the station's Director General,
Oliver Maloney, while sitting through that screening with the
minister. They launched a disciplinary inquiry and moved
one producer, Eoghan Harris, out of television current
affairs into, in his words, 'ridiculous rubbishy programmes'.
Harris was a Workers' Party member and leader of the Ned
Stapleton Cumann in RTÉ, which was wielding considerable
influence, both on air and in the trade unions there. Attacking
the Workers' Party's influence had been O'Brien's objective
since becoming minister. In removing Harris, O'Brien
succeeded wonderfully. Harris re-emerged some years later
as a convinced and permanent convert to O'Brien's anti-
republican view, as the Workers' Party faction focussed on
distancing itself from its republican past. RTÉ management
would also prove its compliance by an excessively cautious
approach – the proof that there was to be no more 'spiritual
occupation' of the organisation.

---

8   Conor Cruise O'Brien, in an address to the Independent Broadcasting
     Authority, March 1979. Quoted in *The Irish Times*, 19 March 1979.

In my early years in RTÉ, the consciousness of Section 31 in both letter and spirit was all-pervasive. People watched each other with suspicion, and 'certain subjects' were largely avoided. I was very active in the National Union of Journalists in the period 1979 to 1982, and then joined the Federated Workers Union of Ireland in 1983, which was the union that represented the station's producers. Both unions nominally opposed the censorship. As Harry Conroy, General Secretary of the NUJ, put it: 'Freedom of expression means nothing unless it includes the freedom of minorities to put forward their views, no matter how unpopular or repugnant those views are to the majority.'[9]

During the 1981 hunger strikes in Northern Ireland, some of the technical operators in radio wore black armbands in support of the dead hunger-strikers. In editorial teams, though, things were different. Roisin Boyd (a reporter colleague) and I had the temerity to question the safety of the Birmingham Six convictions at a *Day by Day* programme meeting in 1984. It was difficult. We were greeted with a hushed incredulity by the other twelve people in the room. People waited to see what Pat Kenny would say. The team had enormous respect for Pat. He was as sharp as a tack, and could be aggressive in pursuit of programme excellence. The team was slightly afraid of him, but he generally tended to be fair and incisive. 'Whether they are guilty of the bombing or not, they were on their way to an IRA funeral in Belfast, so I don't think we should be too concerned to cover that story', he said. Other colleagues around the table breathed a sigh of relief. Roisin and I persisted, and did manage to cover the subject on air many times over the following years. The major investigations in television on both the Birmingham Six and Guildford Four, however, were carried out by British

---

9   *The Irish Times*, 20 October 1988.

television, with the help of British MP Chris Mullin. By the time the Birmingham Six convictions began to be questioned more widely, Pat and other team members were glad of the contacts that Roisin and I had built with the men's families in those years. We got the first interviews with Paddy Joe Hill and Billy Power of the Birmingham Six, and with Paul Hill and Gerry Conlon of the Guildford Four on their release. Arguing for these issues was not easy; we received unwelcome attention from management and colleagues, and lived under a cloud of suspicion.

In 1988, the British government decided to follow the bad example of the Irish government and brought in a broadcasting ban in Britain, which was similar in most details to Section 31. Journalist Ed Moloney wrote of its operation: 'All this had an effect upon the media. When the dominant message coming from so many powerful sources was that no one should talk to Sinn Féin, where did that leave journalists whose work, in theory at least, involved talking to everyone?'[10] I believed that we needed to do that, to continue talking to everyone, even if we could not broadcast interviews, and, through our unions, fight to be allowed to carry out our professional work unimpeded. But it took a toll. In fact, I remember going into meetings in RTÉ with a knot in my stomach when an issue concerning Northern Ireland had to be discussed. Debates were often heated, and sometimes quite personal. I was accused of being a Provo fellow traveller to my face, and friends told me that worse was said behind my back. After many of these meetings, I left the room exhausted, and anxious about what would follow if management decided to get involved.

I felt that it was incumbent on journalists to be aware of how people in Northern Ireland were feeling and being

10   Rolston, *The Media and Northern Ireland: Covering the Troubles*, p. 21.

treated. The story concerned events taking place only some ninety miles up the road. I argued at the National Union of Journalists conference in Ayr in 1981 that travelling from the Republic to Northern Ireland, and spending some time there, should be a prerequisite for journalists in the Republic before they earned an NUJ card. Oddly enough, this suggestion was better received by my British colleagues than by members from the Republic, some of whom told me frankly that it was 'a mad idea'.

In August 1984, an old friend, a teacher from west Belfast, invited me to come up to Belfast to an internment commemoration march to see at first-hand how the security forces treated protesters. I was glad to accept, and invited my new boyfriend at the time, Donal, to come with me. We travelled with photojournalist Derek Speirs. None of us was prepared for what we witnessed. A peaceful protest, marked at the outset by good humour, banter and songs, turned into an unprovoked attack on the crowd by members of the RUC. Everyone sat down in the road to indicate that their protest provided no threat. The RUC opened fire with plastic bullets, and people scattered. A young man of twenty-three, Seán Downes, received a rubber bullet straight to his heart, and was pronounced dead at the scene. We saw the complete terror of the civilians on the march, and understood better why they were prepared to support Sinn Féin.

Derek Speirs courageously took the photographs that appeared in the following day's newspapers. They showed a line of RUC officers preparing to fire into a crowd of seated protestors. Most of the other photographers had run for cover, settling for more distant shots. When the march was over, we went to the top floor of the Europa Hotel, where most of the journalists were in conclave. Many had left before the shootings began, and were cobbling together stories on the basis of second-hand information and police statements. We told them what we had seen. It made an impact, and some reporters began to telephone more widely to ascertain what exactly had taken place. It was a revealing day. I felt that we owed it to communities in Northern Ireland to at least try to understand their situation, to make sense of it. I was aware of the hurt felt by many people I had met that day, who had a sense of being abandoned by politics and journalism in the Republic. When Sinn Féin grew into a major force representing a majority of nationalist opinion in Northern Ireland, political opinion in the Republic was taken aback because the electorate had been given only a partial story for so many years.

Looking back at the minutes of the RTÉ editorial board meetings in the years from 1980 to 1983, Section 31 was discussed regularly. The discomfiture of senior management was clear. On several occasions, they made their unhappiness known to the minister of the time. At the time of the Stardust fire, in February 1981, at which one key witness was a Sinn Féin member, the editorial board noted that there was a 'ludicrous situation where only one broadcaster was shackled by the Section 31 directive.' British broadcasters were not then affected by the ban. On another occasion, it was noted that Gay Byrne had made unsuitable remarks on his radio programme decrying the impact of Section 31. The Controller of Radio agreed to speak to him about the matter.

Reporters and producers were urged to consult with Northern Editor, Jim Dougal, to check whether individuals were subject to the strictures of Section 31, north and south of the border. This led to programme-makers telephoning Dougal and running names past him where there was an element of doubt. Finally, an exasperated Jim Dougal complained strenuously about being inundated with such enquiries. In the future, such queries would be channelled through senior managers. On another occasion, disquiet was expressed at the publicly stated view of the Chairman of the Authority, P. J. Moriarty, that he was in favour of Section 31.

The committee felt that it was a personal view, and no action was taken to distance the organisation from that opinion.

Discussions intensified in February 1981 in the period preceding the broadcast of Robert Kee's landmark series: *Ireland: A Television History*. Embarassingly, two minutes and twenty seconds had been edited out of episode twelve of this co-production with the BBC.[11] There was concern that episode thirteen, bringing history up to date with contemporary politics, contained many breaches of Section 31. Senior management, including the Director General of the day, decided to seek ministerial guidance. They sought approval, on 13 February 1981, to broadcast the episode in its entirety, and noted that RTÉ 'should be seen to endeavour to broadcast the entire programme.' The possibility of 'appropriate deletions was also discussed', although it was felt that these proposed deletions 'could materially alter the thrust of the programme.' Finally, after much correspondence to and fro with the minister, a derogation was allowed so that the whole episode could be broadcast. A humiliating international incident was thus avoided.

The application of Section 31 led many stories to be badly reported or under-reported. Some of the notable topics in this category were the 1981 hunger strikes, the Concerned Parents Against Drugs in Dublin's inner-city communities, the election of Gerry Adams as West Belfast's MP in 1983, the Drumcree/ Garvaghy Road conflicts during the Orange marching season in Portadown, the debate within republicanism about politics and militarism, and the Hume/Adams talks in 1993. I helped to cover many of these. We did the best we could under the Section, and the very restrictive guidelines RTÉ management had issued to journalists and producers.

In 1983, I was in West Belfast covering the British general election when Gerry Adams defeated Joe Hendron and was

---

11   John Horgan, *Broadcasting and Public Life*, p. 191.

elected to the House of Commons. The count was tense. It had been a very closely run contest. The supporters of both sides kept coming out of the closed counting room in Belfast City Hall to give their interpretation of how the count was going. Eventually, late in the evening, the doors flew open. Adams had it. While the international press, including the BBC, crowded around the winning candidate, we had no alternative but to approach the losing candidate, Dr Joe Hendron, who duly gave an interview for *Day by Day*, which was broadcast on the following morning. The same ridiculous exercise was repeated on the television news that night. This was a defining moment in the republican movement, which accelerated the impetus towards the peace strategy. A few years later, the 1986 Ard Fheis saw the split between the Adams/McGuinness wing of Sinn Féin and Ruairí Ó Brádaigh's anti-peace process supporters. RTÉ was in no position to analyse these developments.

Along with other producers, I looked for a temporary lifting of Section 31 at this time, as we had during the 1981 hunger strikes, a point referred to in my own submission to the European Commission on Human Rights, citing newsworthiness and electoral context.

> [We] applied to the Minister for a derogation from the Ministerial Order for example, during the period of the Maze hunger strike in 1981, and during the contest for the West Belfast seat in the general election in 1983 ... so that RTÉ could fully cover those matters ... in each case, a derogation was refused.[12]

Mary McAleese, later President of Ireland, worked as a reporter on *Today Tonight* in the early 1980s, but, as she has ably

---

12 Affidavit to European Commission on Human Rights, paragraph 11.

documented, she was treated with extreme hostility because of her Northern nationalist background.[13] She recounted hearing her colleague Forbes McFall being described at a *Today Tonight* meeting as 'a fucking Provo'. Forbes was one of a few serious and dedicated journalists who, like Mary herself, tried to keep reporting honestly on Northern Ireland during this period. He earned the insult by observing at the funeral of Bobby Sands, attended by 100,000 people, that the prisoners on hunger strike appeared to be supported by the nationalist population.

A memory comes into my mind that epitomised the atmosphere of the time. In 1982, I was having lunch with a group of colleagues from radio in the main RTÉ canteen, and looked over when I heard laughter coming from a table of *Today Tonight* personnel. At the next table to them, eating her lunch alone, was Mary McAleese, who had recently joined *Today Tonight*. I excused myself from my group. I remember that a reporter colleague looked up and said, 'I know what you're going to do, and you're dead right!' I went over to McAleese, reintroduced myself, having interviewed her with Mary Robinson some years previously for *The Crane Bag* magazine, and talked about a recent report she had done. I was outraged at the attempt to isolate someone of her calibre and insights. Later, when she stood for election to be President of Ireland in 1997, Mary McAleese spoke in an interview on *Liveline* with Joe Duffy about how tough that period was. I decided then that I would vote for her, in solidarity for what she had gone through at that time. Eoghan Harris said that, if elected, she would be a 'tribal time bomb', although he was not unduly perturbed. He predicted confidently that she would lose, and concluded that 'if I am wrong, I'll retire, I

13   Mick Heaney, 'The Battle for Political Supremacy in the Newsroom', *The Irish Times*, 3 January 2012.

really fucking will.'[14] Despite the name-calling and a hostile press, Mary McAleese won the election, and went on to demonstrate a brilliance in the role, along with her customary fair-mindedness. To no one's surprise, Eoghan Harris did not retire.

Harris holds a peculiarly distorted view of the whole issue of Section 31, writing as recently as January 2012 that:

> Most RTÉ staff quietly supported section 31, until the late eighties when Trotskyite supporters secured a majority in the two biggest unions, the FWUI and the ITGWU. The NUJ's opposition was somewhat nominal. The real challenge to section 31 came from a minority of radio producers. The two most prominent activists against restricting Sinn Féin spokespersons were Betty Purcell and Alex White.[15]

This analysis gives exaggerated power and influence to Alex and me. In fact, every proposal we put forward was supported by the majority of our trade union colleagues. Harris extends his obsession to include John Bowman and his history of RTÉ Television, *Window and Mirror.* Harris refers disparagingly to page 240, 'where Bowman lauds my principal section 31 antagonist Betty Purcell, "as a colleague for very many years [who] shared many insights with me". Indeed.'

Since I worked closely with John for ten years, this was hardly a remarkable statement, yet Harris sees the comment as evidence of RTÉ's collective plan to denigrate his ideas. There was no conspiracy, led by Alex and me or otherwise. Most

---

14 Eoghan Harris, 'Out of the Shadows – Brenda Power', *Magill,* November 1997.

15 Eoghan Harris, *Sunday Independent,* 'Section 31 saved many young men of 20 from PIRA', 8 January 2012.

trade union members were uncomfortable with the operation of the censorship. Many resolutions were passed, and delegations visited ministers, but only two one-day stoppages occurred over the issue during the whole of the 1980s. There was a passivity instilled by fear. Harris and his Workers' Party comrades contributed to that atmosphere of apprehension. Our colleagues across the water fought more regularly, and intensively, to be allowed to do their reporting job.

All through the 1980s in radio, the censorship of Section 31 stymied us in our duty to report impartially. I remember clearly cases involving the Concerned Parents Against Drugs, who were battling the drug-pushers in Dublin's inner-city communities. Many of the activists were members of Sinn Féin, and we had to ask them the question: 'Are you or have you ever been a member of Sinn Féin?' The reactions ranged from looks of sympathy to acute hostility, and often to outrage. Many times colleagues came back with nothing on tape because people had taken umbrage at the enquiry. Even activists who were not members of Sinn Féin refused to engage with RTÉ.

In her later affidavit in support of the case to the European Commission of Human Rights, reporter Roisin Boyd told of reporting on housing conditions in a flat complex in Dublin's Pearse Street. She had been given helpful background information and introductions to local people by a community worker in the complex. Towards the end of her day's recording, she found out indirectly that he was a member of Sinn Féin. She could not interview him about the situation, despite the fact that he was clearly the person who knew most about the problems in the flats, and had been working to highlight them. 'I was placed in an extremely embarrassing and invidious position as a journalist covering this particular story.'[16] Roisin also pointed to the difficulties

---

16 Affidavit of Roisin Boyd to European Commission on Human Rights, paragraph 2.

of working on stories involving the Concerned Parents Against Drugs, and the heroin epidemic in Dublin:

> It is particularly frustrating for me as a reporter in these situations to note that foreign television stations are at liberty to cover each and every situation fully, and newspaper and other publications can interview and report on whomsoever they wish. I feel that as a journalist I am unable to carry out my proper function in producing to the public a balanced report in connection with every controversial item of the day.[17]

On *Women Today* in the early 1980s, I had the job of convincing a very reluctant Eileen Flynn to give us an interview. She had lost her job as a schoolteacher in a Catholic convent school in Wexford town because she was 'living with a married man'. The head nun claimed that this personal circumstance was contrary to the Catholic ethos of the school. Flynn's partner happened to be a member of Sinn Féin, and so I was instructed to ask her if she was herself a member of the organisation. I had been working hard to convince her to talk to us first rather than to the Sunday papers, and she was agreeable. When the question was put about her possible membership of Sinn Féin, however, she refused to do the interview, sharply putting down the phone. The pros and cons of her case were debated by many people throughout Ireland over the following weeks, but the chance of getting the story directly from the principal herself was jeopardised by a censorship issue relating to matters quite distinct from sexual morality. It later transpired that Eileen Flynn had never been a member of Sinn Féin. A story concerning Church

---

17   Affidavit of Roisin Boyd to the European Commission on Human Rights, paragraph 7.

control of education was covered badly because of fear of the lash of the censor.

I had a strong belief that producers and reporters in RTÉ needed to try to push the boundaries of what we could do. The conflict in Northern Ireland was one of the major news stories of the day throughout the 1980s. Apart from the contemporary importance of the story, there was a growing gap in the archives we were bequeathing to history. On a daily basis I argued over the issue with managers and colleagues. Interviews should be recorded, I argued, even for the purposes of future archives. On 8 March 1981, I took my recording equipment and went north to cover a protest concerning women prisoners that was taking place at Armagh Prison. As an overhang of the battle around political status for IRA prisoners, which had led to the hunger strikes, male prisoners were now being allowed their own clothes and had freedom of association. This did not apply to women prisoners, and a number of them were protesting. A large march had been organised, which would be addressed by trade union and Church leaders. Before I left Dublin, I asked for a Unionist spokesman, and was promised one in Armagh city, but this spokesman did not materialise. I recorded some interviews with family members of the prisoners (vetting each for Section 31, with great trepidation) and some of those who spoke to the marchers from the platform. I did a short report for Monday's *Women Today*.

Senior management was not happy. There was no breach of Section 31, but they felt that I had violated its broader remit in that my piece lacked balancing remarks from the other side. I argued that in features programmes, unlike news, items could be balanced over time under section 18(1) of the Broadcasting Act, but it was no good. There was a determination that I be taught a lesson. The reaction was a product of the feverish atmosphere of the time. I was told that I would be taken out of current affairs and moved to music programmes.

Luckily for me, I had a very decent line manager at the time, Michael Littleton. He was the person who had recruited me. Michael was highly intellectual, severe of countenance, but with a sense of history and context. He had a way of inveigling the truth out of his staff, and he would raise an ironic eyebrow at many of the things we managed to get up to. But he was in difficulty on this particular incident. He made it clear to me that the best he could do was to ensure that I stayed in his department, for eventual deployment back to current affairs should the opportunity arise. In the meantime, I was out of daily programmes, and would be working on a weekly health programme, *Bodywise*. I have recently checked my personnel records, and found that Littleton was doing his best to protect me. That year he wrote on my record that I had made an error of judgement, demonstrating 'a severe lack of maturity', but that I was a committed and energetic current affairs producer. He would be monitoring me elsewhere in his department. A year later, he was able to announce that I continued to show commitment and energy in programme-making, but that, most importantly, I had now developed the all-important 'maturity'. He was allowed to put me back into daily current affairs programmes, first on *Day by Day*, and later as series producer of *Women Today*. Importantly, he had made the case that there was no malfeasance on my part. The 'lack of maturity' argument meant that I could make up this shortfall, and not be lost to news broadcasting.

Jenny McGeever was not so fortunate. In March 1988, she travelled to Northern Ireland to cover the funerals of the three IRA members who had been shot dead by the SAS in Gibraltar. As she edited her report, largely through tiredness, she included the voice of Martin McGuinness, although he was not named. He was heard briefly reporting to family members the result of discussions with the RUC concerning items placed on the three coffins after they arrived in Northern Ireland, an interesting insight into the conduct of such funerals. It was, of course, a technical breach of Section 31, but hardly one that would send people to the barricades. The Minister for Communications at the time, Ray Burke, made public his unhappiness with the item, stating that 'the foundations of the State were shaking'. RTÉ management rushed to sack Jenny McGeever. They could have taken the approach of issuing a stern warning or moving her sideways for a period, as had happened on other occasions where small technical lapses had occurred. But Ray Burke's fury decided the matter. To its shame, the NUJ newsroom chapel accepted that McGeever should be sacrificed, as long as the Programme Editor, who had allowed the item to be transmitted, was not touched. It was an ugly affair. Happily, Jenny McGeever brought her considerable talent and intelligence to bear in a new career as a solicitor in the Four Courts.

Among many initiatives that I took with colleagues in the 1980s to oppose the censorship, one stands out as particularly frightening. It was customary, after the party leader's speech at Ard Fheiseanna, for the Taoiseach to join journalists for a drink and casual chat. At the 1988 Fianna Fáil Ard Fheis I decided to confront Charles Haughey about the continuing difficulties of working under Section 31. As he entered the room, the crowd divided, like the biblical Red Sea, and he moved among us with his customary self-importance. When he came to where I was standing with colleagues, I remonstrated about the censorship. He turned to me with what can only be described as a killing look, listened momentarily, and then, sweeping his arm, moved on. I did not believe that I had convinced him of the need for a policy change! But I was very aware, later, when Fianna Fáil TDs came to oppose his leadership, and spoke of being given a dead-eyed look, that I knew that look well. Charles Haughey did not like to be opposed.

The absence of the Sinn Féin perspective, and of in-depth coverage of the community they represented throughout the 1980s, meant that people in the Republic developed no real understanding of the debates and developments that were happening within republicanism. When the news broke of discussion between John Hume and Gerry Adams in April 1993, RTÉ's restrictions threatened the station's general credibility. Niall Meehan, a lecturer at Dublin City University, researched radio and television coverage of the breaking news that the two main leaders of nationalist opinion in Northern Ireland were engaged in purposeful talks.[18] Out of forty such items in that period, twenty-two were on the Hume/Adams talks. In only three of these reports was a Sinn Féin statement quoted, and a 'health warning', or mention of Section 31, was never referred to. At this key moment in the development of a solution to the Northern Ireland problem, RTÉ was leaving out one component of the debate. It could be said that Gerry Adams's part in the talks represented 50 per cent of the equation, yet RTÉ maintained silence on his perspective, and was not even honest enough to admit the restriction on air. Furthermore, in the years of the operation of Section 31, RTÉ journalists had not maintained contact with Sinn Féin and its supporters, so they were at a significant loss in covering the story, even when it became public.

The ban had become such second nature within RTÉ that it was extended to exclude members as well as spokespersons for Sinn Féin. This led to some ludicrous incidents. A student named Marcus Free rang a phone-in programme to talk about making wine from mushrooms. When he announced that he happened to be a member of Sinn Féin, the call was quickly ended. A similar truncation occurred when a gay rights activist

---

18 Niall Meehan, '(Self) Censoring the Talks: How Section 31 of the Broadcasting Act affected RTÉ's Coverage of the John Hume – Gerry Adams talks' (At www.academia.edu/166367).

was quizzing the Minister for Health about a cut in funding for a gay community helpline. I was in the studio when I received a call from programme management saying that he was a Sinn Féin member and we had to cut short the lively exchange. Lydia Comiskey was censored when talking about her husband going abroad to look for work; Larry O'Toole was prevented from talking about an industrial dispute in a bakery he worked in; and the only eye-witness to a fire in Donegal could not be interviewed for the same reason, such was the fear of breaching the section in spirit or in word.

In March 1992 the Supreme Court ruled that RTÉ had gone beyond the Ministerial Order in banning all members as well as spokespersons for Sinn Féin. Justice Rory O'Hanlon found the RTÉ guidelines to be 'bad in law, a misconstruction of the law, and null and void.'[19] The overcautious zeal to keep on the right side of the government prevailed. RTÉ refused to implement Justice O'Hanlon's ruling, appealed against the judgment, and lost the appeal. RTÉ was seen to have gone further than the Section required in extending the ban to all members of the listed organisations.

Over my many years in RTÉ, I have seen station managers be quite brave in standing up to the government, spin doctors and corporate complainants. This audacity is one of the strong points of public service broadcasting. It is only on the issue of Section 31 that they habitually wilted. Their instinct to go even further than was demanded underlined the fear that surrounded the government-imposed censorship. Lecturer Niall Meehan explained the craven approach of RTÉ's management in this way:

It can be said in RTÉ's defence that when the guidelines were produced on the 21st of January

---

19   Niall Meehan, 'Section 31 Ban Confusion in RTÉ a result of Management Failure', *Sunday Business Post*, 16 August 1992.

1978, by the then Director General, Oliver Moloney, it was only six years since an entire RTÉ Authority had been sacked for not operating Section 31 to the government's satisfaction.[20]

Not all staff in RTÉ were quiescent in their acceptance of Section 31 and RTÉ management's guidelines. In 1986 and 1988 the two unions involved, the NUJ and the Workers Union of Ireland, organised two one-day strikes on the issue. I proposed that first strike at a meeting of radio and television producers in April 1986. The debate in the room was hot and heavy. At this meeting, my honesty and bona fides were brought into question. I was quizzed about my personal politics and student background. When we got down to the way in which a one-day strike would operate, Joe Mulholland, then editor of *Today Tonight*, made it clear that he would keep the programme on air, whether there was an agreed stoppage or not. I then proposed that if this were the case, he was operating foremost as a manager, and could not participate in the union vote. He stormed out of the meeting. That was the heated atmosphere of the time. The two one-day strikes went ahead, and demonstrated that most fair-minded journalists were unhappy with the censorship.

I will deal in Chapter 6 with how the Workers' Party tried, in a consistent way, to damage the credibility of those who opposed them on Section 31 and other issues. Writing later about this period, former broadcaster Colum Kenny asserted that Workers' Party supporters in RTÉ 'helped to create a broadcasting climate that was unfavourable to calm consideration of strong nationalist sentiments.' Furthermore, a number 'benefited personally from the fact that they did not rock RTÉ management's boat on Northern Ireland.' They 'appeared to believe that journalism

---

20   Ibid.

is principally a form of politics, and that ideology is more important than fairness.'[21]

The impact of the Section 31 order was assessed by an International Federation of Journalists' mission to Ireland in January 1987, when the unions invited them to Ireland to examine the effects of the order. Their report ended:

> Our conclusions can be put briefly and bluntly: Irish radio and television are subjected to clear-cut political censorship. And the defence for exercising that censorship, whether it is put by the present or former Ministers, by journalists or by others, does not stand close scrutiny.[22]

We were accumulating a mass of opinion and academic research that undermined the logic and operation of the censorship. I had argued the position to Charlie Haughey on a number of trade union delegations to his office when he was Taoiseach, and, as mentioned, at the media event at the Fianna Fáil Ard Fheis in 1988, but there was no indication of a change of heart at government level. In 1989, Alex White and I decided to up the ante. We would take a case to the European Commission on Human Rights, and hope to get a judgment that would force the government's hand.

The case took a lot of work, collecting affidavits up and down the country, eliciting evidence from presenters and managers, as well as producers and reporters, and convincing the NUJ and the Workers Union of Ireland to support the case collectively. We finally got our hearing in April 1991. It became known as *Purcell* v. *Ireland 1991*, and the solicitor who

---

21   Colum Kenny, 'Censorship, not Self-Censorship', in Mary Corcoran and Mark O'Brien (eds.), *Political Censorship and the Democratic State: The Irish Broadcasting Ban* (Four Courts Press, 2005).

22   'Censoring "the Troubles": an Irish solution to an Irish problem?' Report on an IFJ fact-finding mission to Ireland, January 1987.

took the case was Anne Neary, with Frank Clarke (now a member of the Supreme Court) as our lead counsel.

In my argument to the European Commission on Human Rights, I pointed to the difficulty experienced by producers in covering stories related to Northern Ireland:

> The fact that any of the persons interviewed may be members of, or associated with proscribed organisations, is perceived by me and other producers as a major difficulty and disincentive in the making of such programmes.[23]

I gave a number of examples, including a non-political programme on the effect on rural communities of the closure of border roads. I had specifically ascertained from interviewees that none was a member of an organisation proscribed under Section 31. Nevertheless, one person later turned out to be a member of Sinn Féin, and a long process of investigation by management ensued. Another case to which I referred involved a woman interviewed on *The Gay Byrne Show* on radio, talking about her loneliness because her husband had been forced to emigrate in order to find work. After the interview had been broadcast, it emerged that the woman was a member of Sinn Féin.

> The RTÉ Authority issued a statement apologising for the broadcast on the grounds of mistake, notwithstanding the fact that the woman did not express any view whatsoever about politics or political beliefs.[24]

---

23 Affidavit to the European Commission on Human Rights, paragraph 8.

24 Affidavit to the European Commission on Human Rights, paragraph 14.

In another example of the censorship, Alex White told the Commission that he had been instructed in March 1988 to ask each and every person who phoned in to the *Liveline* radio programme whether he or she was a member of any organisation proscribed under Section 31. He also pointed to his action in sending a reporter to do a story on a counselling service that was giving non-directive advice on abortion services. When the counsellor was asked if she was covered by Section 31, she took great offence at the question, and afterwards wrote to Alex to complain. His conclusion: 'I am not in a position to produce radio programmes which reflect all views on a given topic.'[25]

The difficulties evident in covering events in the Republic were exacerbated for journalists whose main beat was north of the border. Television reporter Brendan O'Brien put it this way:

> I have found it extremely difficult to adequately cover the nationalist perspective in Northern Ireland and to present it with all its subtleties and in all its aspects. There are many Northern Nationalists who believe that the Provisional IRA … is a reaction to the presence of the British Army in Northern Ireland. Many of these nationalists would not however agree with the violent methods used by the Provisional IRA. Many persons who hold that viewpoint refuse now to be interviewed by RTÉ, because they feel that such interviews present them as being 'crypto Provos' because they feel that they are only being asked for interviews because RTÉ is unable to interview members of the Provisional IRA and other proscribed organisations.[26]

---

25 Affidavit of Alex White to the European Commission on Human Rights, paragraph 13.

26 Affidavit of Brendan O'Brien to the European Commission on Human Rights, paragraph 7.

The huge frustration of journalists with being required to work under the restrictions of Section 31 was very evident as we compiled views for our case from across the organisation. Although members of senior management, who had close, regular contact with the government, constantly erred on the side of caution, reporting and producing staff were incensed by the restrictive approach.

The case was well argued in front of the European judges, and we felt confident that they would accept our case. Rather amusingly, the counsel on the government's side was barrister Gerry Danaher, who had been the editor of the Sinn Féin newspaper *An Phoblacht* in the mid-1970s. He now found himself in the opposite corner, arguing the case for censorship on behalf of the Fianna Fáil government.

In the event, by a majority verdict, the European Commission on Human Rights found against the application to repeal Section 31, on a number of grounds. They did not find that voters would automatically have a right to hear the views of all those running for election in equal measure. They found that the State had a right to defend itself against a subversive threat. Despite the fact that the rights of journalists might be undermined by the operation of the section, they believed, on balance, that the State had a right to impose these strictures. The Commission recommended that a new application be made to the Supreme Court to ensure that all domestic remedies had indeed been exhausted, while accepting that the ruling in *Lynch v Cooney*[27] meant that a new outcome from the Supreme Court would probably not be likely.

The case was more than a worthwhile exercise. When Michael D. Higgins moved, as Minister for Arts, Culture and the Gaeltacht, to repeal Section 31 in January 1994, he

---

27 *The State (Lynch) v Patrick Cooney and the Attorney General* [1982] IR 337.

referred to the European case. His rescission of the Section was a politically courageous act, particularly in view of the venom being poured on supporters of the peace process in the *Sunday Independent* every week. The repeal of the censorship was a key piece in the jigsaw that allowed that process to be advanced, and strengthened the voices of those republicans who were arguing for political debate as the way forward.

Article 19 of the Universal Declaration of Human Rights, adopted in 1948, states clearly that:

> Everyone has the right to freedom of opinion and expression; this right includes freedom to hold opinions without interference and to seek, receive and impart information and ideas through any media and regardless of frontiers.

This Article, alongside other human rights, is more than a lofty set of thoughts. It is a statement of one of the basic tenets of democracy. Its perspective, though wide, has a specific application that is for the good of the citizens of states. By contrast, RTÉ and its journalists for many years lived in a blinkered reality. The Irish Broadcasting Review Committee Report in 1974 explained the strictures in this way:

> The problem is to create machinery which will reconcile freedom with responsibility, and ensure that broadcasters are free from detailed interference, while at the same time remaining subject to broad direction and control in the public interest.[28]

---

28 Irish Broadcasting Review Committee Report (Government Publications Office, 1974).

Seán Lemass as Taoiseach famously stated in 1966 that RTÉ should be 'an instrument of public policy'. In no facet of RTÉ's work has this been more evident than in the operation of political censorship under Section 31. The 'broad direction and control' by the government interfered on a daily basis with the work of broadcasters, and with the right of the viewing and listening public to hear all sides and make up their own minds. As political reporter Mary Holland summarised it in *The Irish Times* in October 1993, Section 31 'seriously affected coverage of the conflict in Northern Ireland, and an informed understanding of the problems of the State.'[29] It is still a matter of shame to me that we, as broadcasters, did so little to oppose its sinister operation.

---

29   Mary Holland, *The Irish Times,* 14 October 1993.

4

Day by Day

'Many journalists become very defensive when you suggest to them that they are anything but impartial and objective ... Journalists don't sit down and think, "I'm now going to speak for the establishment." Of course not. But they internalise a whole set of assumptions, and one of the most potent assumptions is that the world should be seen in terms of its usefulness to the West, not humanity.'

— John Pilger[1]

Iworked on the original *Day by Day* programme with Pat Kenny and John Bowman in the 1980s. Pat was, and still is, a sterling broadcaster who can pick up a brief rapidly and turn a fairly mundane interview into a gem, but he had a few weak points. We had arguments about men's role in the family, and about women in the workforce. Pat argued that he would rather be in a plane piloted by a hung-over man than a pre-menstrual woman. These spirited debates would happen in the open-plan office. It was important to be seen to fight your corner articulately. John was more low-key, and entirely

---

1   Cited in David Barsamian, *Louder than Bombs: Interviews from The Progressive Magazine* (South End Press Collective, 2004), p. 38.

driven by journalistic content. He would happily study and add to a brief on a contributor, and his knowledge of current affairs allowed him to turn around stories of the day with great ease.

Programme teams are the backbone of good radio, and it is instructive to look at how they work. As series producer on *Day by Day* in 1985 and 1986, my day began before seven o'clock. I would try to be first in, and peruse the papers before colleagues started to arrive. Then the hectically demanding schedule of a daily programme began: deciding on lead and second lead stories, lining up contributors, finishing briefs, talking to the presenter and recording items with interviewees who were not free during the live programme. Then the programme began, and driving it along, while keeping up with breaking stories, was another challenge.

When I worked on *Day by Day*, it transmitted from ten o'clock to twelve, but later this changed to nine to eleven. There were often tensions within the programme team as to which items merited consideration, and these tensions emerged in the morning in the main open-plan office. Where possible, I tried to make sure that the most fraught discussions would take place behind closed doors, in the meeting after our daily broadcast. It is inevitable in a creative environment, and can be constructive, for colleagues to have strongly argued views regarding items. The only difficulty emerges when rancour or accusations of bad faith come into the equation. It is up to the series producer to try to avoid this. To manage a team consisting of a presenter, three producers, three researchers, a couple of reporters and a broadcasting assistant, the ability to keep everyone in a reasonably happy frame of mind, where they at least feel respected, is the key psychological element. There must be a certain amount of trust between competing colleagues, and a belief in each other's bona fides.

My own view of team leadership is that colleagues need to be encouraged to try difficult things without feeling that blame will attach to them if an item goes wrong. It is up to the series producer to spot problems in advance and attempt to neutralise them.

There were also considerable competitive tensions between programmes, with constant races to book interviews on major topical stories. In those arguments we would 'pull rank' as the flagship current affairs programme to establish our ownership of major, and particularly international, interviews. The ability to win such debates is an important consideration, and one that continues to this day. Now, of course, with increased competition outside of RTÉ, it is not merely a matter of convincing an internal manager. A potential contributor might be asked to commit to an exclusive interview or, at a minimum, to give us the first broadcast of a particular item.

On one of my first days with John Bowman on *Day by Day* in the early 1980s, we had a gap of about ten minutes to fill shortly before the programme began. I rang Bill Attley, who was General Secretary of the ITGWU at the time. I asked him whether he would do a short interview about an upcoming tax march. It would be a straight promotional piece for the march, I said. He agreed to do it. John, who had overheard the telephone call, came over and said to me, very quietly; 'I'm afraid I don't do straight promotional pieces. The interview will be questioning and challenging.' I found a place to ring Bill Attley back, and told him that he could expect a more thought-provoking line of questioning in the interview. 'I'd expect nothing less from John Bowman', he told me. It was a journalistic lesson learnt, and an important one.

On another occasion, in the run-up to the 1982 general election, I had booked Charlie Haughey to do an interview by phone from his office in the Dáil. P. J. Mara rang at fifteen minutes to air to tell me that Mr Haughey had decided to come into the Radio Centre and would be there in ten minutes. As he was the incumbent Taoiseach, protocol demanded that he would be met by the Director of Radio, or at a minimum by the Controller of Radio Programmes. I ran to their offices, but both were unreachable and at meetings. I went out to the steps of the Radio Centre. When Haughey arrived, I explained why there was no senior manager there to greet him, and wondered why he had changed his mind and decided to come into the studio. 'I want to see the whites of the fucker's eyes', he said, referring to John Bowman. When the programme was over, I told John what he had said. He laughed with some mischief. 'I suppose I should take that as a compliment', he said.

One of the programmes I was very happy about was a special *Day by Day* where I invited all the Dáil deputies to agree to exchange their lives with a single mother in Ballymun for one week. Geraldine Kennedy, then a Progressive Democrat TD, was the only parliamentarian to take up the challenge. It made for very interesting programming. Geraldine found it a real struggle to exist on the paltry single mother's allowance, and her daily broadcasts quickly showed how a person's reality shrinks to obsessing about money and the lack of it. She couldn't even sit down and concentrate on reading a book, she told us. She was too busy thinking of recipes involving turnips and cheap cuts of meat. I phoned her during the week to monitor her progress, both on and off air. On one occasion she asked me whether her boyfriend could bring a roast chicken when he came to visit the following night. I had to refuse. He could visit, but could not shore up her supplies. Geraldine Kennedy learnt a lot from the experience, and I had to applaud her rigour in taking on the challenge. The broken lifts, the lack of public transport close by, the closure of the local library – all were having a huge effect on that beleaguered community. All her colleague TDs refused the experiment. One replied that she would have liked to do it, but was having a barbeque for her constituents that weekend! We read out all the negative replies.

I worked on a number of general elections on radio in the 1981 and 1982 period, and directed the main studio during the February 1987 and June 1989 elections. This involved predicting each of the constituency counts, and being aware of what was happening and upcoming in every part of the country. While I was focused on this operation during the 1989 election, which demanded considerable concentration, then Minister for Communications, Ray Burke, came up behind me, patronisingly tapped me on the shoulder, and said, 'Yes, dear, the Minister will have a cup of coffee, white, no sugar.' I was beyond fury, but, more importantly, all the constituency details flew out of my head. I literally could not remember which count was due next, and which were the next dozen constituencies I was watching out for. It was only the assistance of my colleague, sound operator Mick Wright, which allowed me to refocus and get back on top of the task in hand. As I looked at him blankly, he said, 'We were waiting for Dublin South and Limerick East.' I remembered, and slowly got back in control of the information. This was the kind of unnecessary stress that could be brought into a live broadcasting situation by a difficult politician. We just had to grit our teeth and try to get on with it.

Later, in the mid-1990s, I was invited, along with my colleague, former radio producer Bernadette O'Sullivan, to travel to Brussels on a European Union trip concerning the introduction of the euro. These 'junkets' were not all the fun that they seemed. Certainly there were dinners in quaint restaurants in the evenings, but the days started early, and consisted of one lecture after another by speakers from the European institutions. At one of the question and answer sessions, the lecturer insisted on the timeline and process for the introduction of the euro. Bernadette had the temerity to ask a very straight question: 'What if the monetary integration doesn't work?' He rounded on her in an extremely hostile fashion. 'We will not contemplate the possibility of failure' was his rather puerile response. The other journalists in the room looked at one another and lifted an eyebrow. It did not augur well for intelligently facing up to the difficulties involved in a monetary union. In recent years I have often thought of the angry response of that bureaucrat to a simple and reasonable question as the uneven development of countries in the union, and banking scandals, posed questions for the survival of the new currency.

Bernadette was one of many lifelong friends I met through work in radio. Other colleagues of straight integrity who brought their considerable gifts to the process of programme-making were Kintilla Heussaff, Anne Daly, Roisin Boyd and Pat Coyle. They were a formidable group of women, each with their individual insights and strengths, which they contributed without reservation. I was also fortunate to make friends with Jackie Parkes, daughter of orchestra saxophonist Charlie Parkes. Before her untimely death, she and I shared a love of jazz and went to dozens of concerts together, as well as exchanging music in one another's homes. Her son Glenn and my daughter Katie were born in the same week. We were firm friends.

When I turn on the radio now, as a listener, I cannot help seeing the work that goes into every item. Each book needs to be read, and a brief written for the presenter. Stories of the day demand international contacts, and the ability to pursue the appropriate person closest to the action. Debates require an understanding of the dynamics of a good argument, and recognition of the best talkers in each field. Talk radio gobbles up items, and with a two-hour programme to fill, five days a week, the demand to fill the time intelligently is the paramount one.

I was always concerned at the societal impact of any particular item, and therefore would resist addressing any 'tabloid' item that would add to discrimination or prejudice.

(For this reason, I was always against covering stories of 'faith healers', who would falsely raise the hopes of people suffering in the most difficult circumstances.) The personality dynamics of presenters and programme staff were the next consideration, but still important to address and get right. The final concern had to be the impact of the story on the organisation for which I worked. Complaints were to be expected, but thorough homework and a sense of fairness resolved most concerns.

Most importantly, in my many years in radio and television, we never lost a legal case or had a finding against us from the Broadcasting Complaints Commission. It is a minimal source of satisfaction, but a relevant one. All of us who worked on *Day by Day* in the 1980s had huge opportunities to bring issues before the public. We tried to do so fairly and ethically, imbued as we were with the principles of public service broadcasting. We did not have a set of commercial interests trying to skew the debate in favour of any individual or company, which is an important and fundamental principle. I will always be immensely grateful to RTÉ for the opportunity to engage with issues, host debates, support artistic endeavour, and to learn more from contributors about the world we live in. Alongside the sometimes exhausting business of making programmes happen, there was constant stimulation and fulfilment in working in radio.

5

Questions & Answers

'I don't think a tough question is disrespectful.'

— Helen Thomas[1]

I had worked with John Bowman on *Day by Day* in radio before I saw the job advertised as 'Editor of *Questions & Answers* in Television'. John was the most kind and intellectually generous person I ever worked with. He was steeped in the Irish political tradition, and had an encyclopaedic knowledge of current affairs, Dáil constituencies, the RTÉ archive and broadcasting history. When I saw the ad for *Questions & Answers* in 1991, I felt a sense of homecoming. This would be a natural way to make the transition to television.

I applied for the job of editor of *Questions & Answers*, and after a rigorous set of interviews found myself packing my bags for the television building in the late summer of 1990. I had some concerns: I was leaving behind a cohort of great friends, and a way of working that suited me well. Television was rumoured to be a much more unfriendly place. The fears were unfounded. I would add to my radio friends with new

---

1   Quoted in Robert Shetterly, *Americans Who Tell the Truth* (Puffin, Reprint Edition, 2008).

colleagues and companions in television. But the step across the RTÉ campus was nerve-wracking enough.

Before I left the Radio Centre, John Bowman gave me very good advice. I was under pressure to occupy a desk in the main open-plan office in current affairs. This would make my job of negotiating with government and senior figures in society extremely difficult. Hard talking was often required in negotiating for the most eminent and controversial panel possible. 'Don't move over until you secure an office you are happy with', John told me. 'Once you are in the door, you have less of a negotiating position.' I waited for an office to be offered, and I soon got one.

I was to spend ten fruitful years on *Questions & Answers*, and managed the debating run-up to three general elections in that time. I was attracted to the democratic possibilities of the programme, which was the only format in television that allowed for the 'plain people of Ireland' to question those in authority on issues of the day. I was very happy to be working again with John, with whom I had many great discussions about politics and history over the next decade. We certainly came from very different backgrounds, his academic and scholarly, mine educated but activist, and our political emphasis was distinct, especially on Northern Ireland. But what Michael Littleton had described in radio as 'worthwhile creative tension' worked extremely well for us. Our conversations were wide-ranging and respectful, and helped to shape the agenda, panel and audience for upcoming programmes.

In that decade I also filled the contributor tables for the post-general election programmes. As well as working on the content, I was happy to witness John's superlative and unsurpassed understanding of the Irish electoral system. He knew the issues, personalities and geography of each constituency, and could predict with precision the outcome of many late counts as the election coverage went on into the night. No other current affairs presenter could match him on that detail. I was looking forward to learning a lot in close-up editorial work with John, and in holding my own when it came to the broader political canvass, where I was fairly confident of my instinct for politics.

On the first night I edited the programme, a far more mundane crisis emerged. A panellist rang to say that his car had broken down in the country on his way in, and he would not make it. It was one hour to the programme. The editor of current affairs at the time, Peter Feeney, assured me that there was no panic. We went through a list of nearby journalists who would be up to speed on the events of the week. One agreed, and a taxi was dispatched. I learnt quickly that the need to fill slots, which dominated so much of my radio work, was in essence the same in television. The only difference was that the person had to be physically brought to the studio, and into make-up before transmission.

It worked out, and I knew quickly that Peter was a department head who was not afraid to get involved when a programme's needs required him to do so. He was capable of representing the organisation at any level with charm and distinction. He handled politics and current affairs with an assurance that made the task look easy. He was not one to throw blame around when things went wrong; his instinct was to put things right and save RTÉ from any censure.

In November 1992 we brought *Questions & Answers* to New York to cover the Clinton/Bush presidential election. On the night we arrived there, from a plane that landed at 6.30 p.m. (11.30 p.m. Irish time), the five of us who formed the team at the time: myself, John, researcher Kathleen Magee, assistant producer Margaret Keenan and director Niamh White, went looking for a restaurant. John had kindly looked for good places to eat in one of the guidebooks, and we went walking in the city. The place, when we found it, was indeed spectacular. It was in a basement that had housed one of the early wine-storage caverns of New York, and the vaulted roof was intact and atmospheric. Sadly, a recent change of ownership meant that it was now a burger joint, staffed by 'pirates' with patches over one eye, who addressed us in the salty language of the sea. The kids around us seemed to be having a great time. We laughed, and thought, 'the best laid plans of mice and men...'. Next day we woke up and it was time to get to work.

The panel on the programme consisted of writer Jimmy Breslin, former US ambassador to Ireland Margaret Heckler, New York Police Chief Ray Kelly, and journalist and author Pete Hamill. The audience had no compunction about putting strongly argued questions to the panel, and, because this was New York, they correctly predicted a Democratic victory in the election. The topics covered extended to include the visa issue for Irish immigrants to the US, and the Irish-American view of politics in Northern Ireland. I was struck by the more direct form of debate evident in US political culture. Irish people tend to be quite friendly towards political figures, and that easiness was missing. It made for some very lively exchanges.

American attitudes to politicians may be related to the size of the society. In Ireland, many people know their politicians personally from school, community or university, and are seldom in awe of them – an easy familiarity is far more likely. In fact, people see it as a badge of honour not to be intimidated by the powers that be. On the other side of that familiarity is a willingness to please, often with an attendant casual regard for probity in public life. To put it at its very mildest, this lack of distance between political and other institutions and voters has its dangers for the resulting country.

We watched the election results in a bar on West 34th Street. The patrons were Irish-American, and the excitement was palpable. Clinton was a huge favourite among the New York Irish. The State results came in slowly, and began to accumulate. Bill Clinton and Al Gore won comfortably against George Bush and Dan Quayle, and as the night went on, the bar crowd grew excited and happy. Many of them recognised John, since RTÉ programmes were relayed in the Irish bars via Cable and recording. People wandered over and gave us their interpretation of the significance of particular State results. When the final result was delivered, Clinton/ Gore had 43 per cent of the popular vote, 44,900,806, and had carried thirty-two States and Washington DC. Bush/ Quayle had 37.4 per cent, or 39,104,550, and had won in eighteen States. It was an exciting experience to witness that moment in US history at such close quarters. When we got back to Ireland, we were all exhausted, but exhilarated. And then it was time to try to get enthusiastic about Irish political nuances again.

Every Tuesday morning John and I would have a long chat, usually by telephone, where we would decide on the likely political agenda for the following Monday. Once we knew the probable subjects, we would pick a panel to suit, trying always to have a government minister and a prominent member of the Opposition. The other two seats were always more fun to fill, in that the magic of the programme depended on these independent voices and how they would interact with the politicians on the night. The other unknown was, of course, the audience, and particularly the questioners, who were chosen at short notice on the night. It was a particular skill to spot where a person was coming from by the wording of their questions. We could then ensure that we had a fair spread of views in the questioners. The agenda that seemed apparent on the Tuesday often changed as the week went on, and even over the weekend. Panellists got very nervous towards the programme deadline, ringing me to see if I could predict the likely topics. Some of the best performers were also the biggest worriers. Tony Gregory, an original thinker on most issues, was constantly apprehensive about his performance and about letting down his constituents.

Others, like Wicklow Fianna Fáil TD Dick Roche, had no self-doubt or concerns before the show.

My first two years on the programme were in the period when Charles Haughey was Taoiseach, and his press office played hardball with us every week, trying to influence the agenda and withdrawing ministers at short notice. For a whole three-month period in 1991, we did not succeed in having a minister on our panel. Inevitably, things changed when an election drew near, and the competitive nature of politics demanded a skilled and articulate representative from the government side. It was also the case that leadership heaves led to impassioned presentations from the colleagues of the individual under threat. Politics was always a fascinating business to be involved with, up close.

In 1994, we broadcast *Questions & Answers* from South Africa on the eve of the first free elections there. We arrived in Cape Town to find a city in a state of palpable excitement. I had previously done some work in Johannesburg, and found that city to be menacing and divided. The white suburbs were policed by roving security teams, and the walls were high and electrically monitored. The city centre belonged to the poor blacks, crime was high, disadvantage obvious and widespread. Cape Town had a different history, with some racial mixing in the bohemian District 6 area. But it also had racially based division. The beautiful centre and waterfront area belonged to the whites. The 'coloureds' (people of Indian or mixed-race colouring) lived in the nearest townships outside the city centre. Farther out again, the black people lived in real privation in other townships. When we went to the South African Broadcasting Corporation to meet the colleagues who would assist in our broadcast, all the editorial and technical personnel were white. The cleaners in the corridors were black and of mixed race. A huge process of transformation was about to take place, and the first step in that development was the simple act of a free and fair election. There was no doubt that the outcome would be a victory for the African National Congress, led by Nelson Mandela. It was what would happen then that was on people's minds.

John and I discussed the huge expectations that lay on the ANC. There was also a real concern that the tiny but militant white supremacist AWB (the Afrikaner Resistance Movement, taking its initials from the Afrikaans version) would engage in military action. F. W. de Klerk's Nationalist Party's engagement with the democratic change was critical. We proceeded to finalise our panel and audience. Representatives of the Nationalist Party and the AWB would be joined by Kader Asmal, who had lived in Ireland during the years of ANC exile, and former Nigerian President Olusegun Obasanjo.

I chatted about politics with our local driver, and he told me in great excitement that Nelson Mandela would be speaking in Khayelitsha township's football stadium on the day before our programme. It was a busy time, but I was determined not to miss this opportunity. I canvassed team members. John was completely snowed under with the preparation for our programme and with radio work he was undertaking while in South Africa. Other colleagues were apprehensive about the implicit dangers of being the only white people in the stadium. I consulted with our driver, who confirmed that there would be little chance of trouble. He would drive me there, and attend the rally with me. Next morning we would set off at 9.30. Five minutes before we left, our researcher Liam O'Flanagan rang my room to say that he was coming too. I don't know if it was a sense of gallantry that caused him to decide to go, or the historic nature of the occasion. In either case, he and I were not disappointed. The event began with individual singing and a gospel choir. This was followed by Zulu dancers with spears, before finally Nelson Mandela's car and entourage arrived into the stadium and drove around its perimeter. He then emerged and spoke, to tumultuous applause. I remember the atmosphere, people holding up babies, chanting, crying and cheering. His message was one with which we would become familiar: tolerance, multiracialism, forgiveness, change, progress. We returned to our hotel feeling euphoric.

The next day we did our programme, which went without a hitch. The last question was for the panel to come up with one word that represented South Africa to them. The AWB councillor said 'braai', the South African word for barbeque. The woman representing the Nationalist Party opted for 'diversity', Obasanjo said 'struggle'. It was left to Kader Asmal to voice the word 'hope'. Over the next number of years it was his responsibility to turn some of that hope into observable change, as he worked as Minister for Water Affairs to attain clean water availability for all South Africans.

The day after the programme, we woke early. It was election day. John was planning to go out on the polling queues to interview electors about their feelings on the day. I went with him. We started at a white neighbourhood, where people were quite reserved about speaking. Some did look forward to a more fair and multiracial society. They maintained confidence that Mandela's message would prevent civil war. Next we went to a 'coloured' township. The people in these areas had an ambivalent view of apartheid. They resented discrimination on grounds of race, but had been advantaged as a 'labour elite' by the white population. Many of them had worked in domestic service in the big houses in Cape Town. They were worried about a victory for the ANC, and whether or not new prejudice would apply to them in a changed South Africa. Most were voting for the Nationalist Party. Finally, and with some trepidation, we went to a black township. Our driver warned John that people might be resentful and angry to be asked how they would vote by a white stranger – after all, surveillance and spying had been a major part of the arsenal of the white South African State – but John was not to be deflected. With journalistic curiosity, he approached the queues and asked people how they felt, and how they intended to vote. One or two eyebrows were raised, but then the excitement of the day took over. Enthusiastically, they talked about their dreams of change. One man had his two small children with him, wanting them to witness this great occasion. Some women, with babies in slings, sang songs into John's recorder. All went well until a police truck arrived on the scene, and our driver suggested we make good our escape – and quickly. As we drove back to the city, John checked his recordings. He had the elements of an excellent additional radio programme for his return home. It was an extraordinary day, and we were very fortunate to bear witness to that moment of history.

We had many memorable insights during my period of stewardship of *Questions & Answers*. Mary O'Rourke challenged Caroline Simons about the Pro-Life Amendment campaign monopolising the term 'pro-life' for themselves. 'I am pro-life too', she asserted furiously, 'but I don't want women's lives to be put at risk.'

Padraig Flynn came to an outside broadcast in the Burlington Hotel, and argued Albert Reynolds's case as his leadership became untenable in 1994.

Michael D. Higgins welled up with tears as he recounted his experience in Somalia in 1992: 'The constancy of death has robbed the people of their ability to grieve', he said.

Emily O'Reilly savaged Ivan Yates about the treatment of Brigid McCole by his Fine Gael-led government, and extracted an apology from him to the family.

In early 1996, Veronica Guerin called for the assets of drug dealers to be targeted as the best method of undermining the gangs. I asked her afterwards in the hospitality suite whether she was ever fearful for her safety. 'You can't allow yourself to think about that', she responded. Five months later, she was murdered.

Mary Holland, among many wise contributions, pleaded with John Bruton to be patient with the peace process, and not to jeopardise talks by polarised point-scoring.

Charlie McCreevy angrily proclaimed, following the ousting of Albert Reynolds, 'The sale sign on Fianna Fáil is now taken down. We paid the price, we lost our leader, we ain't paying no more.'

In a Protestant town hall in Macroom in the mid-1990s, I watched in surprise as people queued after the programme to get an autograph from Sinn Féin's Martin McGuinness.

Tony Gregory argued with total passion for the legalisation of cannabis as one of a series of measures to undermine the drug traffickers.

The victims of child sexual abuse used the platform of the programme to demand justice from a Church hierarchy in denial.

The wide range of issues we were able to cover, and the unique way in which we were able to hold government and opposition parties to account, made the programme relevant and striking. John Bowman's incisive interviewing often unearthed truths that politicians would have preferred left uncovered. Politicians were afraid of *Questions & Answers* in a way that they were not intimidated by ordinary studio interviews. The reason was that they could not be guaranteed easy delivery of a prepared answer because of the unknown quantity of the audience. This led to a particular nervousness in the period before an election, local or national.

The June 1997 election saw *Questions & Answers* in a number of disputes with the political parties. This was as it should be, and never caused me great anxiety. Sometimes, however, senior managers became involved, and they tended to support the integrity and fairness of the decisions we were making. The election was declared for 6 June, and soon all the parties were willing to put their major candidates forward. We travelled to Tralee on 12 May for a programme

featuring Dick Spring, who was then Tánaiste and Minister
for Foreign Affairs. The other panellists were Fianna Fáil's
Finance spokesman Charlie McCreevy, historian Joe Lee and
journalist Mary Holland. When we were out on an outside
broadcast, everything was a little more fraught. Without
the known elements of the Donnybrook studio, we had to
contend with hotel rooms, a travel set, wires, vans, and a
different kind of audience, anxious to welcome us to their
home town. Dick Spring, while charming, could be a difficult
enough politician, and, four weeks out from an election, he
and his advisor Fergus Finlay were particularly apprehensive.
They were comfortable enough about fielding the main
questions of the week without any notice. These were fairly
self-evident at the time: the election issues, Michael Noonan
in trouble over Hepatitis C, the Dunnes tribunal and the
revelations about Charlie Haughey, the peace process. What
provided the nightmare for the politicians was the 'quirky
question at the end', where they could be shown up as lacking
in humour or humanity, or appear to be out of the loop on
some light-hearted element of which the general public
would be well aware. This was the question that Spring and
Finlay pushed me to divulge. I refused to reveal the question
in advance, and things were quite tense as we made our way in
to begin the programme. Dick Spring need not have worried.
The final question was fairly straightforward: 'With Bertie
Ahern peering out of the darkness, and John Bruton holding
the baby, what will Dick Spring be doing on the billboards of
Ireland during the election campaign?' Of course, he and the
other panellists acquitted themselves easily and with humour.
After the programme, the tension was gone. Dick Spring was
back to his witty self, and well supported by constituents,
who were delighted to see the programme in Kerry.

Our problems were not yet over; the campaign continued
intensely. Two Sundays later I was in Louisburgh, in County
Mayo, for the annual AFRI Famine Walk. The programme

for 25 May was set up and ready to go. It was a sunny day, and I was enjoying the walk in good company, glad to be away from work pressures. One of the organisers drove up to say that there was an urgent message at the hotel for me, and he took me there. It was the Fianna Fáil press office, telling me that they were pulling out of Monday night's programme. We had a Fine Gael and a Labour representative, along with a journalist, and they felt that the programme was unbalanced against them. I suspected that Bertie Ahern was behind this; he had quite a reputation for trying to influence programmes. I rang my head of department, Peter Feeney, and told him that I would be back in Dublin in a few hours, when we could meet.

As I drove, I mulled over the problem. The number of outings for each party in the run-up to an election was decided by RTÉ's Election Steering Committee on the basis of former votes cast. While it was true that Fianna Fáil was apparently 'outgunned' on this occasion, I had spoken to the journalist on the panel to ensure that there would be no 'ganging up' in an unfair way. On other weeks, Labour or Fine Gael would be left out of the panel, and so, numerically, the programme would be fair and balanced over the whole election period. All this meticulous planning and attention to detail, however, was now thrown out by Fianna Fáil's refusal to participate in the second-last programme before the election.

There was only one thing to do. I had no intention of standing down either Fine Gael or Labour, and to give the minor Progressive Democrats an extra seat, in lieu of the journalist, would cause a new set of reverberations. We would have to run a programme with no politicians taking part. When I arrived in Dublin, I proposed this way forward to Peter Feeney, who agreed that it was the best option. And so the *Questions & Answers* of 25 May 1997, just twelve days before the general election, was a politician-free zone. A week later, on 1 June, we had our pre-election finale as planned, with an array of heavy-hitting speakers: Bertie Ahern, Ivan Yates, Ruairí Quinn and Mary Harney.

Looking back, this decision seemed at the time to be the only possibility, with Fianna Fáil en masse ruling themselves out of participation. Our big worry was the upcoming election. Yet, in reality, RTÉ and I gave in to what was essentially a veto by a powerful political party. We should have withstood that pressure, and explained Fianna Fáil's absence as being due to their own choice. They probably would have come in at the last minute if such an 'empty chair' technique had been threatened. Yet no one in senior management would contemplate such a scenario, even though I had offered a non-controversial solution. It was a galling political victory for a bullying tactic by Fianna Fáil.

I was also involved in contributing ideas and stories to the wider current affairs department. In late 1991, during what was only my second year in television, I was given a lead on a major story by a contact in the Electricity Supply Board. A small wind-powered generator was supplying, with great consistency, the electricity needs of the people of Cape Clear Island, a community of 200 families. Charles Haughey, who was Taoiseach at the time, was looking for just such a generator for his own private windswept island: Inishvickillane. He had enquired about the cost of installing such a generator from a German company, and had been given a price of £135,000. After some time, the company contacted him to see if he wished to go ahead with the work. Haughey wrote back that it was not now necessary, because the head of the ESB was going to give him such a facility for free. I spoke to the managing director of the company in Germany, who was prepared to give an interview, and he supplied me with a copy of the rather sharp letter from the Taoiseach. In the meantime, the people of Cape Clear had their generator removed and taken to Inishvickillane. The replacement they received was much less reliable, and they had already experienced an early winter of periodic breakdowns in supply. They were dying to talk.

I was given permission to proceed with a report on the issue, and was given a director, John Masterson, to film it. John and I decided to hire a helicopter and fly over the two islands to get aerial shots. This would have provided the wonderful visual image of one island, deserted except for a mansion, and another, which showed the clusters of houses demonstrating a vibrant community of islanders. Unfortunately, our ambition to film this meant alerting the Department of the Marine to our intentions to film over the Taoiseach's island. Soon, questions were being asked. I was called into a meeting one Sunday morning to meet the Controller of Television Programmes. He told me that he had never, in all his years in television, had such a difficult piece of news to relate. Charles Haughey had made it clear that the negotiations at the time on the licence fee would be severely affected if this film were made. He had no alternative but to think of the wider organisation. The report could not go ahead. He was pale and embarrassed in delivering this news. I was very angry, and considered going public at the time. But a promise that we could return to the subject later, when the licence fee issue was settled, held my ire. I would wait for a better time. Looking back, it was a mistake, and I should certainly have taken the issue to the wider public. By the time we came back to looking at the film again, in the following year, Haughey was a spent docket, and no one would have been surprised at the story. A year is a very long time in politics.

Current affairs can always be relied upon to deliver drama, and I found myself centrally involved in one at the time of the double referendum, on the Amsterdam Treaty and the Good Friday Agreement, on 22 May 1998. The Good Friday referendum was, naturally, a historic moment, and the vast majority of the current affairs department decamped to Belfast to cover it. Seán O'Rourke and I argued that we needed to maintain studio facilities and some team members in Dublin to monitor and cover the Amsterdam Treaty result, which was building into quite a serious contest. The Fianna Fáil and PD government, supported by Fine Gael and Labour, were in favour of a Yes vote, with only the tiny Greens and Sinn Féin questioning the proposition, along with civil society anti-Europe campaigners. All European referenda up to this point had been passed by a majority of about 80 per cent, and there was no sense of danger to the referendum passing. Seán and I argued at meetings that opposition was growing, not least around neutrality and the perceived arrogance of the European establishment. It was also felt that the weighted voting initiative (which would give Ireland seven weighted votes to twenty-nine each for Germany, the UK, France and Italy) would marginalise smaller States. While a defeat was unlikely, a tighter margin would be quite a story. In the event, we were overruled on the studio issue, but we said that we would operate some coverage of the European referendum from the small TV news studio.

As the results started to flow in, it was clear that the Good Friday Agreement referendum would pass by approximately 95 per cent, but the Amsterdam Treaty was in difficulty. Seán and I jumped into action, and started to appropriately fill the programme from the broom cupboard that was the TV news headlines facility! All the major leaders of government and opposition parties, including Taoiseach Bertie Ahern, had to come in to defend the outcome, while squeezing past one another, in our tiny, cable-strewn box. We filled about a third of the air time of the special programmes, and had tremendous fun in doing so, against the odds. The final result, of 61.74 per cent for the proposition to 38.26 per cent against, was a shocking harbinger of a growing unease in the population with the forward trajectory of Europe. The trend that began to be demonstrated in 1998 had by June 2001 grown to a full-on defeat for the Nice Treaty by 54 per cent to 46 per cent. This was the referendum that had to be re-held a year later in order to achieve the government's desired result. It made an appalling charade of the democratic process, and the decision to hold a second referendum indicates a widespread disdain for democracy. Ireland was given the slight concession of the choice of opting out of EU Defence policy before the second vote in October 2002.

During my time editing *Questions & Answers*, I also instigated a programme on development issues, *Divided World*. This was international issues done economically, consisting mainly of bought-in reports from the excellent community of film-makers working in developing countries. Viewing and editing their pieces was extremely educational, and they worked with us to include an 'Irish angle' where that was possible. Myles Dungan presented the programme, which included vigorous discussions in the studio on subjects such as racism, 'charity begins at home', the Rwandan genocide and post-apartheid South Africa. Occasionally we travelled ourselves, making an interesting film on the Lesotho water dam, which was changing an ancient mountainous region of that country into a huge industrial landscape of engineering and pipes. This was being done to provide water for drought-stricken South Africa. We put the hard questions to Kader Asmal, South Africa's Minister for Water Affairs. He was, as always, charming and truthful, emphasising the complexity of the issue. He personally oversaw the provision of wells and pipes into the vast townships of South Africa. He admitted that there was a price paid by the rural communities in Lesotho: their landscape and historic way of life was undermined.

I filmed in Cuba, for *Divided World*, on the subject of the US embargo, and saw the substantial effects on children and the vulnerable of the difficulty in accessing pharmaceuticals. Despite the blockade, Cuba had the world's most exemplary health system, based on community hospitals, with free access for all to the care they needed. Cuba also had a remarkable education structure, and the highest level of literacy in Latin America, despite its low GDP. Already, though, the distortions of the market were causing unease. We interviewed a trained doctor who had been earning thirty dollars a month as a qualified medic in the Ear, Nose and Throat Department of Havana hospital. Although she was committed to this work, she had recently given it up to become a waitress in one of the central hotels, where she could make four times her salary from tourist tips. She hoped to return to medicine after a year or two. *Divided World* allowed us to bring educative and beautiful films to the Irish public on a television shoestring, thanks to the contribution of freelance film-makers. In 1996, I received the European Community Broadcasting Award from the European Community Humanitarian Organisation for *Divided World*.

Not all our times in current affairs television were serious and sombre. In the mid-1990s two colleagues, *Questions & Answers* researcher Liam O'Flanagan and current affairs reporter Jerry O'Callaghan, were about to retire. I got the job of arranging their party. I invited the senior managers of the organisation, and Joe Mulholland, who was then Controller of TV Programmes, was one of those who agreed to speak. He told a hilarious story. Back in the 1970s when Annie Maguire was wrongly accused of being an IRA bomb-maker, Joe went to London to do a story on her, accompanied by researcher Liam and reporter Jerry. He was, at the time, close enough to the Workers' Party line on Northern Ireland. Liam was very anti-republican and a supporter of Section 31, while Jerry was a west Cork nationalist. Each had their own distinct view of the Maguire story. They looked forward to arguing their positions over a glass of wine later in the hotel, but first they had to visit Annie Maguire for the pre-interview chat. She spoke to them in great detail, and they looked forward to filming a good piece in the morning. When they then got up to leave, Annie Maguire, a hospitable Irish woman, would have none of it. She had a stew in the pot, and beds made up in the spare room for the three of them. They could not demur. The image of these three large, opinionated men lying down side by side on single beds, after stew and pots of tea, is one that still makes me smile. Their plan for a convivial debate had to be held over for another day.

6

Battles with the Workers' Party

'No honest journalist should be willing to describe himself or herself as "embedded". To say, "I'm an embedded journalist" is to say, "I'm a government Propagandist".'

— Noam Chomsky[1]

When I joined RTÉ in 1979, I was excited at the prospect of making programmes about, and for, the real Ireland I knew; a country that was in need of fundamental change, with a dominant Catholic Church and a backward and inequitable social and economic system, but I soon found myself up against a different force.

The Workers' Party had emerged from a split in Sinn Féin and the IRA at the outset of the Troubles. Their background was in secretive militarism, and indeed the Official IRA travelled with them out of the split. In addition to this paramilitary base, they had adopted a form of socialist rhetoric, but one that was imbued with Moscow-based Stalinism. They were spoiling for a fight, and RTÉ was their major strategic target.

---

1   Cited in *Imperial Ambitions: Conversations on the Post-9/11 World, Interviews with David Barsamian* (Metropolitan Books, 2005), p. 34.

The place where the battle took place was in the unions, and specifically in number 15 branch of the Workers Union of Ireland. There I would meet union activists who became firm friends, and with them would take to task the infamous Ned Stapleton Cumann of the Workers' Party.

Conspiracy theorists, particularly in Fianna Fáil, have argued that RTÉ was totally under the control of the 'Stickies' in this period. The reality was more complicated, but they did attempt to exercise a stranglehold on the organisation and the programmes within it. They often did this by engaging in activities that were, in my opinion, diametrically opposed to their espoused respect for workers and their rights.

I had been very active in the National Union of Journalists in my years as a reporter on the *Irish Medical Times*, and had been a delegate to conferences in England twice. I now had to leave the NUJ, and became involved with the union that represented producers: the Workers Union of Ireland. When I walked into my first meeting, I found myself in the middle of a cauldron of intrigue and debate. The Workers' Party people, led by John Caden and Tish Barry, had dominated the Section Committee of the union during the late 1970s. They had won representation from the 200 programmes people, who were entitled to five committee seats. The clerical and administration members, who numbered 300, were entitled to only four seats on the committee. This piece of gerrymandering was enough in itself to cause resentment in the clerical administration grades. Their fury was added to by the refusal of the Workers' Party committee members to support their pay battle in 1979, telling them that the offer from management of 3 per cent was more than fair. Some felt that it was because they thought that conflict about money for cash-strapped grades was beneath them. Others saw it as more straightforwardly careerist.

I arrived at RTÉ in time to see the rise of a new and more representative leadership. Brian Higgins and Josephine

Hogan were committed trade unionists without political party baggage. They were taking on the aggressive and vociferous Workers' Party activists fearlessly, and were inspiring. They engineered change in the standing orders, to allow the committee to become six clerical/administration members with just three from the programmes side. I was elected as one of the programme representatives. Soon, this conflict within the RTÉ section was played out in the wider number 15 branch.

I have detailed elsewhere the long battle with the Workers' Party people who favoured the censorship involved in Section 31. But here, on straightforward industrial issues, their influence was equally negative. When in 1980 radio producer Pat Feeley made a hard-hitting documentary about McElligott's Garage in Castleisland, County Kerry, he ruffled important feathers, and RTÉ management decided to move against him. A tribunal of enquiry was set up and, in a disgraceful development, RTÉ employed a private detective to follow Feeley to ascertain who his contacts in the garage were. At a meeting of radio producers, I proposed a resolution of strike action in support of Pat Feeley, which was widely supported. John Caden virulently opposed any such action. Feeley had exasperated him by supporting the clerical admin grades in 1979. In what was to become characteristic name-calling, Pat Feeley was dubbed a 'Provo' and a 'Trotskyite' by Caden and his followers. Nothing could be further from the truth. Pat Feeley had been in the Limerick Labour Party for many years, where he was a supporter of Jim Kemmy, and he rejoined that party later after he had left RTÉ.

Looking back on the minutes of the Section Committee in the early 1980s, it is instructive to see how busy and dedicated we were on the bread and butter issues of trade unionism: casualisation, new technology, pay improvements, shift allowances and the correct boarding of promotions. My colleagues on the Section Committee came from all political backgrounds and none. We became bound together by the work we did in maintaining an eagle eye on the management. For instance, when it was proposed that count assistants in the 1982 general election should be paid a small fee, instead of the overtime to which they were entitled, the minutes said it straightforwardly: 'Brian Higgins and Patricia Grennan put them right on that.' The other members of the committee were Eilis Boland, Ian Wilson, Paddy Goode, Pat Malone, Jo Wheatley, Nuala Gormley, Muriel Carney, Marian O'Neill and Katherine Cahill. They diverged in personality as they did in politics, ranging from polite to outspoken, grey-suited to hippies, from meticulous to passionate, and all places in between. It was an honour to work with each of them. Reading back on those minutes, it is apparent that service to members, and in particular dedication to the lower-paid grades, was the overriding consideration.

While we in the majority of the committee busied ourselves with issues of pay and conditions, the Ned Stapleton Cumann of the Workers' Party was laying its sights on a much bigger prize: control of the fledgling television current affairs programme *Today Tonight*. Founded in 1980, *Today Tonight* would quickly earn its nickname of '*Today Tonight*: the Workers' Programme.' As *Magill* magazine reported in 1982: 'out of a total of 16 editorial staff on *Today Tonight*, 6 hold views very similar to the positions of the Workers' Party. These are Joe Mulholland, the Editor, Tish Barry, Gerry Gregg, Barry O'Halloran, David Blake Knox, Joe Little.'[2] In their in-depth study of the Workers' Party, *The Lost Revolution*, Brian Hanley and Scott Millar gave the following view:

> Although Mulholland never committed himself to movement discipline, he did recruit a number of

---

2   Vincent Browne, 'SFWP 7 – The Slanting of a Programme' (*Magill*, 1982).

young reporters and journalists to the programme who were closely aligned with the Ned Stapleton Cumann. These included (Gerry) Gregg, Barry O'Halloran, Joe Little, David Blake Knox and later Una Claffey ... critics complained that SFWP members were regularly interviewed on *Today Tonight* without their party affiliation being revealed.[3]

Mary McAleese, who worked as a reporter on the programme at the time, told her biographer Ray McManus that her time on the programme was 'the worst period of her life.'[4]

Today Tonight did some interesting programmes, mainly on economic issues, such as youth unemployment and the Stardust fire in the early 1980s. The blind spot about Northern Ireland, however, was manifest, and the Workers' Party's battle with Provisional Sinn Féin for votes was played out on the national canvass of RTÉ's current affairs flagship. We can only now wonder at the scenario in April 1981, where Bernadette Devlin McAliskey, just a few months after being riddled with UDA bullets, found herself sitting opposite Glenn Barr, then a UDA leader, in a *Today Tonight* studio. He was allowed to hold forth, justifying the loyalist campaign, while his republican opposite numbers remained silenced.[5] Joe Mulholland later stated that the programme was a grave error and should not have happened.

Colleagues who worked in current affairs under Joe Mulholland, and later under Eugene Murray, describe the Friday meetings where plans were thrashed out and

---

3   Brian Hanley and Scott Millar, *The Lost Revolution: The Story of the Official IRA and the Workers' Party* (Penguin Ireland, 2009), pp. 374-375.

4   Gerry Gregg, 'RTÉ, The Stickie Myth and Falling Standards' (*Magill*, 2005).

5   Vincent Browne, 'SFWP 7 – The Slanting of a Programme'.

decided as essentially Workers' Party vetting arenas. Some independent team members tried to reflect honestly what was going on in the country. Jerry O'Callaghan, then a reporter in *Today Tonight*, tells of a brilliantly articulate argument put forward by Brendan O'Brien on the day after the Gibraltar shootings in March 1988, for a programme on the issue. His pitch was met with stony silence. Some debate ensued, and finally editor Eugene Murray commented that it would be too difficult to find a Spanish translator, despite Gibraltar being almost entirely English-speaking. Jerry felt compelled to name what was going on: 'You just don't want to do it, isn't that right, Eugene?' Murray agreed that was the case. ITV went on to make the award-winning *Death on the Rock* programme. RTÉ current affairs was deeply damaged, and not for the first time.

Meanwhile, the number 15 branch of the Workers Union of Ireland was having its own dramas. The meetings took place in a hall at the back of Parnell Square, and they were heated and difficult. As well as the RTÉ section, the branch included other semi-State staff, and academic staff from the university and third-level sector. We discussed national pay bargaining and East Timor, women's rights and higher education funding. At one national conference of the union, General Secretary Paddy Cardiff, in accepting our resolution that a crèche should be provided at the National Conference, said that yes, he thought that a crèche would be a good idea, for the delegates of number 15 branch! There was not much space for women in the trade union representative movement.

There was a mix of people in the branch, most of them left-wing and radical to varying degrees. In 1981, the Workers' Party's Una Claffey was branch chair at the annual general meeting. A year later, she was defeated for that role by Brian Higgins. John Caden had been on the union executive, supported by the Workers' Party caucus in RTÉ, and by wider 'Stickie' support in the union. By 1983, the growing unpopularity of the Workers' Party clique allowed Brian Higgins to wrestle the Executive seat from Caden. There were emotive speeches and dramatic votes to be taken. The backdrop was the Workers' Party losing control in the RTÉ section because of their controversial support for Section 31, and because they had served staff interests there so badly.

In 1988 I ran against John Caden for the union executive position, and defeated him. I then served on the Federated Workers' Union of Ireland executive for a number of years, up until the amalgamation with the ITGWU, and the merger into what became SIPTU.

These seemingly distant bureaucratic squabbles for the leadership of the union branch were watched with huge interest back in RTÉ. They were a sign that the Workers' Party faction was susceptible to defeat. Eoghan Harris, a capable orator, had dominated RTÉ union meetings for over ten years. He had an enormous capacity to bully and charm to get his own way. I had myself received a hugely effusive card from him following a debate I had on television in 1982, where I defended *Women Today* against criticism by Desmond Fennell. My interview was 'brilliant', and 'exposed Fennell entirely', he said. He would flatter individual colleagues and try to get them into his network.

Many friends told me stories over the years of being taken for a drink by Harris, who would regale them for hours with entertaining stories, before asking them if they wished to work with him on some party project or other. On the other side of this charm was a loud, intimidating presence at meetings, where anyone who disagreed with him was denounced and shouted down. I soon became a victim of the second mode. Those of my colleagues in the Radio Centre who opposed him, and I, found ourselves described as 'Hush Puppies' by Harris, by which he meant supporters of Provisional Sinn Féin. Among the people who withstood this barrage were

Roisin Boyd, Patrick Farrelly, Ronan O'Donoghue and Alex White. It was extremely damaging to people's careers, but Harris, and his colleagues John Caden and Gerry Gregg, merely considered this to be collateral damage in their battle for supremacy.

By 1986 the hegemony of the Workers' Party in the RTÉ trade unions was in decline. Caden had been defeated for the executive once already, Claffey had moved to the NUJ, and Harris and Gerry Gregg were on their way out of RTÉ, preparing to set up an independent production company with Soviet Union backing. The ambition remained large and vainglorious. Seán Garland, who was General Secretary of the Workers' Party at the time, wrote to the central committee of the Communist Party of the Soviet Union. The letter introduced the 'talented team' of Gregg, Harris and Caden and their project, 'ISKRA – a Marxist film-making enterprise which commands this party's full support.' Without any sense of irony or self-doubt, the company was named after Lenin's Bolshevik newspaper of 1917, *Iskra*, meaning 'spark'. The letter went on to explain: 'Some members of the WP had formed ISKRA [which] fosters in an environment hostile to a Marxist analysis of many of the problems confronting Western society.' Such an analysis would be delivered through their programmes, it argued. It is worth remembering that part of the hectoring of the previous years in the trade unions, and by solicitors' letters to *Magill* and other publications, was a constant denial of membership of the Workers' Party by these individuals, under threat of legal redress. Now, however, RTÉ was being left behind and honesty to benefactors was required. Yet, extraordinarily, and to this day, Gerry Gregg continues to get major commissions from RTÉ for his programmes. When Eoghan Harris finally left the Workers' Party in 1990 after a number of strained battles, he was interviewed by Jerry O'Callaghan for *Today Tonight*. 'I'm a propagandist and always have been', he said, 'that's what I do.' It is hard to argue with that self-assessment.

By 1987, many of the activists on the Section Committee were the same names as earlier in the decade. They were joined by other capable and dedicated people, Alex White, Brigid Ruane and Eibhlín Ní Ghabhláin. John Caden was on the section committee, at this time, the only member of the Workers' Party faction who was still so involved. A bitter row erupted concerning industrial action taken in pursuit of the twenty-sixth pay round in October 1987. There had been a two-to-one ballot for industrial action, and the strike committee had decided on targeted stoppages in radio and television. *The Gay Byrne Show* was the radio programme selected. On Wednesday, 30 September, according to the minutes of the section meeting of 8 October, it was put to John Caden that he had turned up for work, along with Gay Byrne, on the day of the stoppage. He said that he had come in to meet with his union rep. Other members of the section committee pointed out that John Caden had said that he was turning up for work, and instructed members of his team to so do. The branch secretary said that he found it strange that someone would turn up to see him, since he had no plan to be in RTÉ until he was informed by Nuala Gormley/O'Neill that people were coming into work. When John Caden continued his denial, Alex White suggested that John write to the *Sunday Tribune*, which had said that he had attended for work, to repudiate this claim. He could make it clear that he had supported the union's stand. This he refused to do. He then circulated a petition to look for a re-examination of the way in which the dispute would be run. Branch secretary Bernard Browne pointed out that this petition, in the middle of an industrial dispute, undermined the union's position:

> The reality was that John Caden stands above and outside the wishes of the membership. We have a

mandate, and even if you think you know better, you have no right to undermine that mandate.[6]

Brigid Ruane said that there was a difference between arguing your point of view, and waiting until action had been taken and then starting to go around with petitions. That was divisive and undermining. As a trade unionist she said that she would be ashamed if anyone caught her at that during a strike. There was no point in voting for industrial action if it could be so easily undermined.[7] Feelings were understandably impassioned, and the issue taken very seriously.

The section committee voted to pursue a Rule 12 against John Caden, for action injurious to the interests of the union. This was proposed by Alex White and seconded by Josephine Hogan, and was passed unanimously. The enquiry was requested for the following reasons:

1. That allegations have been made that the member in question turned up for work on the occasion of industrial action by this union, contrary to express instructions.

2. That allegations have been made that the member in question encouraged other members of staff on the Gay Byrne Show to turn up for work on the same occasion.

3. That the member in question has refused, during a meeting of this Section Committee, to repudiate a statement in the national press that he did in fact turn up for work on the occasion in question.

4. That the member in question has confirmed, during a meeting of this Section Committee, that he was

---

6   Section committee minutes, Federated Workers' Union of Ireland, 8 October 1987.

7   Section committee minutes. 8 October 1987.

instrumental in organising a petition calling for a general meeting of the union. This petition was compiled during the course of the industrial action – action which had been duly mandated, in line with the democratic procedures of the union. This [Section] Committee asks the General Executive Committee to make a determination as to whether the conduct of the member in question constitutes 'conduct injurious to the interests of the union and its members' as set out in rule 12.[8]

The resolution was proposed by Alex White and seconded by Josephine Hogan. It was passed unanimously.

In the weeks that followed, Eoghan Harris got involved by mounting a major attack on the union. He said that the members had been called out on strike against their wishes (despite a two-to-one vote for the action). He also said that the section was being run by a 'Provo Faction'. Harris was asked to attend the next section committee to substantiate his allegations. He replied by stating that he was resigning from the union, and going to the press with allegations of a 'Provo faction' running the RTÉ union. In my opinion this was a gigantic distracting tactic, to take attention away from the very serious Rule 12 investigation against his comrade, John Caden. But it was also very damaging to the union, and to individual members on the section committee.

The committee responded with a statement that it was an elected industrial committee of the union, whose sole responsibility was to represent the interests of its members. It invited any member to inspect the minutes of the previous years to demonstrate the committee's concentration on normal industrial issues. The notion that they were preoccupied with Section 31 was undermined by the fact that it had been almost

---

8   Section committee minutes. 20 October 1987.

a year since the issue was raised at the committee. At a meeting of the general union membership nine months before, a motion reaffirming opposition to section 31 (in common with other unions in RTÉ) was passed by an overwhelming majority of the attendance at the meeting. Mr Harris was asked to withdraw his defamatory remarks.

Eoghan Harris replied by withdrawing his resignation and determining to continue his fight within the union. The General Secretary, Bill Attley, wrote to him saying that he could not rescind his resignation until he had unconditionally withdrawn his allegations against the union and the section committee. Bill Attley wrote to Bernard Browne in February 1988 to say that Eoghan Harris had now withdrawn his letter of resignation. Attley stated that this did not in any way excuse his attack on democratically elected representatives, and that:

> ... the General Executive Committee has directed that I inform the Section Committee that it has the full support and confidence of the General Executive Committee, and regards these unwarranted attacks as damaging to the interest of the membership in RTÉ.[9]

The investigating committee on the Rule 12 proceedings against John Caden found the case to be unproven. The allegation had been that he had come into work with the intention of working. As the branch secretary Bernard Browne explained to the Section AGM in February 1988, the investigating committee found that you can't try a person on their intentions, and the case was therefore unproven.[10]

---

9   Letter from B. Attley to B. Browne on behalf of the General Executive Committee. Recorded in section committee minutes, 2 February 1988.
10 Minutes of Section Annual General Meeting, Federated Workers' Union of Ireland, 11 February 1988.

At the Section AGM held on 11 February 1988, I proposed a motion of thanks to the Section Committee for their work in the previous year. The attacks on the committee were reminiscent of McCarthyism, I said. This was vocally opposed at the meeting by Gerry Gregg and John Caden. The motion read:

> That this meeting offers a vote of thanks on behalf of the members to the officers of the union for all the work they have done on our behalf this year, and condemns the campaign of vilification against the officers and members of the Section Committee.

This was passed by an overwhelming majority, with only two votes against. A few months later, in a reflection of that mood, I was elected to the Federated Workers Union Executive to represent the branch for the next three years. One of many issues with which the Section Committee in the late 1980s was involved was that of Section 31, to the chagrin of the Workers' Party faction.

In 1994 began the next stage of my personal battle with Eoghan Harris. In late February of that year I had invited Harris to appear on *Questions & Answers* to debate the issues of the week. My memory of his inclusion was that it was my idea, though my head of department took some convincing, being concerned at the possibility of his libelling people. I was therefore surprised, but not amazed, to read Harris's analysis of his inclusion, written in an article in *The Sunday Times* entitled 'Time for the Media to Get Tough', published on 13 March. In an extraordinary, and untrue, set of convoluted arguments, Harris claimed that a three-year boycott of his appearing on the programme had been ended only with the intervention of the Director General of RTÉ, and that I was using my position as editor of *Questions & Answers* to keep him and his arguments off the airwaves. It was a very damaging piece, and one that I could not allow to stand unchallenged. The case was taken by me personally, and the Controller of Programmes at the time, Liam Miller, made it clear that he thought it unwise. If I lost the case, my position would be untenable and I would lose my role as editor. At home, I worried that the costs might mean losing the house, but I was determined to press ahead to clear my good name. The case was against *The Sunday Times*, not Harris himself. I had no interest in pauperising someone who was a political opponent. I was fortunate to have Hugh Carty as my solicitor in the case, and he instructed Adrian Hardiman as counsel.

The implication of Harris's piece was that I was a Provo sympathiser and did not relish disagreement with their position. Hardiman asked me just one question at our counsel briefing: 'Have you ever been a member of Sinn Féin, even at college?' I replied that I had not, although I had been a member of many left-wing and socialist groupings at that time. He was satisfied that the attempted witch-hunt would not succeed under court questioning, and proceeded to take on the case. In the meantime, I collected affidavits from people who saw me as damaged by the piece. I also had to approach the Director General to ask him to appear, to challenge the central mistruth that I had been instructed by him to invite Harris on the programme. Joe Barry told me that he would be happy to clear up the matter, and the preparations for the case continued.

Two and a half years later, on 13 December 1996, *The Sunday Times* settled the case on the steps of the court for a five-figure sum and, most importantly, a front-page apology. John Bowman, always the kindest and most loyal friend, came to court with me without knowing that the case would be settled. He took a huge risk with regard to his own reputation by so doing, but then he knew the truth of what had happened. Harris had been just one of the names we had discussed that morning in 1994, and I had been anxious to have him on as a highly entertaining panellist. There was no conspiracy.

What is more difficult to understand is RTÉ management's approach in continuing to give major political and historic subjects to these people to make programmes. RTÉ got itself into serious hot water when it commissioned a four-part series on Des O'Malley from Gerry Gregg and Eoghan Harris's company, now renamed Praxis Pictures, in 2001. O'Malley had been Minister for Justice in Jack Lynch's government of 1970, and had supported the Lynch line that Charles Haughey and Neil Blaney had acted independently in their plot to import arms for the nationalist community at the time. The evidence now suggests that the wider Cabinet was involved, and there is strong evidence to suggest that Jim Gibbons, Lynch's Minister of Defence, knew of the plan. As the *Sunday Business Post* put it on 6 May 2001:

> What is so remarkable about the O'Malley documentary is that Gregg succeeded in peddling his views through one of the most important and costly political profiles that RTÉ has broadcast in decades. What is even more remarkable is that RTÉ let him. No one at senior level in RTÉ was unaware of Gregg's politics. Apparently some also knew that Harris was a co-director of Gregg's latest production company, Praxis Pictures.
>
> Harris and Gregg are not just ideological soulmates. Harris has also provided a chorus of approval through his *Sunday Times* column for virtually all Gregg's productions over the last few years. One was described as 'spellbinding', another as 'brilliant', another as 'worthy of an award'.[11]

---

11 Unnamed, 'Peoples Workers' Friend', in the *Sunday Business Post*, 6 May 2001.

It was always highly unlikely that an ideologue like Gregg was going to produce a balanced view of Des O'Malley. He was the figure chosen to represent in the most simplistic terms Gregg's own battle with republicanism and nationalism. From the opening of the first part, O'Malley was referred to in chummy terms as 'Des', and as 'the boy from Corbally ... with a gleam of mischief in his eye.' Gene Kerrigan, in the *Sunday Independent* of 6 May, brilliantly dissected the first programme, in which he had been invited to participate, as a 'token dissident'. It would be a 'warts and all' profile, he was told by Gregg.

> I did not subscribe to the view that O'Malley is a moral or political giant, and tried to provide Praxis with the requested warts. It crossed my mind, as I was pushed to say something positive about O'Malley and the Beef Tribunal, that the stuff about the warts might be cut. Nah, I told myself, don't be paranoid ... Watching the first part of the documentary last Sunday night, I got a sinking feeling. Not a wart in sight.[12]

Referring to the description of O'Malley as 'the boy from Corbally' with 'a gleam of mischief in his eye', Kerrigan remarked that he then knew 'we're straying from documentary into a branch of show business.'[13] The lack of objectivity was entirely predictable, and many of us in the producer group had warned management about the dangers inherent in this undertaking. We were told that the programmes had been commissioned by Joe Mulholland when he was Controller of Television Programmes, and that the series

---

12   Gene Kerrigan, 'Fluffing over bruising realities', *Sunday Independent*, 6 May 2001.

13   Ibid.

would be scrutinised to maintain objectivity and credibility. Cathal Goan, Head of Television, said at the time, 'I have seen the first programme and I am reasonably happy that it is objective. There is an editorial line to be detected in it; it is very anti-Provo, but it is not strident.'[14] In the event, the series was to cause major problems for RTÉ's reputation for being fair to all concerned in that it canonised O'Malley and whitewashed any conflicting evidence of his actions. While it might be bureaucratically understandable that a programme commissioned by a former Controller would be considered for broadcast, there was a major dereliction of duty on RTÉ's part in allowing the broadcast of these simplistic and propagandistic programmes.

The biggest problem posed immediately for RTÉ was that its current affairs programme *Prime Time* had a big scoop. It had unearthed evidence that O'Malley, as Minister for Justice, had signed a certificate of privilege in October 1970. It directed that a file containing a contentious witness statement, alleging that Jim Gibbons knew about the plot to import arms, be withheld from the court. This had the effect of allowing the trial of Haughey to go ahead, since it would otherwise have been aborted. The evidence was from a very senior figure in the Irish Army, Colonel Michael Hefferon. Des O'Malley exercised a political judgement when he ordered the file to be withheld.

O'Malley had been pursued by *Prime Time* and other news sources for a response to this suppression of material, and had so far declined to comment. With his own credibility now in question, he decided to speak exclusively to Gregg's documentary to clear the issue once and for all. There would be no other interviews given. Gene Kerrigan commented with his usual insight and accuracy:

---

14   E. O'Reilly, 'RTÉ bosses angry over O'Malley article', *Sunday Business Post*, 6 May 2001.

The series should have been postponed, perhaps for months. There was no hurry. It purported to be an assessment of a 30-year career. The chips are still falling. Instead the transmission date was brought forward and a ten-minute section, allowing O'Malley to respond to the revelations, was hurriedly inserted.

A supposedly reflective documentary was allowed to take on a clumsy news and current affairs role. Appearing as though he was in the hands of fans with cameras, O'Malley used the documentary to hide behind. This was his one exposure to the media, the one occasion on which proper answers could be sought to valid questions. He could refuse to answer anyone else, saying he dealt with that in the documentary.

Here's how tough the questioning was: 'You have nothing to fear?' Trapped by this relentless probing, O'Malley conceded that the revelations gave him nothing to fear.[15]

The reason I have dealt with this subject in such depth is that it provides a real example of how the management of RTÉ continued on a course of action with Praxis Pictures that could end only in disaster. They were in the hands of propagandists who were determined to use their expensive commission to push a party line. And the facts, as Eoghan Harris had argued in his training document *Television and Terrorism*, were not sacred, whereas opinion, or perspective, was. Second only to *Mission to Prey* in its fallout, the Des O'Malley series undermined RTÉ's authority to deal fairly with the highly contentious and sensitive subject of Northern Ireland, and it left Fianna Fáil politicians, in particular, feeling that they had been the victims of a skewed political analysis

---

15   Ibid.

that was out to denigrate them. Gene Kerrigan's summation was apposite:

> That Praxis chose to act as it did neither concerns or surprises me, given that in this newspaper last week, Gerry Gregg denounced *Prime Time*'s 'so-called' revelations. An unwillingness or inability to recognise a genuinely troubling development suggests that Praxis simply isn't up to dealing with its subject matter in an adult way.
>
> What is of concern is that RTÉ, as the commissioner and broadcaster, has been a party to allowing a central figure in a controversy, Dessie O'Malley, use a rather fluffy documentary series to blur the record on issues that are of both historical and current importance.[16]

As the hostile fallout to the documentary series gathered pace, Gerry Gregg's partner in Praxis Pictures, Eoghan Harris, leapt to his defence in a familiar way. Anyone who disliked the documentary had to be guilty of 'bad politics', or by implication be sympathetic to the Provos. This was the way in which Harris prevented legitimate debate about issues in his heyday in RTÉ. The suggestion of bad politics was enough to worry staffers on their way up the career ladder in RTÉ. But the riposte to Harris's contention on this occasion came from an unlikely source, *Irish Independent* TV reviewer John Boland. Writing on 12 May 2001, he said:

> This is probably going to get me into all sorts of trouble (in fact I know it is) with Eoghan Harris, who is one of the people behind the series and who

---

16   Ibid.

suggested in his *Sunday Times* column last weekend that only those with 'bad politics' could possibly take issue with Des O'Malley's stance on the current Arms Trial controversy.[17]

Boland went on to say that he was largely on the same page as O'Malley and Harris on many issues, but he refused to accept Harris's contention that 'if you're not totally with him, you're against him.' He went on:

> If I say that the first two instalments of *Des O'Malley: A Public Life* were a hysterical mess, it's not because I hate the Stickies (to whom Eoghan Harris and director Gerry Gregg once belonged, as if I care, though they obviously do) or because (God Forbid!) I'm some crypto Provo, but because the tone struck me as embarrassing, the structuring as inept, and the intention disingenuous, if not dishonest. Does that make me guilty of 'bad politics'? I don't think so – it just makes me resistant to bad programme-making or bad journalism, or whatever you want to call it.[18]

This is a fair assessment of a pitiable series of programmes. More importantly, from the point of view of an understanding of the influence and power of certain Workers' Party individuals in RTÉ, it demonstrates the power of intimidatory tactics in attempting to silence dissent. Happily, on this occasion, some columnists decided to resist this approach, and many did speak truthfully from their varied perspectives. Even so, the judgement of senior members of RTÉ's management in allowing the programmes to be completed and broadcast

---

17 John Boland, 'Glenroe: Dozing off into the sunset', *Irish Independent*, 12 May 2001.
18 Ibid.

indicates the extent of the influence the Workers' Party continued to have in RTÉ up to 2001. It should have been the role of the management to prevent such a hijacking of the airwaves, in the public interest. Instead, they facilitated the commission and broadcasts.

Over my thirty-odd years of working in the unions in RTÉ, more than half of those years were locked in combat with the forces of the Workers' Party and their supporters. Some colleagues gave them backing out of fear, others because they were broadly sympathetic to their views. But the large number of union activists who worked with me on section and branch committees during those years, and who worked primarily on issues of trade union conditions, but also in opposition to State censorship, knew a fundamental truth about the members of the Ned Stapleton Cumann: they could not be relied upon to support staff interests.

When Bertie Ahern called a general election in April 2007, Eoghan Harris was first in line to cheer him, and to denounce consistently the work of the Mahon tribunal, which, he said, was based on 'the ravings of Tom Gilmartin.' On *The Late Late Show*, just before the election, Harris, on top form, poured scorn on commentators who were criticising Ahern over his personal finances. It was a performance that many believe won Ahern the election. On 3 August 2007, Bertie Ahern, returned to power as Taoiseach, appointed Eoghan Harris to the Senate for the next four years at a salary of almost €70,000 per annum. Back in RTÉ, the section committee of SIPTU continued to defend its members against the onslaught of cuts brought about by the severe economic recession, primarily caused by Fianna Fáil policies. In 2013, as in the 1980s, the job of defending staff interests fell to unpaid genuine trade union activists. Some things just don't change.

7

The RTÉ Authority

'There is a saying that no institution is large enough to house one human soul.'

— Lelia Doolan[1]

I have sat at many desks and tables in my years in RTÉ. In the Radio Centre I had held forth in many pulpits in the open-plan office among my colleagues. When I went over to be editor of *Questions & Answers* in television, I shared a tiny ten-by-eight office with my researcher colleague Liam O'Flanagan for seven years. After the new building, known as Stage Seven, was built, and my empire had expanded to include a programme with Brian Farrell, called *Farrell*, and a development programme, *Divided World*, I moved to a larger office of my own, overlooking bamboo trees and a water feature. Later again, in *The Late Late Show*, *Would You Believe* and *The View*, I was back to an open-plan office with a pedestrian view of the side car park.

---

1   Lelia Doolan, *Institutions and their Use of Power*, RTÉ Radio lecture, 2003. Quoted on Aislingmagazine.com (accessed 28.01.14).

Perhaps the strangest table I ever sat at was the French-polished mahogany table of the boardroom on the third floor of the administration block, where I sat on the RTÉ Authority for five years. Here we would be pampered and cajoled by the most senior executives in RTÉ, in the hope that we would allow them to run the organisation in the way they believed was best. We nine members would be given detailed documentation, tea in china cups, and lavish lunches where we could talk with members of staff. It was all rather surreal to someone who had worked at the coalface of programme-making for over twenty years. It gave me a tremendous insight into the complex nature of the work of RTÉ's Director General, in particular. To maintain the agreement of a board of relative innocents, while also placating the minister and his officials, and keeping the staff feeling upbeat, was a huge and demanding role. Seeing it up close, despite many strange moments, was revealing and educative.

In April 1995, I ran in an election to be the staff member on the RTÉ Authority. This was a new initiative, instigated by Minister for Arts, Culture and the Gaeltacht, Michael D. Higgins. There was great interest in the role, and over twenty candidates. I was fortunate to be chosen by my peers, receiving 731 first-preference votes, and in due course I received a call from the minister. He congratulated me, and asked me to serve on the board. He stressed that my role would be primarily to serve the public interest, as well as reflecting the views of staff at the boardroom table. In the next five years I would often be asked to comment on how my colleagues would react to a particular policy or development. I did what I could to contribute in an honest way, and to look after both their interests and broadcasting in a wider sense.

The Authority was chaired by Professor Farrell Corcoran, an esteemed academic and a serious advocate for public service broadcasting, about which he had written extensively. Former Taoiseach Garret FitzGerald was there, and I was surprised to find myself in agreement with him on many things during our term of office. Trade unionists Des Geraghty and Bill Attley were a formidable pair of voices, often huddled together at the end of the table. Anne Haslam, a tax consultant with Fine Gael connections, was a proponent of a classical music station, and articulated, among other things, a strong liking for Formula One racing! Anne Tannahill was a soft-spoken Belfast publisher, who was later replaced by the warm and wise Pat Hume. Fine Gael businesswoman Maureen Rennicks was with us briefly, and then was replaced by the loquacious and populist voice of Patricia Redlich of the *Sunday Independent*. Bob Quinn, the Connemara film-maker, was a member, and determined to make a difference. I applauded his enthusiasm and commitment, but often wished he would go about things with more deftness and diplomacy in order to convince other members. The management was already distressed by his appointment, and some spoke to me in apocalyptic terms about the damage Bob could do. I surveyed the room as we were introduced at the first meeting in June 1995, and thought: here was a group with mainly positive intentions. We could probably do some good.

The Director General at the time was Joe Barry, a Cork man of easy charm, who had been appointed by the previous Fianna Fáil-appointed Authority. His term of office had eighteen months more to run, and he proved adept at seeing off challenges. He would take members aside individually to argue a particular case, and he was robust in the meeting room. The first battle I had with him concerned the publication of a newsletter for staff.

One of the promises I had made in my election literature was to connect the Authority with staff by way of a monthly newsletter. People were not cynical about the role of the Authority, but felt that it was remote from their concerns. I was determined to initiate a connection between the most powerful body within the organisation and the staff on the ground. I raised this at the first meeting. Joe Barry said that it simply could not be done: there were commercial sensitivities, and members of the Authority had to feel free to express themselves without fear of being quoted. I argued the position, and made it clear that I could not renege on a solemn undertaking given in the course of an important poll. Joe Barry asked for some time to consider the situation, a tactic that I would see used over many subjects in the coming months. I agreed to give him some time, but underlined the urgency of the matter, in that staff would expect a report on this first meeting, and I intended to give it.

Over the next two weeks, Joe and Farrell Corcoran entreated me to drop this demand. Farrell offered to do his own newsletter, but I insisted that this would be seen as a corporate fudge. At the end of the two weeks I said that I had my copy ready to print, and if there was an attempt to prevent publication, I would go to the minister on the issue. This caused the Chairman and DG to shift their position. They asked me whether I would be amenable to the Chairman reading my newsletter each month before it was published, to ensure that commercial information might not be gleaned by the broadcasting opposition. Since I had no intention of leaking such material, this was not a difficulty. The newsletter was permitted. I had won an important battle, but I was now aware that any attempt to modify things would be hard-fought.

We were entering a changing landscape in broadcasting. Public service broadcasting, perceived as 'an instrument of enlightenment' by BBC Director General John Reith in the 1920s, was facing competition on a number of fronts. It had been six years since former minister Ray Burke had vindictively capped the number of advertising minutes RTÉ was allowed per hour, causing a budgetary crisis for the organisation. He had also sanctioned two new national radio and television channels, and twenty-one local radio channels.

TV3 was firmly on the map, while the minister's favourite, Century Radio, had been replaced by Radio Ireland. The local radio stations were winning up to 50 per cent of the listening audience. Now we would be facing more competition in the new digital television age, and the issue of how to construct that digital future became a central concern for us each month. There were rumours that the transmission network was about to be privatised. Michael D. Higgins, the new minister, was a friend of public service broadcasting, and would have shared the view of Huw Wheldon, former BBC Director General, that 'multiplicity does not mean choice'. He wanted to support the public service ethos of quality programmes underpinning Ireland's national identity, while also ensuring plurality, fairness and impartiality. He had proven his principle of supporting free speech by his abolition of Section 31 the previous year. Now he was to set out his perspective on broadcasting change with his Green Paper of 1995. It was entitled *Active or Passive? Broadcasting in the Future Tense.*

Senior management were aghast at some of the provisions. An Irish-language television service would be set up, but RTÉ would be forced to provide one hour of free programming to the fledgling station each day, with no new money provided for this. While RTÉ's senior executives were largely sympathetic to the inauguration of a new Irish-language service, this was a huge financial hit, of the order of €5m per annum. The position of independent broadcasters was to be placed on a statutory footing, with up to 20 per cent of TV programme budgets to be spent on independent production. The Independent Radio and Television Commission was to be superseded by a Broadcasting Authority of Ireland, which would cover both RTÉ and the independent broadcasters. The RTÉ Authority would be replaced by a new 'super authority', with responsibility for both sectors. Most importantly, the digital future required regulation. It was proposed that a new body, DTT (Digital

Terrestrial Television), would oversee this transition. It might not be led by RTÉ, or even by a national consortium. The danger of players such as Rupert Murdoch's Sky Corporation coming in and controlling access to the airwaves had to be forestalled. The minister's proposal saw RTÉ lose control of the transmission network.

RTÉ began its counter-attack. It was imperative that continuity of service would be guaranteed by national control of the network. RTÉ needed to have exclusive control of one digital multiplex. In addition, it was vital that we would maintain as many important sports fixtures as possible as national, free-to-air events, to allow the audience to view these live. RTÉ, with Authority approval, began to push on all these fronts.

Over the next few years, we spent many fractious hours attempting to ameliorate proposals on broadcasting developments, as Michael D. Higgins gave way to a new Fianna Fáil minister, Síle de Valera, in 1997. She was slow to see the need for Ireland Inc. to grasp the opportunity provided by digital television, and to support the public–private partnership, DIGICO, that RTÉ was proposing. But we did have some success on the designation of major sporting events such as All-Ireland finals, the opening matches of the European (UEFA) soccer championships and the Aintree Grand National as free to viewers. The list is constantly updated, and recently the Rugby Six Nations championship was added.

There were a number of individuals sitting at the Authority table who, I believe, had a deep commitment to ethical broadcasting. They were Garret FitzGerald, Des Geraghty, Bob Quinn, Farrell Corcoran, Anne Tannahill, Pat Hume and me. We were each individually concerned about the invasive and destructive power of advertising to children, and we were determined to see something done about it.

There was no one more tenacious on the subject than Bob Quinn. At the second meeting of the Authority in July 1995, he began an onslaught, which would continue over the next four years. His diligence concentrated minds. Bob proposed an outright ban on advertising and sponsorship during children's programmes. The Director General, Joe Barry, pointed out that this would cost the organisation €4m and, in his estimate, fifty jobs would be lost at the station. This assessment, at best a conjecture, caused trade unionists Bill Attley and Des Geraghty to assert that nothing should be done without a full awareness of the financial implications. They made the only serious argument in favour of toy advertising: Irish manufacturers would be disadvantaged in the competitive toy market, while large and better-funded international companies would remain free to advertise on other television channels.

My view was that Bob's principled but extreme position could not win the day, so I proposed something that I considered would be achievable: a moratorium on advertising to children during the six-week run-up to Christmas. As a parent myself, and having broadcast many programmes on the issue, I knew that this period was when disadvantaged families were put under severe pressure because of the illusory promises of toy advertising. I also pushed for a more detailed and properly prepared debate on the subject at the September meeting, giving the Chairman and Director General time to make some concrete proposals. Garret FitzGerald seconded my resolution for a temporary ban. I noticed the DG and Bob Collins (then Assistant Director General) exchange a look. This campaign could develop momentum.

In September, Joe Barry was back with a detailed and considered response. He proposed:

- No advertising in programmes aimed at pre-school children;

- No sponsorship of children's programmes;
- A maximum of two ad breaks per hour in children's programmes;
- A minimum of 20 minutes between each advertising break; and
- The preparation of informational commercials explaining the enhanced promises of advertisements for transmission in the pre-Christmas period.

This was a step forward. The proposals were thoughtful. They excluded the most vulnerable tiny children who believed trustingly in the advertisers' depiction of their products. Many critics of advertising to children point out that the smallest children cannot distinguish commercial messages from programme content, so they are particularly susceptible. The ban on sponsorship was welcome, as were the gaps between ad messages. The infomercials would attempt to counter the propagandistic value of the advertising message, but were unlikely to compete with them in terms of spending or production values. Bob Quinn was unimpressed, and argued for an outright ban, but he was largely unsupported. I did not feel the proposals went far enough, and continued to push for the Christmas ban. The best I could achieve that day was the promise that we would discuss the Christmas embargo at the next meeting, and although Bob and I wished to delay the publication of the Director General's proposals until after that meeting, so that they could be considered as a package, we were overruled. The Director General's proposals would be passed and publicised, stealing the momentum from the later consideration of the issue.

When, in October, I reintroduced the idea of the Christmas ban, I was vociferously supported by Anne Tannahill, Garret FitzGerald and Bob Quinn. But the arguments against were based on realpolitik. The strongest one was that since all our competitors would continue to advertise, and since children

At school, aged 7.

Mary's Communion, 1960, with Mam, Mary and Tony.

2   The Oracle of Apollo at Claros

3   The tomb of Achilles on the Trojan plain

4   Yenişehir village above the Trojan plain

With Brigid Ruane and David Neligan at an SLP party
conference, 17 October 1978. Courtesy of Derek Speirs.

Mam on strike outside Clerys, 30 June 1983.
Courtesy of Derek Speirs.

9 Odysseus receives wine from Maron, priest of Apollo at Ismaros

10   Land of the Lotus-Eaters

Quizzing C. J. Haughey on Section 31 at a reception after
1986 Ard Fheis. With Kintilla Heussaff, Roisin Boyd (seated),
Kathleen O Connor and Leo Enright.
Courtesy of Derek Speirs.

With Garret FitzGerald at Iveagh House for the recording of
the series *FitzGerald at 80*, 26 May 2006.
Courtesy of Derek Speirs.

zapped between channels constantly, our sacrifice would be of little avail. I have always felt that such an argument is not enough to justify doing nothing, but the four of us were outflanked and outvoted. The best we could achieve was a request to *The Late Late Toy Show* to include low-priced items, and to mention the toys' real qualities, rather than the superlatives showered upon them by advertising. It was only a little gratifying to see this advice in the programme in early December.

There were many more skirmishes on this subject, including major debates in 1997 and 1999. Even with a new Director General, Bob Collins, the principle remained the same. To cut off a revenue source of €4m could not be justified. Children would see ads elsewhere, including on RTÉ programmes after six p.m. (10.7 per cent of RTÉ One's audience and 33 per cent of the Network Two viewership was made up of children in the six to eight p.m. period). Where would we be satisfied to make the cut-off? My own feeling was that we could live with non-toy advertising, if reluctantly (the pushing of sugary cereals, for instance, was invidious). This would bring the revenue loss down to €1.69m, or €480,000 if we confined the ban to Network Two. With the displeasure of the executive evident each time this subject was raised, however, we were ultimately doomed, despite making substantial and sustained efforts to change policy.

Joe Barry was due to retire at the end of 1996, and a competition to replace him began in the autumn of that year. Bob Collins, as Assistant Director General to Joe Barry, was known to the whole Authority and was the front runner. Other major contenders were Liam Miller, Joe Mulholland and Eugene Murray. Each wrote documents that laid out their vision for the job and the obstacles facing RTÉ in the next five years. A sub-committee was established to interview the candidates and report back to the Authority. I was happy to be excluded from the sub-committee; it would be undesirable to have a role in such an appointment, given my position on the station's staff.

When the sub-committee, after much deliberation, came back to us, having interviewed each candidate a number of times, they had a rather odd proposal to make. They envisaged giving the position of Director General to Bob Collins, while insisting that he take on Liam Miller and Joe Mulholland as Assistant Directors General. They concluded that change was required in certain management responsibilities related to programming, organisational management, policy development, opportunities for revenue enhancement, cost management and public affairs. Of the two posts at Assistant Director General level, one (Joe Mulholland) would concentrate on programming affairs, talent development, regional programmes and the schedule; the other (Liam Miller) on organisational change and the commercial side. Bob Collins would have the central role of developing corporate policy and liaising with the government and the Authority.

I was frankly gobsmacked at the proposal. I had hoped that Bob Collins would be the emergent candidate, but was sanguine about the alternative candidates. I told the Authority that I believed this outcome was a disaster, and quite unworkable. These candidates were in competition with one another, and had different, if overlapping, proposals to take the organisation forward. The imposition of a double Assistant DG set of roles, with prescribed functions, and many of the important editorial functions divested to Joe Mulholland, would undermine the Director General's role as editor-in-chief of the organisation. It would be a recipe for division and confusion. Staff would also be unhappy with such an outcome. I proposed that the sub-committee should reconvene and suggested that Bob Collins, who was emerging as the preferred candidate, needed to be given the title and the power to decide on structures to take RTÉ forward. I had no doubt that he would find a way to use the available talents of the other applicants, but the way in which he would use them could not be prescribed to him without fundamentally undermining his authority and leadership. Garret FitzGerald, who had been on the interviewing sub-committee, agreed with the thrust of what I was saying. He said that the issue needed to be reconsidered, and that we should adjourn.

When the meeting reconvened some time later, I proposed that we should make just one decision at the meeting: to appoint Bob Collins as Director General, and that the other candidates should be informed that they were not being recommended to the minister for appointment. It would be up to the new DG to discuss his plans with the Authority, including how he would envisage using the talents of some of the defeated candidates. This was agreed. I don't know what Bob and the other candidates made of the Sistine Chapel-style deliberations, or what the Authority secretariat told them during that period. Suffice it to say that we had white smoke, and a clear victorious candidate to lead the organisation forward.

Joe Barry retired and Bob Collins replaced him. I had great hopes that things would change significantly under Bob, a progressive and intellectual person of great integrity. In truth, the organisation chugged along very similarly to before. I learnt a lesson: in large organisations the system is bigger than the contribution of any well-meaning individual, even if that person is Director General. Similarly with the Authority, despite many debates that felt as if they were matters of life and death, we could claim only a small number of victories. As an Authority we established Lyric FM, which still contributes in a significant way to the broadcasting landscape, and has become a respected focus for listeners who appreciate serious music, yet its audience remains small.

We also vetoed a proposal to knock down the beautiful period building on RTÉ grounds, Mount Errol, and earmarked some funds for its refurbishment and upgrading.

The most important issue that came before us for consideration in our five years as Authority members was what became known as the Coughlan judgment. I was very aware of this upcoming legal decision, having lived productively in current affairs with the related McKenna judgment. In 1995 Patricia McKenna had won her case in the Supreme Court relating to the coverage of the divorce referendum of that year. She had argued that the government had no right to spend taxpayers' money on promulgating one side in the referendum campaign, in this case the Yes vote. When it came to a referendum on the Constitution, the people are sovereign and uppermost and 'are taking a direct role in Government either by amending the Constitution or refusing to amend it.' The McKenna judgment held that the scales should be held equally in a referendum, allowing the citizens of the State to form their own opinion without public money being spent to convince them of the government's position. To me, the right of people like Green MEP Patricia McKenna and Irish Sovereignty Movement campaigner Anthony Coughlan to test the fairness of State organs in the courts was a positive good. It kept the government under proper pressure to act fairly in pre-referendum debate. And it was no harm that RTÉ should have a counterbalance to the 'prevailing political wisdom' that dominates thinking in the higher corridors of power. John Pilger, in his book *Heroes*, remarked that 'the consensus view is often a euphemism for the authorised wisdom of established authority.'[2] Where the people had been asked for their solemn opinion on an issue, it was quite wrong to expend public funds on the side of that established authority. Irish people had a tendency to

---

2   John Pilger, *Heroes* (Random House, 2010), p. 509.

be very independent of their political masters in referenda, whether on the abolition of proportional representation or on European issues. And it was awareness of this public volatility which had led governments, and subsequently broadcasters, to try to tip the scales in favour of a Yes vote.

Governments are made up of political people, but they are also human. They want to succeed in winning votes. It is all too easy, as happened again in 2013 in the Children's Rights referendum, to spend public money to argue one side of an argument. In broadcasting terms there was a direct parallel in granting an imbalance of time to each side, to the government's earlier spending of funds to shore up its argument. Bearing in mind the admonition to the government to hold the scales equally, RTÉ was waiting with serious concern to see how Anthony Coughlan's case would go.

In the 1995 referendum, RTÉ had taken the view that it should allow for party political broadcasts by the Yes and No sides in the referendum campaign. However, the station had also decided, because Section 18(1) of the Broadcasting Act expected them to be 'fair to all interests concerned', that they should give the political parties time to transmit their own party political broadcasts. The upshot was that forty-two minutes of time was given to the Yes side, and only ten minutes to the No side. It was blatantly unfair. RTÉ's legal opinion was that equal treatment might happen where the Yes and No camps were similar in size, but where a greater body of opinion is arrayed on one side of the debate, including all the main Dáil parties, that they should be allowed a proportionately larger coverage in terms of time. Many of us in current affairs had felt that this was an incorrect verdict. The people should be allowed to reach their decision in a free and democratic manner, without feeling that they were being railroaded by a near unanimous political system.

On 24 April 1998, Judge Paul Carney of the High Court passed down a judgment that supported Coughlan in his contention of RTÉ unfairness:

> I am satisfied that RTE's approach has resulted in inequality amounting to unconstitutional unfairness which would not have arisen had their starting point been to afford equality to each side of the argument to which there could only be a YES and NO answer.[3]

He elaborated that he wanted his judgment to be as narrowly based as possible (applying to referenda, but not to broader political debate or elections), and that the significantly unequal allocation of time had added to his view that RTÉ had been unfair to the people at large.

The judgment was reported to the Director General as we sat at an Authority meeting. I had known Bob Collins over many years, and he was fairly unflappable. He was a conscientious public service broadcaster, and the instinct to be fair would be deep in his consciousness, yet this judgment seemed to take him by surprise. He visibly paled. The advice that had allowed the main political parties a special place, and unbalanced time, in the divorce referendum was wrong. To me it proved only that the most learned legal people can find any argument logical. Common sense dictated that fairness demanded equality in party political broadcasts in a referendum. The Constitution as tested on this question had clearly been found to favour the people having an unfettered access to both sides of the debate. It did not seem controversial. And the judgment referred only to party political broadcasts.

---

3   The High Court, Judicial Review no. 1997 209 J.R., *In the Matter of the Broadcasting Authority Acts between Anthony Coughlan (applicant) and the Broadcasting Complaints Commission and RTÉ (respondents) and The Attorney General (Notice Party) 24/4/98.*

The news would still cover all the news conferences on both sides, and would therefore reflect the fact that all the political parties favoured a Yes vote. Judge Carney was not suggesting that the provision of equal coverage should apply to other political controversies, or to the run-up to elections.

The Director General immediately informed us that the judgment would have to be examined, and urgently, given that referenda on the Good Friday Agreement and the Amsterdam Treaty were imminent. My immediate suggestion was that there was no need for any party political broadcasts on these issues, and if there were to be, one for and one against seemed appropriate. Within weeks, that suggestion was acted upon. Bob Collins rang each Authority member individually to get agreement to drop party political broadcasts on this occasion. The question of whether to appeal *Coughlan* would be left to another day.

Over the next number of meetings, we argued long and hard about the suitability of an appeal. Our decision seemed to be pre-empted by the deadline. The Director General decided to submit the appeal on 17 June, the last day it was possible. His major concern was that the judgment might be allowed to extend to other aspects of current affairs programming, and that an identity might be established between the concept of equality and RTÉ's statutory obligation of fairness to all concerned. Our discussions intensified. At the June meeting, Bob Quinn and I made it clear that we had not given our assent to this appeal. Other members, in particular Des Geraghty and Pat Hume, were concerned about the wisdom of the proposed petition. Farrell Corcoran, the Chairman, pointed out that we had asked the executive to pursue further information regarding an appeal. The application did not commit us, and could be withdrawn at any time. The Director General had acted in good faith, in view of the remit he had been given in April, and the urgency surrounding a decision had dictated a course of action. We would be furnished with two Senior Counsels' opinions before our next meeting, when there would be a full debate.

When we received the detailed legal opinion, I was even more worried. The learned counsels argued that a preponderance of support on one side of a referendum obviated the need for equality in the espousal of points of view. Their emphasis was on fairness to all concerned, and they felt that the political parties had a particular place in that debate. They were entitled to give their views by way of party political broadcasts. They were very concerned about the proposition of fairness equalling equality, and one even referred to 'the straitjacket of equality', which I found alarming. Although both counsels and the RTÉ Head of Legal Affairs were in favour of appealing, at least one lawyer emphasised that there was no guarantee that RTÉ would win in this high stakes venture: 'There is a state of uncertainty in relation to the potential attitude of the Supreme Court and I could not advise with any degree of confidence that RTÉ would be successful on appeal.' Despite this lack of certainty, the Counsel recommended an appeal.

This was a political minefield for RTÉ. My biggest concern, which I stated at the Authority meeting on 24 July 1998, was that RTÉ would be seen to be siding with the political parties in opposition to an ordinary citizen who had won the right to equal coverage. RTÉ's reputation for fairness would be seriously undermined. There was some argument that the appeal would give us certainty, allowing RTÉ to decide on a case-by-case basis how much time each side was due in a referendum. This appeared to be the view of both the Director General, Bob Collins, and the Authority Chairman, Farrell Corcoran. I considered that this was a freedom we did not need, since it would lead to the political parties pressing us for their say in every instance. In each future debate, for instance, on a European referendum, RTÉ would be left to second-guess the result of the vote, and try to apportion time on that basis. In such referenda, historically, the stated views of the political parties were not reflected in the popular vote, which tended to break down on a 70:30 or even a 60:40 basis.

The Carney judgment left us in a situation where more or less equal time would have to be given to the Yes and No sides in referendum political broadcasts. Our news and current affairs remained free to cover newsworthy events and debates. (The estimate was that the major parties would receive up to 70 per cent of news coverage just by weight of their numbers and ex officio positions.) The judgment seemed ring-fenced to apply in referenda only, which appeared quite acceptable to me. I was also concerned that there was no certainty of winning, and that RTÉ would then be seen as the 'cat's paw' of the political parties, fighting on their behalf. The appeal could lead to the copper-fastening of equal time in broader political circumstances. It was better to leave the situation as it was, until or unless a specific case would later merit a fight. Bob Quinn was equally adamant that the appeal could damage RTÉ's reputation, and other members expressed deep unease.

At the September meeting, the Director General himself proposed that the appeal be withdrawn. He had taken further legal advice, and did not feel that RTÉ would be damaged by letting the judgment in *Coughlan* stand. The reaction of members of the Authority was baffling. Having been listened to by the Director General, they now started to waver in favour of an appeal. Perhaps they worried that their position would appear inconsistent if they now withdrew the case. Or perhaps they were concerned about the ire of the political establishment. In either case, the members who were closest to political parties, Garret FitzGerald, Des Geraghty and Farrell Corcoran, all argued for continuing the appeal, on the basis of clarifying the broadcaster's position. I was taken aback, and found myself in the now familiar position of being in a minority of two with Bob Quinn. Occupants of the middle ground were silent. I proposed that we delay our final position until the October meeting, in the hope that Bob and I could convince some of the other members back to their original concerns. It was that important.

By the time the October meeting came, the Broadcasting Complaints Commission and the Attorney General had joined themselves with our appeal. This only made things appear worse for the RTÉ position. It seemed that the station was lining up with the government and State to overcome a worthwhile victory by an ordinary citizen. Bob Quinn came in with his arguments well prepared, and he and I tried to argue the toss against the Executive and members of the Authority. It was hopeless. We were outgunned by the weight of the opinion of counsel, which argued for the continuation of the appeal, and the sense that it was now too late to withdraw. I was very depressed leaving the meeting that dark October night. I felt that it was not yet over, and that RTÉ would actually lose in court. The organisation's humiliation would be complete.

So it transpired. I woke up on my birthday, 27 January 2000, to the news that RTÉ had lost its appeal. Anthony Coughlan had been right to argue that the allocation of party political broadcasts to all the parties, alongside the Yes and No sides in the debate, was flawed. It was unfair that RTÉ had given forty-two minutes to the Yes side and only twelve minutes to the No side. Referring to the *McKenna* judgment, Chief Justice Hamilton stated:

> The principles upon which it was based are of general application, being based on the constitutional rights of the citizens and the requirements of fair procedures, [which dictate that] the scales should be held equally between those who support and those who oppose the amendment.[4]

---

4   *Coughlan v Broadcasting Complaints Commission* [2000] IESC 44 (26 January 2000).

RTÉ's coverage could 'by no stretch of the imagination be regarded as maintaining a proper balance.' Justice Susan Denham in her judgment added that RTÉ 'must exercise the overall – broad picture – of impartiality and fairness', particularly in a case where 'direct democracy is invoked', i.e. a referendum. The judges could not have been clearer. All the opinions we had received that indicated that unequal coverage could somehow be fair were rejected emphatically.

In future referenda, RTÉ decided not to give free political broadcasts in the run-up to referendum votes, thus allowing the sovereign people to adjudicate for themselves on any Yes/No proposition. Since May 1998, citizens have been helped to make up their minds, with varying amounts of success, by the Referendum Commission, which has attempted to give fair and equal coverage to both sides. RTÉ was damaged in the public's perception by its appeal against *Coughlan*. It has learnt to live with the Supreme Court judgment, which is the final word on the matter.

There was now a feeling that, as an Authority, we were limping towards our final months. We had nearly all felt instinctively opposed to appealing against the judgment in *Coughlan*, yet we had allowed the Executive and lawyers to have their way, and the result was undesirable. Bob Quinn gave in to his long-held instinct in June 1999, and resigned from the Authority. Perhaps his view that the board is no more than a rubber stamp to vet decisions of the Executive is correct. I found myself worn out with trying to maintain integrity while making practical alliances that would get things achieved. It was slow and problematic.

In March of 2000, with just three months to go in office for the Authority, one of those dramatic 'events, dear boy, events', occurred. Joe Mulholland, as Managing Director of Television, had been in hot water several times over the previous eighteen months. There had been a large budget overrun of €1.2m in spending on the Soccer Premier League in 1999, which had annoyed the Authority. Then RTÉ lost the bid to broadcast the Champion's League to TV3. Members were still aggrieved by Mulholland's dramatic insistence that only one name would be offered for discussion as *The Late Late Show* presenter: Pat Kenny. There had been an embarrassing attempt to dumb down the weather forecast by replacing the popular, trained meteorologists by young women. But now there was a crisis at television management level, which I felt had to be brought to the notice of the Authority.

In early 1999, Helen O'Rahilly had been appointed from the BBC as Director of Television, essentially as Joe Mulholland's deputy. She arrived like a whirlwind, making it her business to engage with many members of staff, and thus found out promptly the scale of the problems faced. (She had, for instance, visited the tiny office where Liam O'Flanagan and I were preparing *Questions & Answers* one evening, to ask how things were.) Most importantly, she had the energy and commitment to help solve those difficulties. There had been a certain strain with Joe Mulholland, which had been evident even at general meetings with television staff. But now, in March 2000, after many battles with Joe Mulholland, Helen felt that her position was untenable and she felt forced to resign.

There was despair among the staff. I requested an item on the agenda to deal with the crisis, feeling that it merited a discussion of more importance than an item of 'Any Other Business'. This was granted. I outlined how devastated programme staff were by the loss of O'Rahilly, and proposed, reluctantly, a resolution that Joe Mulholland be asked to step aside as Managing Director of Television. Garret FitzGerald listened solemnly to the arguments, and then, with a sad nod, seconded the proposal. There was now a flurry of activity on both sides of the table. Des Geraghty, who had up to now been a loyal supporter of Joe, made clear a new ambivalence, and Bob Collins and the Chairman Farrell Corcoran felt that an adjournment was required to examine the implications. Having proposed many items that had been quickly or ponderously shovelled towards the rubbish bin, I had the real feeling that this was not one of those occasions.

Over the following hours, an action plan was put in place. A meeting was held with Mulholland, and he was content to retire with a generous package, so the way was clear for new blood at the top of television. Cathal Goan, who had done an inspirational job at TG4, was the Director General's choice, and the Authority supported that nomination. The change was accomplished seamlessly, and Cathal went on to replace Bob Collins as DG four years later. In such a way do large organisations protect themselves from damage, and marshal change into the future. Joe Mulholland was free to develop his McGill Summer School project, which many people considered to be his real passion.

The five years I spent on the RTÉ Authority were educational, shocking, boring, interesting and amusing at various times. It gave me a great insight into how a large organisation works, from the essential task of maintaining budgets, to the reality of working with the government and civil servants, to the key question of editorial programme-making, and the staff and industrial relations issues that emerged. I met some great people on the Authority, not least the incorrigible Bob Quinn. His own book *Maverick* makes a worthwhile contribution to any analysis of RTÉ during this period.[5]

It was enlightening to see the Director General and his team proficiently handling each and every threat to the organisation, and having the patience to explain matters to a quite naïve group of non-broadcasters. I am not convinced that a board, meeting monthly and reading documentation in

---

5   Bob Quinn, *Maverick: A Dissident View of Broadcasting Today* (Brandon Publishers, 2001).

between, can really fulfil the oversight of a large and complex organisation. The Authority is too easily outfoxed by the Executive. But there were moments where we cared enough to influence the direction of policy. Perhaps the interference of a group of well-meaning outsiders can contribute to the strategy being developed at the top table of a state-sponsored body. For myself, when my five years was up, I was happy to slip out of the boardroom door, and continue doing what I loved most: making programmes with my colleagues. I was back to that consuming and all-important question for programme-makers: will this actually work on air?

8

The Late Late Show

'In the High Court, one upset Catholic wanted the Late Late item outlawed, claiming it would greatly undermine "Christian moral values" and "the respect of the general public for nuns".'

— *Irish Independent*[1]

Friday afternoon, and the sound is pumping in Studio Four for *The Late Late Show* rehearsal. A bizarrely hectic week of work inevitably leads towards the big day, every Friday. Pat Kenny is in the studio, and at his most demanding. He is always very calm by the evening of transmission, but here, in the studio during the afternoon, every possible problem is examined meticulously. The researchers and producers are on hand. All the film clips are lined up. The cues for guests are planned. The script is on autocue, and every move that will be made that night is gone through at full speed.

The programme is described as the most important show on RTÉ television, and certainly it has delivered in ratings and advertising for the organisation for nearly forty years. When I joined the team in June 2001, colleagues stopped me in the corridor to shake my hand and offer congratulations. I

---

1   7 October 2008.

was slightly bemused by this. After all, I had been in television current affairs for over ten years, and had covered several vital general elections. But the pumping sound summed it up. There is serious money in Entertainment.

Revered as it is by senior management, *The Late Late Show* is viewed far more critically by the television audience, many of whom regard it as past its sell-by date. Numerous commentators have argued that it should never have been allowed to outlive the tenure of Gay Byrne as presenter. In its earlier years, in the 1970s and 1980s, a phrase was coined: 'It started on *The Late Late Show*.' Gay Byrne had an instinctive rapport with the television audience, and he had a journalistic disposition that allowed him to target fundamental topics and make them his own.

Famously, a woman admitted that she had worn no nightie on her honeymoon night, which led to the programme being denounced by a Catholic bishop. John Feeney condemned the hoarding of wealth in the Church while congregations went hungry. There were rows about crime, the EEC and the political system, among many others. *The Late Late Show* was the must-see programme on RTÉ, and in those decades had audiences of up to a million. But the years had seen some decline, and a major crisis was caused when Gay Byrne retired from the show.

I was a member of the RTÉ Authority in 1988 when then Controller of Programmes, Joe Mulholland, was asked to bring a list of possible successors to Gay to the Authority for discussion. Joe came into the meeting and, rather dramatically, opened his folder. There was just one name on the sheet: Pat Kenny. Three years later, Pat was being derided for his presentation style. The most wounding criticism described him as 'the plank' – an epithet that stuck. It was believed that his manner was stilted and awkward and that he was unable to relate easily to guests. In addition, the programme was seen as having become 'too soft'.

Cathal Goan, the Managing Director of Television, approached me to say that he wanted to expand my experience in the organisation, and that *The Late Late Show*, as RTÉ's flagship programme, would be a good development for me in my career. He also felt that I could give the programme some serious heft by increasing the number of debates and controversies on the show. He was concerned that the programme had become rather lightweight. I told Cathal that I knew very little about Britain's soap stars and celebrities, and indeed I had little interest in much of the programme's stock in trade. He intimated that those items would be well covered by the regular researchers on the programme. My role would be to help to get the programme back to being talked and argued about in the homes and workplaces of Ireland. I had no problem with any of that, but I was a little underwhelmed at the prospect. I considered my real home to be in current affairs.

I joined my colleague producer, Brian Hayes, and five researchers that summer, and we prepared to work out our strategy for the autumn. We would have regular debates, as well as more substantial interviews to satisfy the audience of people over forty, which was *The Late Late Show*'s core viewership. I strongly believed, as did many colleagues, that Pat Kenny was being underused in the programme's light agenda. He had been a gifted broadcaster on political issues on television, and remained so in radio. He was quick to assimilate a brief, was a natural debater, and had an unerring instinct for politics and social debates. I saw it as my task to place Pat's analytical strengths at centre stage. The major criticism of his style was his interviewing technique with actors and comedians. Given a subject in which he was interested, Pat was a superlative broadcaster, and was greatly feared by politicians of all parties. Many of us mourned his loss from current affairs television, and wondered why he had made the move to entertainment. The most obvious reason was the huge fees paid to entertainment presenters over their colleagues in current affairs, such as Miriam O'Callaghan and Seán O'Rourke. The issue of presenter salaries embroiled RTÉ in a continuing controversy from 2005 on. Deputies and Senators, perhaps miffed by trenchant criticism of their expenses and trips, demanded details of star contracts, and would soon insist on a significant reduction in those fees. When presenter salaries were at their highest point, in 2007, Pat's remuneration was close to €1m per year. If he had stayed in current affairs (arguably a more difficult and intellectual role than *The Late Late Show*), his salary would have been nearer to €200,000. These kinds of anomalies helped to give *The Late Late Show* its image as the place to be in Irish television.

The programme was also sponsored. During my time producing the show, the sponsors were Renault Ireland. One of the comforts of public service broadcasting is that advertisers and sponsors have no say in a programme's content. Items are decided by producers without fear or favour, which is as it should be. There is a rigid separation between programme management and the commercial side of the house. Although the Director General clearly has to focus on the financial realities, I have never come across an example of advertisers' concerns being brought to bear on programme-makers. I remember that when Bill Cullen, Managing Director of Renault, brought out his book *It's a Long Way from Penny Apples*, it was assumed by the publisher and its publicity personnel that the memoir would be automatically covered on *The Late Late Show*. We decided that there were more pressing items during the week of the launch, and the book was not featured. I know that Pat came under some pressure to push for that interview to take place, but he backed our decision strenuously.

The content of the programme was mapped out at the weekly programme meeting on a Monday afternoon. Researchers would pitch for ideas, which Brian and I had already positively assessed. It was a highly competitive and often argumentative session. Ideas were discussed intensively, and any flaws in a subject were scrutinised. Debate and conflict were important for content, and ensured a lively edition of the programme. Most of the subjects were mapped out a few weeks in advance, but there was always room for a topical debate of the week, and this would sometimes be instigated as late as the day before the programme went on air. No matter how well planned we were, it was extremely busy right up to programme time on a Friday night.

Tuesdays, Wednesdays and Thursdays were given over to setting up items and writing briefs for Pat. On those midweek days, the office was like a schoolroom, everyone at their desks until late, heads down, each person working on their individual programme items. As producers, Brian and I would be supervising this content and working out how each item would come together on the studio floor. One of the considerations was to keep movement in the programme, so that an important interview would be followed by a game in which the audience participated, followed by music, and maybe a debate. It was a complex running order. On Thursday evening, at about seven, director Niamh White and broadcasting co-ordinator Deirdre Horlacher would make sense of it all, writing up the details for the crew on Friday. Niamh was responsible for mapping out the shots for speech and music content. The order of events and shot lists would be printed, and became the 'bible' for programme day. Everyone – cameras, sound, design, lighting, staging and electrical services – knew where they had to be and at what time on Friday. It was only with this extremely regimented understanding of the running order that the programme would run like clockwork.

Friday morning would allow us to put any finishing touches and flourishes into programmes. Prizes for the audience would be prepared. Research briefs would be finalised to include detail from last-minute phone calls. Then Pat would come over after his radio programme, at eleven o'clock, and go through everything with that night's producer. He would take his briefs to study until the afternoon. Two o'clock was presenter rehearsal, and this was followed by the music rehearsal. Then, around 5.30 p.m., team members would change for the show. Some female colleagues would even dash down to the hairdressers to get a blow-dry. Friday night was that kind of evening. It was Showtime, and everyone was tense and excited. It was important that each item and segment would work well. By the time the programme finished at half past eleven, and we sat down in the hospitality suite to analyse obsessively each and every subject, there was always a huge sense of relief, but sometimes also of despair, where a well-planned item had just not worked. A comforting glass of wine would take the edge off the pain on those nights.

The hospitality post-mortem was the first look at how the programme had gone. This would be followed by a detailed dissection of the programme at the following Monday's meeting. And then we would, of necessity, move on to the next one. Each item and programme mattered enormously, and we were all fully involved and committed.

On Tuesday, 11 September 2001, just before two o'clock Irish time, I was sitting at my desk working on a document. 'God, look at this!' shouted researcher Bill Malone, and we watched as the first plane hit the Twin Towers. Commentators wondered if the pilot had had a heart attack. Ten minutes later, as the second plane hit, the nature of the attack became evident. It was a horrific attack on ordinary American civilians, yet also a symbolic attack on corporate America. As news of the attempt to hit the Pentagon reached us, it was clear that this was a political attack on the United States, which would have huge global repercussions. I called together the team members who were in the office that lunchtime, and instructed them to stand down the agreed programme for that Friday. This could not be one item in a programme mix with celebrity chat and music. We would have to start from scratch.

That week was one of the most memorable in my years at RTÉ. It demonstrated the way in which RTÉ staff can work under a pressing deadline to produce a programme of quality. To put together a *Late Late Show* from zero in three days was quite a task. Everyone worked flat out, and the programme, which I had the honour to produce, was the highlight of that broadcasting year. Pat got fully involved, and mucked in with other colleagues. It was a great feeling to drive such a dedicated team.

I rang Mary McAleese, President of Ireland, for an interview to open the programme. I knew that she would deliver a sympathetic and nuanced discourse, while also demonstrating the importance of this event to an Irish audience. This was the essential tone to strike at the outset. The President was followed by Mark and John Clifford, whose sister Ruth and niece Juliana had been killed in the Twin Towers. Despite their heartbreak, they were also capable of analysing the reasons behind the attack. They gave their perspective on the flaws in American foreign policy that had led to this terrible tragedy. It was clear that Irish people were not going to suspend their critical faculties in the face of this atrocity. Difficult things needed to be said about the treatment of Palestinians and the role of the US administration as Israel's closest ally. The programme became a demonstration of the Irish capacity for genuine sympathy for those affected, but also examined the context for this crime against the citizens of the United States.

The clear thinking of the Cliffords was further exemplified by other analyses from historian Tim Pat Coogan, American journalist Katherine Holmquist and comedian Des Bishop. We also had a thoughtful reaction from a representative of the Muslim community, Farouk Ameen. There were impassioned views from a number of Americans living in Ireland, and members of the Dublin Fire Brigade. The firemen had been on a visit to their New York colleagues that summer, and they knew some of the men who were at that moment fighting the fires in the buildings and saving civilians from the towers. It was also becoming evident at that time that the New York firemen would become central heroes of the tragedy. Many of them went into clearly perilous situations with no thought except that of saving their fellow New Yorkers. A great number died as a result. There were a lot of Irish-American names on the list of firefighters who had lost their lives. The Dublin firemen were able to describe the qualities of their American colleagues. Their contribution to the programme was moving and memorable.

The Late Late Show is, of course, not just a discussion programme. The choice of artistic contributors had also to be carefully curated. When I contacted writer Joe O'Connor, because he had lived in New York, he suggested that he would read W. H. Auden's poem 'September 1, 1939'. It was a perfect choice, written as it was on the day when Hitler invaded Poland, and World War II began. On that day, Auden was sitting in a New York café as people went about their business, oblivious of the new dispensation of war that was happening in Europe. The apposite first verse declared:

> *Waves of anger and fear*
> *Circulate over the bright*
> *And darkened lands of the earth,*
> *Obsessing our private lives;*
> *The unmentionable odour of death*
> *Offends the September night.*

As Joe O'Connor read these profound words on the programme, the ability of art to transcend a political moment and make emotional sense of an event was manifest. The effect in the studio was haunting.

Brian Kennedy, Maria Doyle Kennedy and Paul Brady also contributed timely and pertinent tributes to the victims. At the end of the programme, we interviewed US Ambassador Richard Egan. I was anxious that this would not be a straight political interview. The Ambassador mentioned the number of drawings and paintings that had been flooding into the Embassy from Irish schoolchildren. We brought those pictures into the studio. This was the element that took the interview onto a different level. The item became a measure of the spontaneous compassion that Irish people felt for the innocents who had lost their lives.

When the credits rolled, we made our way up to the hospitality room with some of the remaining guests, and fell into the armchairs, shattered, but content with a job well done. Nita Byrne and Katherine Cahill, two of the researchers on the programme, had worked until eleven o'clock every night that week. As well as being exhausted, we were also a bit shell-shocked by the enormity of the occurrence. We debated among ourselves for several hours how the Twin Towers attack would affect the global political situation. Eventually, we all returned to our homes, where I slept until two o'clock the next day.

That programme was just the second in the series, and we had over thirty more to go in the season, including the behemoth that is the annual Toy Show. So it was back in on the Monday to start again, piecing together the different elements for the following week's programme. We were to have a varied agenda in the coming season, and I was very aware of my role to initiate and fight for more serious content on *The Late Late Show*.

One debate we featured that September was on the subject of intervention in childbirth. Feminist controversialist Naomi Wolf had just brought out a book arguing that intervention in childbirth was often unnecessary, and represented male power politics in the delivery room.

She debated her views with Peter Boylan, master of the National Maternity Hospital, and midwife Marie O'Connor. Marie pointed to the practice of symphyseotomy, whereby a woman's pelvis is broken to ensure ease of childbirth. This practice had horrendous implications for the subsequent health of the woman, who would find it difficult to walk, would suffer extreme pain, and many women were destined to become wheelchair-users later in life because of the procedure. Symphyseotomy was promoted by the Catholic Church, which saw it as simplifying later childbirth, and had been widely used in Irish hospitals up until the 1980s. This example was a perfect illustration of the point that Naomi Wolfe had made in her book. It was also the type of debate that *The Late Late Show* did very well.

Some of the other discussions with which I was particularly happy during that season were dialogues on the difficulties of raising teenagers; young priests talking about their lives; a drugs debate focusing on the easy availability of Ecstasy; rural planning and the proliferation of bungalows; internet pornography; and personal injury claims and the growing incidence of ambulance-chasing lawyers.

In 2002, Ireland was once again racked by a proposal to amend the Constitution to tighten the constitutional ban on abortion. The amendment, if passed, would have removed the threat of suicide as a ground for legal abortion in the state, as well as introducing new penalties for anyone performing an abortion. We fielded a significant debate on the abortion issue in the run-up to the 2002 referendum, featuring Dr Berry Kiely and Fianna Fáil's Mary Coughlan arguing for the new amendment, and Labour's Liz McManus and Fine Gael's Nora Owen arguing against. This programme needed the meticulous balance of time and structure, as required by the 1995 *McKenna* judgment governing broadcasting for referenda. RTÉ's management saw this programme as a key element of the television debate preceding the referendum.

A few weeks later, days before the vote, we had six protagonists on either side of the issue explaining their most contentious posters. Confusion had been caused by the fact that the most extreme of the anti-abortion groups were lining up with pro-choice campaigners in calling for a No vote. Our item certainly helped to clarify the debate, because we had six campaigners standing in front of their strongest placard, each explaining their particular position.

I was a bit of a poacher turned gamekeeper on the issue of *The Late Late Show* covering matters of political controversy. When I was in current affairs, in both radio and television, we were strongly opposed to such programmes getting involved in coverage of this nature. We felt that entertainment programmes lacked the rigour for a fair consideration of the issues. But with Pat in the chair, I was successfully able to argue that *The Late Late Show* could adequately fulfil this function. A public service role would be addressed by the larger audience who could witness debates.

We had lots of standout individual interviews too. There was a ripple of excitement in the office when Paul Newman came in to do a pre-recorded interview. Director Niamh White and I were determined to maintain our professional distance, and record the insert item without going down to the floor of the studio. In the event, we were so bowled over by the actor's charisma and his down-to-earth charm that we both came down to shake his hand and chat after the interview. He spoke to each member of the crew, and had his photo taken with many of them. Colin Farrell was similarly disarming. His parents accompanied him, and his primary concern was to see that they were well looked after. I reassured him on that point, and after his interview he was chatty and warm to the team and other guests in the hospitality room.

Hospitality was where each of the guests was brought before and after their interview. It gave them a chance to relax after their television performance. Bob Fisk came in to talk about his latest book on the Middle East, and proceeded to kiss Victoria Beckham's hand. Gerry Adams and Ruairí Quinn debated the future of the Irish left in the studio, but did not engage with one another afterwards. Footballer Paul McGrath chatted with boxer Chris Eubank. Anne Doyle swapped fashion favourites with our hospitality supervisor, Angela Kennedy. Such was the nature of the mix on *The Late Late Show*.

Two of the most popular interviews in that season were with Mary Robinson and Bob Geldof. One of the first things Brian and I would do on a Monday morning was to look at the audience for each segment of the preceding Friday's programme. The results were often as we would have expected. In Mary Robinson's case, the ratings increased for her interview, even though she was in the third segment of the programme, traditionally a time of night where audiences began to decline. It was a few months after the Twin Towers attack, and Mary Robinson analysed the fallout from that event. Her concerns were about the increase in racism and xenophobia throughout the world. She also pointed to the difficulties engendered by the UN Security Council's focus on countering terrorism. Many governments were using the security context to undermine opposition politicians, the press and trade unions. Mary Robinson was insistent on a wider definition of human rights to include not just political freedoms but also the right to food security, education and health. As I chatted to her before and after the interview, I was surprised to note that she was profoundly shy, almost bashful. She worked to overcome this characteristic by her focus on her world-improving agenda. A few years later, I was to get to know her well as we worked together on a documentary about her life and role in human rights. It was my job on that occasion to get past her diffidence, and encourage her to speak personally about her motivation. She remains a figure of national importance, and a principled and fearless advocate on behalf of the world's most oppressed people, in her many political and social campaigns.

When Bob Geldof came onto the programme, he spoke very truthfully about his relationship with Paula Yates and their break-up. He was a champion of children's rights, and believed that many fathers were denied their parental role after a marital breakdown. He spoke openly about loneliness and feeling suicidal in the period following his divorce, and of the importance of friends in pulling him through. Despite his outspoken and even belligerent image, Geldof was courteous and approachable to everyone who dealt with him backstage.

After the success of the programme on the attack on the Twin Towers, we decided we would do a *Late Late Show* from New York during the week of St Patrick's Day. In October 2001, I travelled there with researcher Nita Byrne to meet people for the special programme, and to set up interviews. One evening we were sitting in a pasta restaurant near Harlem that had been recommended by my old friend, Patrick Farrelly, now a film-maker in New York. He had said, 'If you're in luck, Bill Clinton might come in. If not, you'll at least get a reasonable plate of pasta that's very edible.' We certainly thought it would be unlikely, but showed up on the appointed night to meet Patrick and his partner Kate, who were both helping us to research the New York programme. (Because of their contacts with the New York firemen, we were the only international crew who got to film on Ground Zero when we came to New York in March 2002.) As we sat and ate our food, to our astonishment Bill Clinton walked in with his entourage. I lost no time in approaching his security minder, and said that we were from Irish television and that I would appreciate a word with President Clinton, whenever he had finished eating. He said that he would see what he could do. About an hour later I was called over, and Bill Clinton left his table and spoke to me enthusiastically about Ireland and the peace process. I told him about our St Patrick's Day programme. He replied that he would be in the Middle East at that time in March, so, with regret, he could not appear on the programme. I then mentioned a special programme we were doing with John and Pat Hume in November. He said that he was a huge fan of John, and would definitely make himself available on the night to do a phone call about Hume's unique contribution to peace. This he duly did, one month later. People speak about the charisma of Bill Clinton, and I can vouch for it. For the time we spoke, it seemed to me that I had his undivided attention, and that nothing was more important to him than the success of our project. When I finished the conversation and returned to our table, people in the restaurant continued eating and left him alone. It was only when he and his party got up to leave that the diners stood up and gave him a standing ovation. He made a point of going into the kitchen and thanking the staff, and was then applauded out the door. I imagine that this ritual happened each time he visited this very ordinary Italian restaurant, which happened to be near his office in downtown New York.

The Late Late Show was a very busy programme. The team lived around the schedule of the programme week, with little space for a normal social life. I was happy to be part of the obsession that the programme became for all of us, but there were times when I really missed having an input into political programming, and moments, too, where an audience game or entertainment interview felt like a chore to deliver. I sometimes found myself wondering whether I was in the right place.

The programme was going from strength to strength, and we were all busy getting on with it, when I had a major row with Pat Kenny. Many broadcasters have their blind spots, and in Pat's case it was an intense critique of what he would call the 'feminist agenda'. He fundamentally believed that fathers were frequently treated unfairly following a relationship or marital breakdown. I, and other members of his teams, had often argued these points with him, subsequent to programme interviews.

Dr Maura Woods was one of the early pioneering doctors who had taken seriously the issue of sexual assault and rape. In the 1980s, through her work with the Rape Crisis Centre, she had set up a sexual assault unit at the Rotunda Hospital to give specialist help to women and children who had been sexually violated. The unit became central in the collection of forensic evidence for criminal cases, and was under the aegis of the Eastern Health Board from the 1990s onwards. For the programme of 1 February 2002, an interview had been planned with a man called Eddie Hernon, a representative of two men's advocate groups, Vocal Ireland and the Accused Parents Aid Group. The interview followed the Medical Council's finding that week of professional misconduct against Dr Woods. The Council had found that she had failed to follow rigorous medical practice in her diagnosis of sexual abuse against five particular fathers who had been referred to the Sexual Assault Unit by the gardaí and social workers. Eddie Hernon was one of those fathers.

Eddie Hernon's estranged partner had referred their five-year-old child to the authorities, having noticed blood on her daughter's pants after a visit with her father. This happened in England, and the British doctor who examined the child found no evidence that the bleeding had been caused by sexual trauma. Later, on their return to Ireland, the mother sent the child for a second evaluation, and she was treated at the Sexual Assault Unit, where she was examined and psychologically assessed using anatomical dolls and other procedures. It was found there that she had indeed been sexually abused. The Medical Council had now concluded that Dr Woods was 'excessively definitive in her report'. I had not been involved in the item for broadcast, but I had no difficulty with covering this development in the fraught and emotive subject of accused parents and sexual abuse. Child abuse is a very serious allegation for a mother to seek to have investigated, and it is entirely wrong for a father to lose visiting rights on any spurious or inconclusive basis. It seemed that Maura Woods had, on this occasion, erred in her diagnosis of these assaults.

I was busy working on a separate subject for the following week's programme when the phone rang in the office at five o'clock on Friday evening, just a few hours before the Maura Woods item would be aired. The caller was a senior social worker from the Eastern Health Board, whom I had known for many years. We had worked together on a number of programmes that highlighted difficulties faced by disempowered people, and I knew him to be a passionate and fair advocate for his clients. He spoke to me in outraged terms about us giving an open platform to Eddie Hernon, which he would use to vilify Maura Woods in a highly contentious way. He told me that Hernon was a controversial person within the accused parents lobby groups, and that the social worker himself had been subjected to a vile postering campaign accusing him of being a paedophile because of his involvement in removing children from homes where he and the courts considered them to be at risk. He also pointed to Vocal Ireland's connection to Vocal USA. The founder of the organisation in the US, Ralph Underwager, had been accused of controversially defending paedophilia. When asked whether choosing paedophila was a responsible choice for individuals, he had answered:

> Certainly it is responsible … Paedophiles spend a lot of time and energy defending their choice. I don't think a paedophile needs to do that. Paedophiles can

boldly and courageously affirm what they choose …
as a theologian I believe it is God's will ….[2]

Hernon had referred to the 'child sex-abuse industry' in an
attempt to undermine the work being done on behalf of
children at risk. I asked the social worker whether he would
come in to studio that night and debate the issue, but he was
precluded from doing so by his official position. He warned
me, however, to be very careful about unleashing Eddie
Hernon into public debate without any restraining element.

I immediately spoke to Pat Kenny about the phone call,
in a spirit of pursuing a correct balance in the item we were to
transmit. He told me that he saw no reason to be careful about
the interview, but if I wanted to include an extra element in
the segment, then I was free to do so. I rang a journalistic
colleague, Susan McKay, an award-winning writer who had
also written an acclaimed book with Sophia McColgan, who
had been raped by her father from the age of six. I explained
the situation to Susan, and wondered if she would oblige
me by providing a balance to the item by speaking about the
character and groundbreaking work of Maura Woods. She
agreed to come in at very short notice, on condition that she
would not sit on the panel with Eddie Hernon (whom she also
knew), and that she would not discuss his particular case, but
would talk only about Maura Woods and her work. I agreed
to this format, and then told Pat that this was our agreement.
'Fine', he said. Such an agreement about a controversial
interview was rare enough, but, given that Susan was saving
us from a potentially perilous situation, it seemed little to ask.

Live in the studio, however, things took a very different
turn. Pat interviewed Eddie Hernon as though he were an

---

2   Ralph Underwager, the *Padika* interview (a European pro-paedophile
    publication), cited in Jennifer Freyd, *Betrayal Trauma: The Logic of
    Forgetting Childhood Abuse* (Harvard University Press, 1998), p. 38.

innocent abroad, despite being a vocal and experienced spokesman for a lobby group. Pat encouraged Hernon to say that he had been maliciously accused, and that Maura Woods was operating an agenda, in which she was happy to make false allegations against him. It is important to note here that, while the case against Eddie Hernon was clearly flawed, it was wrong to accuse Maura Woods of making false allegations. As Emily O'Reilly put it on the following Sunday, 3 February:

> Some media reports on the unpublished committee report have stated that it found that Woods had made false allegations of sexual abuse. However, it is understood that while Woods was found not to have observed proper protocols, it makes no claim about the validity of the accusations.[3]

We were in a complex field, and while the interviewee could claim much comfort from the Medical Council's findings of professional misconduct in her diagnosis, it was going close to libel for Pat to encourage Eddie Hernon to denounce Dr Woods. I had made this clear to Pat earlier in the evening before the programme was aired.

When he finally went to Susan, Pat's opening question was: 'Given all that this innocent man has been put through, how do you account for Maura Woods getting it so wrong?' As Susan tried to steer the conversation in the direction of Woods's professional work more generally, Pat said, 'Even if she was Mother Theresa in most of her work, it does not counter the wrong she has done this man.' The interview continued in this vein, with Susan McKay being pilloried for doing exactly what we had asked her to do: provide a broader context for the work of Dr Maura Woods.

---

3   E. O'Reilly, 'Woods: Zealous Campaigner who has lived with controversy', *Sunday Business Post*, 3 February 2002.

I was livid. A respected contributor had been denigrated on air, when she had gone out of her way to oblige us at short notice. The programme segment was unbalanced, if not libellous. It was tabloid in the extreme, despite Pat being very well aware of the nuances of the case. When Susan came out of the studio, I immediately apologised on behalf of the programme. She did not want to come to the hospitality suite and, despite being obviously upset, she handled the difficult situation with consummate professionalism.

When the programme was over, I approached Pat in hospitality. I told him angrily just what I thought of what he had done, and how unfair he had been. I also told him that I considered that his approach was the most dumbed-down simplification of an issue, and his attitude was what I would expect only of the trashiest of tabloid newspapers. I told him that I would be removing myself from the programme at the earliest opportunity. It was most unusual for me to berate a colleague in the hearing of programme contributors, but I was not prepared to wait until everyone had left. Of course Pat gave as good as he got, saying that he stood over the tone of the interviews in the context of the Medical Council's findings. We exchanged views loudly, and then I stormed out and went home.

I was determined to walk away from *The Late Late Show* because I had lost trust in the presenter's judgement. The following Tuesday, the Director of Television Programmes, Clare Duignan, invited Pat and me to a meeting to try to conciliate between us. Unfortunately, the meeting was held in the Oasis television canteen at lunchtime, so when the debate started again, many of our colleagues were treated to a stand-up shouting match while they ate their lunch.

I was anxious to leave the programme immediately, but Clare handled the situation with some finesse. At a subsequent conversation in her office, she convinced me that the upcoming programme I was doing from New York could not be carried as effectively by another producer. She did not ask me to forgive Pat for what he had done, but she wanted to 'park' the controversy for a couple of months, and for me to see out the season. This would avoid embarrassing headlines for RTÉ in the newspapers. Clare assured me that she would give me a new assignment in the summer. It was a clever compromise because, by the end of the season, having done another ten or twelve programmes with Pat, we both started to mend fences and get on together, even though any warmth between us had been diminished. The situation was also helped by the fact that Cathal Goan asked me to draft a reply to a complaint from Susan McKay, and he sent that reply to her almost word for word as written by me, including criticisms of Pat's approach. Susan rang me delightedly about a week later to read out the great letter she had just received from the Managing Director of Television. I recognised it very well, but said nothing about who had composed the words of apology. It included the following paragraph:

> Pat Kenny has been spoken to about this issue and he accepts that by asking you a number of times about the individual cases in the Medical Council report he went against the agreement you made with the programme. Friday night is a very busy night for him and he did not take in the importance of the commitment made to you. He apologises that this happened and that you were upset by it.

As a postscript to this episode, Professor Muiris Houston and fifty other doctors signed a letter to the press on 12 April 2002 in which they argued that the intemperate items that had been written in the press about Maura Woods had created 'a climate of fear among professionals working with sexually abused children.' It was, and remained, a subject of intense controversy.

Pat Kenny and I continued to make programmes together for several months, and among them were some that were significant. We did a piece about the Church on trial following the Ferns Report and the resignation of Bishop Brendan Comiskey in March 2002. The interviewees included the three men whom Father Seán Fortune had abused when they were young boys in Wexford: Colm O'Gorman, Pat Jackman and Donnacha Mac Gloinn. They gave powerful testimony about the culture of ignoring complaints and suppressing evidence of abuse, which had gone on for decades in the Catholic Church. Marie Collins and Andrew Madden told of similar cover-ups in the Dublin diocese, and the failure of Bishop Desmond Connell to act on their complaints. The programme concluded by calling for wider national enquiries into other dioceses to mirror the shocking events that had happened and been concealed in County Wexford.

On 15 March, *The Late Late Show* broadcast a special programme from New York. It was clear that, six months after the attack on the Twin Towers, the city was still in shock. There was an uncanny burning atmosphere in the air; it seemed like the smell of death. We discovered in the weeks coming up to the show that it was not going to be easy to get big stars for our programme. While *The Late Late Show* was the best-known television programme in Ireland, and a phone call was enough to ensure the attendance of most invited guests in Ireland or Britain, in New York things were different. Bookers working for the big television companies planned the appearance of celebrities months in advance, and for large fees. We did not pay contributors, and most people had not heard of *The Late Late Show*. Still, with the help of Kate O'Callaghan and Patrick Farrelly, we managed to make a credible New York tribute programme. Along with writer Pete Hamill, we interviewed comedian Joan Rivers and actors Tom Wilkinson and Denis Leary. President McAleese joined us to do a follow-up to her interview on the week of

11 September. There was music from Cuban legend Arturo Sandoval and the Harlem Gospel Choir. In a fitting example of the resurgence of that great city, we had a spirited rendition of 'Danny Boy' from the New York Police Department Pipe and Drum Band. It was not easy to bring all these elements together in front of a local audience while broadcasting from a small commercial studio in downtown Manhattan. We were all relieved when it went so well.

April 2002 marked the second anniversary of the death of *Sunday Independent* journalist Jonathan Philbin Bowman. I had been working with his father John at the time of his tragic accidental death. It had been a devastating blow for John and his wife Eimer, and was a nightmare they had to face every day. John had brought his historian's mind to bear on the subject, and published a wonderful biography of Jonathan. We covered it on *The Late Late Show*, and as I trawled through film clips of Jonathan on various programmes over the years of his short life, I had to agree with John's summation of him, as 'entertaining, exasperating, and hugely mischievous'. I was not at all surprised to find a huge number of calls on the phone log for that evening, with people expressing their sympathy with John and Eimer, and telling parallel stories of tragedies in their own families.

One of the last big discussions I oversaw at *The Late Late Show* followed a controversial attack by gardaí on a Global Resistance March in Dublin on 6 May 2002. Global Resistance, and their sister organisation Reclaim the Streets, were part of a new international movement of protest organised in opposition to corporate capitalism and the banking system. Word came to us that gardaí had attacked peaceful protesters in Dame Street, Dublin. I checked the footage on the website Indymedia, and certainly the assaults seemed unprovoked. I spoke with the news cameraman who had covered the event. He agreed that the footage was genuine, and was only sorry that he had not been closer to the fracas. We ran a spirited discussion of the event and the reaction of the Garda Síochána on our programme that week. On the Monday, the Garda Commissioner apologised for the overzealousness of the gardaí on duty. It was a good outcome for us.

Although I worked on *The Late Late Show* for only one season, it gave me great insight into the complexity of making a programme that needs to be light, entertaining, hard-hitting, controversial and touching in equal measure. Many people find themselves at home watching television on a Friday night, and *The Late Late Show* still manages to keep enough of them impressed to stay watching. The format is under increased threat from the well-resourced chat shows in Britain, which can tie down the big Hollywood stars and A-list celebrities. Perhaps there is no one correct answer to the perennial question: is it time to wind up *The Late Late Show*? I suspect that as long as it provides RTÉ with large advertising and sponsorship, it will continue to be scheduled.

9

Would You Believe

'Is there any point in public debate in a society where hardly anyone has been taught how to think, while millions have been taught what to think?'

– Peter Hitchens[1]

It is August 2002, and I am in a boat on a lake at Muckross House, Killarney. The mist is damp and the light ethereal. I am with philosopher John Moriarty, a great spiritual writer, and as we drift towards a site of early Christian worship, he is giving me insights into the nature of forgiveness. Anger and resentment are like screaming wounds of the soul. Compassion, even for those who have wronged us, is the balm that will heal. The action is ours to take, and the feeling that it engenders brings gentle calm. It makes perfect sense, and in the hypnotic company of this benevolent and religious man, it also seems easy to do. We talk through some examples, and muse over historical possibilities. Then the left brain takes control. We have a television programme to make. Work mode takes over.

---

1   'The Deserving Poor, and Being Booed in Norwich', *Mail on Sunday*, 13 June 2011.

Making documentaries for RTÉ is probably the best job in the organisation. Every week you are immersed in the story of an individual's life, sharing their insights into the lessons they have learnt in their own particular struggles. And you have the privilege of trying to shape a programme that organically reflects that person, using imagery to help tell their story. I made documentaries over two periods. The first was from 2002 to 2004, where I worked on a series about ethics called *Drawing the Line*; a series on marital breakdown, *For Better or Worse*; and with fellow producer Kevin Cummins on the programme *Would You Believe*. Later, from 2007 to 2009, I was the series producer of *Would You Believe*. In this role, I concentrated on stories with a spiritual or learning aspect.

The programme on John Moriarty was the first television documentary I made. Before I left Dublin I had read some of John's impenetrable spiritual writings, and I had also been talking to him about a new project he had in mind: to build a hedge school in Kerry, where people could go and reflect on the fundamental questions of life. He was steeped in the Celtic tradition, finding true comfort in poets and scholars of an early era.

When I arrived down to film, with reporter Mick Peelo, we found his house in a remote lane of wild fuchsia, at the foot of MacGillicuddy's Reeks. The spectacular landscape was complemented by the well-tended garden of shrubs and flowers. A black and white collie welcomed us in with tail a-wagging. John's own abode was spartan, with a battered, tiny bed with images of St Teresa of Ávila on the wall. The kitchen was adequate to the needs of this modest, contented man, and the camera crew, the reporter and I were soon eating soup with rustic brown bread, and admiring the number of books, balanced in piles that threatened to tumble. As John talked us through his routines, two things were salient: the fireside with books, and the Kerry landscape. These were the essence of the man, and they would become the visual framework of the documentary.

For the next week, we talked about philosophy and spirituality. He was a devotee of the Christian Mystics, believing that individuals can find their true nature only by contemplation and solitude. We filmed in John's beloved landscape of ancient Celtic crosses and churches. We followed him, walking in forests and boating to ancient islands. We discovered surprising elements. In his forties, he had been deeply in love with a young woman, but had found the impetus towards family life too much of a distraction to his spiritual searching. He had reluctantly let her go, and moved on through the thorny woodland of heartbreak. He recited an *aisling* poem of the eighteenth-century bard Eoghan Rua Ó Súilleabháin at the ruin of Eoghan Rua's cottage in Sliabh Luachra. Shaking with emotion, he spoke about his dream to reflect the *spailpín* traveller of old, who would bring people together to study the ancient Celtic heritage and belief. He introduced us to various species of butterflies and different types of thistles, and spoke about where they had travelled from over time. At the end of an intense week, we had a life in images and conversation. It was time to head home to Dublin to edit the footage.

This is how it was in my time making documentaries. We had a tight schedule, with just a three-week turnaround. The first week was filming, the second preparing for the edit while also planning the next shoot, and the third week was an intense edit, leading to a documentary of twenty-six minutes' length. In the first week, the cameraman and reporter were central to the programme's vision and production. In week two, a producer worked largely alone to shape the programme, cutting back the shots and interviews and finding other images to enhance the programme. In the same week I would also be working with the researcher and reporter for the subsequent programme. In week three the editor took control, crafting beauty from the available shots and archive photographs and footage. I remember that one of my favourite editors, Mercedes Garvey, once revealed that every Wednesday, in the middle of a documentary edit, she would feel that this one was not going to work. By Thursday, the magic always seemed to happen, and she was feeling, 'maybe…'. By Friday, we would have threaded together the footage and script to create something of value. A documentary edited in a week is never going to be perfect. The treadmill was intense, but we did have the honour of reflecting very varied Irish lives, and making some sense of Irish society. At the time when I was working on *Would You Believe*, three of us were producing twenty documentaries each year, on that three-week turnaround. One week we would be talking to Seán Kinsella about cooking and losing his fancy Mirabeau restaurant to the bank in the 1970s; three weeks later, the story was how a Labrador dog was helping a child to live with autism in County Louth.

A couple of months after my trip to Kerry, I was driving into a housing estate in Lucan, County Kildare, at half past six on one Sunday morning. I had decided to look at a Nigerian family's commitment to their evangelical church by spending a Sunday in their company. The pre-dawn start signalled the regular Sunday morning breakfast time for this immigrant family. When cameraman Ronan Lee and I arrived at the Olopade house, the estate was still in darkness, but it was all systems go. Two-year-old Toby was having her hair plaited and her shoes polished by her mother, Taiwoo, while her father, Israel, was serving breakfast to eight-year-old Fernie. By seven o'clock we were on our way to Prussia Street in Stoneybatter, where the service was due to commence at half past seven.

All day long the Pentecostal religious congregation prayed, sang and gave testimonies of God's goodness. We filmed the proceedings over the day. The preacher spoke for an hour or more. Then, echoing the evangelical modus operandi, members of the congregation came up and gave testimony of the battles fought and difficulties overcome. When the service broke for lunch, this devout group of people chatted and exchanged their stories of the week. Most were working long hours in low-paid jobs, despite bringing skills and experience from their own countries. Taiwoo herself answered phones in a call centre for long hours during the week while her husband worked in an office. Neither they nor the children had any qualms about giving over their whole Sunday to devotion. They were lovely people, highly disciplined and committed and, although we were mystified by the long hours of worship, we came to admire them as the day went on. At lunchtime we joined the children at their Sunday school, and recorded the singing, dancing and games in which they were involved. The service finished at half past four, and we went back with them to film their evening meal and then on to RTÉ to look at what we had in the can.

The footage, as it happened, was wonderful and very colourful. The interviews gave an insight into the sense of community and support among this largely Nigerian group of worshippers. The resulting documentary was called *Praising the Lord All Day,* and I won a Metro Ireland Broadcasting Award for it the following May.

The highlight of my early years making television documentaries was a programme I made on Marian Finucane's work with AIDS orphans in South Africa in 2004. Marian was a good friend from my early years working with her on *Women Today.* She had suffered a terrible personal tragedy when her daughter Sinéad died of cancer at the age of eight. The illness began with Sinéad's almost casual observation, as the family drove home from a weekend in Mayo, 'I've got a lump under my arm.' From there, it was the shocking revelation of cancer, with the attendant hospital visits, operations and a bone marrow transplant. None succeeded, and Marian and her husband John were faced with the decision to leave Sinéad in hospital or take her home for her final weeks. They opted to bring her home and make her comfortable. Sinéad lived for another six weeks, and during that time she did a number of things she had always wanted to do, such as riding a horse and going sailing on a boat. She died, at home, surrounded by Marian, John and her brother Jack, in 1990.

People have very individual ways of coping with extreme grief. Marian needed to keep going. Even after Sinéad's death, she rarely spoke about how she was coping, although her husband John was much more open to talking about their beloved daughter.

It was now fourteen years later, and Marian had not spoken publicly about Sinéad in that time. From her involvement with the hospice movement, who had helped her to cope with Sinéad's medical needs at the end of her life, Marian had become a committed advocate of hospice care in Ireland, and was regularly involved in fundraising for it. In 2003 she had gone one step further, setting up a charity with John, which would bring hospice care to individuals suffering from AIDS in Cape Town, South Africa, where she was also building an orphanage for AIDS orphans. The charity was called Friends in Ireland.

It struck me that the work that Marian and John were engaged in, dovetailing as it did with my own interest in development issues, would make for a vivid documentary. It would popularise the work and help the charity. I knew that getting the documentary passed in RTÉ would mean convincing Marian and John to speak about Sinéad. She was adamant that this would not happen on screen, and I respected absolutely her decision. I proposed the documentary within Factual Programmes, laying out a very tight budget, and with the focus on the South African children and the nuns in the township where Marian was building her orphanage/hospice. I was subjected to intense pressure from my head of department about including Marian's personal loss within the programme. It was even suggested that we could secretly film photos of Sinéad from the walls of Marian and John's home. I was outraged by this suggestion. Marian was a colleague and friend, and was due the consideration that I would accord to any subject of a programme: the right to maintain boundaries to the subjects covered. This was not a political interview where such accommodations were rarely contemplated; it was a deeply personal portrait of the work of the charity, and we would have complete access to Marian and John's home and journey to South Africa, from arrival to departure. I could see the point of public interest in the family's tragedy, and spoke candidly to Marian and John about the pressure. We agreed that John would do the 'heavy lifting' in talking about Sinéad, and would even talk on camera at her graveside, which is in an ancient cemetery adjacent to the family home.

Marian gave us her total commitment at home and when we arrived abroad. I was fortunate to involve one of RTÉ's best cameramen, Kieran Slyne, to craft the shots. Kieran was a keen photographer and lighting cameraman for documentaries. We had worked together a lot in the documentary unit, and I knew that he would bring a painterly quality to the filming in Africa. The brilliance of the natural landscape and the sunny dispositions of the children also gave the programme richness and vitality. Marian visited some patients who were within days of death from the virus. We had the moving faith of the hospice manager and Sister of Nazareth Sister Brenda, who talked us through each of the difficulties that had to be faced when caring for the adults and children in the hospice/orphanage.

We filmed at the official opening of the orphanage. Chickens scattered on the dusty path, and giggling children rehearsed their dancing and singing. There were choirs composed of the children from the area, the Khayelitsha

Township. In the midst of dire poverty and illness, the people were intent on enjoying this rare moment of celebration. They intended to have a good day. We worried about microphones and camera angles. We would only get one shot at this.

Sister Brenda gave us a walk through the hospice, and introduced us to patients and staff. Suddenly, she took Marian by the hand and led her to a veranda at the back of the building. There, in the sunlight, was a bench, with an inscription in memory of Sinéad. 'This is just to show you that Sinéad will be with us every day in our thoughts and prayers', she said. We ran with the camera to keep up, Marian with tears in her eyes, and then we went into the marquee to film the proceedings. I took care to clear with Marian that we could use the footage at the bench, as I knew it was a key moment for the documentary. 'Go ahead', she said, understanding that it is such spontaneous moments that bring a programme to life.

The programme was broadcast, and was extremely well received. The beautiful footage of the children dancing was in stark contrast to the abject poverty in evidence throughout the township. As we drove back to our hotel one evening, the sun was dipping in the hurried way of an African sunset. We passed the train station at Khayelitsha just as thousands of exhausted residents were pouring out of it after a long day's work in the city. Kieran got out of the van and captured the scene on camera. It was such scenes that gave the documentary its stunning look. But it was the commitment of Marian and John to their South African project that made the programme truly shine. Nearly half a million viewers watched it on its first transmission.

It was good to hear that in the months following the broadcast, funds flowed in to help the admirable work of Friends in Ireland.

One of the most controversial and examined programmes we did in 2009 was on the debate in Erris, County Mayo, about the Shell gas pipeline. There had been a lot of coverage alleging political manipulation of the issue, and we were eager to reconnect with the people behind the story. We went down to film a human interest story about Willie and Mary Corduff, and their reasons for opposing the pipeline. They were measured and compassionate contributors, and Geraldine Creed, who directed the programme, did a stunning job in showing the landscape they were trying to protect. Hard questions were put to the Corduffs, and their answers were convincing. Of the twenty-one documentaries we did between September 2008 and June 2009, this was the one that had to be the most tightly argued. Management and RTÉ's legal office were under severe pressure from Shell's public relations department to stop the programme. At one stage, their head of PR, John Egan, formerly a reporter with RTÉ, sat in the RTÉ canteen and summoned us over to talk. It was a concerted effort to frighten us off, but the programme went out unchanged. Willie Corduff, along with four other residents, was later jailed for his peaceful protest.

I spent two memorable and gratifying years from September 2007 to 2009 in charge of the *Would You Believe* series. Although the programme was under the remit of the religious affairs department, it had a wide canvas, covering human interest stories and items of social or political importance, under a broad umbrella of 'the deeper life'. I had assembled a dedicated group of very varied individuals, who each brought something of their own lives and experience to the output. The other producers were the beautifully cinematic Geraldine Creed, the insightful Stephen Plunkett, and Alan Robinson, a programme-maker of artistic vision. For reporters, we had Roisín Duffy, who had been in the newsroom in Northern Ireland all through the Troubles and was a spirited and gifted colleague; Mick Peelo, who had worked with Mary Raftery on *Cardinal Secrets*; and Anna Nolan, formerly of *Big Brother* and interested in moving towards serious journalism. On research, we had the wise and wonderful Janet Couchman, and that woman of many contacts and energy, Nita Byrne. Our programme departmental assistant was Anne McCoy, and she managed to stay upbeat and organised even when the rest of us were losing our cool under pressure. When a new Head of Religious Programmes, Roger Childs, came in at the beginning of 2008, he was truly amazed by our significant output of twenty documentaries a year. 'If it ain't broke, don't fix it', he remarked at our first meeting. Yet by September 2009, we were all scattered. I was back in Arts programmes, Alan was on *Fair City*, Stephen on *Winning Streak*. Anna and Geraldine, as freelancers, were out looking for other work, Roisín was back in the newsroom, Nita and Anne were up in Entertainment and Janet had taken early retirement. Only Mick remained in Religion. Our regular cameraman Kieran Slyne remarked that it was the end of a golden period of documentary-making. We all felt a little lost. There is too little recognition in an organisation like RTÉ of the importance of a creative team who can work together to make programmes efficiently and well. Too often teams and individuals are moved on to other projects that are less suitable to their particular talents. By the nature of the creative process, people are not equal and interchangeable. But this factor is often overlooked by managers intent on filling rosters.

Maurice Neligan was a senior cardiologist in the Irish health service, and one of the biggest critics of the plan to co-locate private hospitals on the sites of public hospitals. He was a vehement opponent of the scaling down of real capacity in health care, and of the waiting lists, which grew for public patients while doctors were asked to do less. Operating theatres were left idle so that anaesthetists did not have to be paid. Consultant numbers were kept low to suppress the demand for ancillary services. Hospital administrators were turning vulnerable people into clients and customers; the system constantly pressed for quicker discharges for unwell patients; and doctors and nurses were being asked to spend more and more time on administrative tasks, leaving less time to concentrate on medical issues. The Minister for Health at the time, Mary Harney, moved through the health system like 'an avenging angel', according to Maurice Neligan in a documentary I made with him in November 2007.

When Roisín Duffy and I approached his ample and comfortable home in Blackrock, County Dublin, we felt hugely for him and his wife Pat. Their daughter Sara, a nurse, had been murdered by her drug-addicted boyfriend six months earlier. For this kind and genial man, committed to his philosophy of patient care, to be struck by such a tragedy seemed unjust and outrageous. We were going to have to bring him through it all again, and, although he was anxious to talk about Sara, it was a sensitive interview to conduct.

As we walked through the rooms of the Neligan home, filled with artistic mementoes of travels abroad and in their beloved Kerry, we came upon a photograph of the whole family taken some years earlier. Sara stood out in the photo because of her reticence. Maurice agreed that she could be a reserved girl. He and Pat were thrilled that she had found a happy place in the profession of nursing. A relationship misjudgement, though, led her to that place of extreme danger, and she was brutally and mindlessly attacked and killed. He talked frankly about how Sara's death had challenged his own Catholic beliefs, although he held to them still. He was grateful to be part of a profession that demanded his full commitment, because otherwise he might have lost his mind with grief.

As we sat in his library of gilt-edged medical volumes, filming him at work with his books, we worked through how we could show aspects of his life in Dublin and Kerry. At the family's holiday home he showed us a bench in memory of Sara, at the end of the garden where she loved to sit. We had driven down from Dublin and managed to shoot footage at the bench, just as the sun sank into nightfall. Maurice Neligan was an unstinting professional who gave so much of his energy to his patients, and to trying to improve a health system that had become seriously dysfunctional. He died just a few years after our programme was made, at the early age of seventy-four, prematurely leaving his treasured wife Pat and his remaining family.

Another doctor who made a difference was the unorthodox and caring psychiatrist Ivor Browne. A committed Buddhist, he approached psychiatry not as a discipline to cure people, but rather as a route that helped patients on an emotional journey for change. In the documentary I made with him, writer Colm Tóibín commented: 'He was just a good doctor, a kind man who would get up in the middle of the night for people.'

As chief psychiatrist in the Eastern Health Board back in the 1970s, Ivor had opened up the locked wards of the large mental institutions like St Brendan's and reintroduced patients, where they were able, to life in the community. He was an opponent of the heavy use of drugs to placate patients, arguing that their journey to emotional and spiritual growth would be stunted by the soporific effects of psychiatric medicines. We filmed in the grounds of the old hospital and, looking at the now closed massive stone buildings, Ivor spoke of his recurring terror that a fire would break out, when 400 female patients would be stuck together in one cavernous old building. He was visibly moved as he remembered his anxiety.

He had treated Phyllis Hamilton as a patient, and encouraged her to be open about the father of her son Ross, who was the Catholic priest Father Michael Cleary. Father Cleary and his siblings denied the paternity, and were happy to vilify Phyllis in the public press. Ivor Browne spoke up for her. In an interview for the documentary, Ross Hamilton called him 'a life saver'. If Ivor Browne had not supported Phyllis's version of events, 'no one would have taken us seriously at all', Ross said.

At eighty years of age, Ivor was a believer in Indian philosophy and a vegetarian, living in a modest house in Ranelagh. He was looking after his partner of many years, the feminist and writer June Levine. He was baking bread, playing music, and occasionally taking a rowing boat out to Dalkey Island. Most of all, he was reading books. In the latter years of a life lived in battles with authority, he had found a true contentment.

In my time with *Would You Believe,* I got to know many remarkable people. Felicity Heathcote actively worked against the spread of Israeli settlements in the West Bank. Peter Mulvany campaigned for exoneration for the twenty-six Irish teenagers who were shot at dawn during the First World War. (They were charged with desertion after refusing to move forward in the trenches because of shell shock caused by dreadful combat conditions.) Father Peter McVerry went out on a limb for the homeless boys he looked after, himself living modestly with his dog in a flat in Ballymun. And John O'Donoghue brought solace and support to many through his Celtic philosophy and poetry.

In 2006 I had begun planning a documentary on Mary Robinson for broadcast in December 2008, to mark the sixtieth anniversary of the Universal Declaration of Human Rights. It would be entitled *Promises to Keep: Mary Robinson's Fight for Human Rights*, and would take in her early life in Ballina, County Mayo, her political work in Ireland on issues from family planning to asylum-seekers, her domestic life in New York, the difficulties she encountered as the UN Commissioner on Human Rights, and her role as one of Nelson Mandela's 'Elders'.

I had known Mary Robinson from our time together in the Women's Movement in the 1970s, and had been on a working group when she was preparing her Family Planning Bill towards the end of that decade. There was an amount of trust between us, which was vital for a documentary that would be intimate as well as inspirational. By early 2008 I had an agreement from her to participate, and I began to work on a budget and the logistics for the filming of a major documentary of this kind. I had been keeping various managers abreast of developments, and there was support for the project in principle. I had to ensure that the various personnel needed for the programme would be free to work on it that summer without interfering with their commitments for *Would You Believe* the following autumn. Most importantly, I was liaising with Roisín Duffy, whose extensive foreign-affairs experience and personal warmth would ensure an optimum result for the programme. I had also checked the availability of Kieran Slyne for release to the project during the summer period. One of the key scenes would be filmed in South Africa in July, when the Elders, including Richard Branson, Archbishop Tutu and Kofi Annan, would be in Cape Town for Nelson Mandela's ninetieth birthday. When the permission came for this filming we would have to move fast, so I had blocked out the possible requirements during that time.

April came quickly, and I was liaising with Mary Robinson's former Assistant, Bride Rosney, who was by now the Director of Corporate Affairs in RTÉ. In one of those extraordinary turns of events, which happen to people in large organisations, I was suddenly called in by my head of department and told that I would not be needed for the summer filming on the documentary and that I should take my leave in July, leaving me ready to come back with my leave cleared for the autumn series of *Would You Believe*. He further informed me that he was assigning an independent producer to be director on the project. I was appalled at this suggestion. Firstly, I knew that Mary Robinson's agreement to do the documentary, and particularly the requirement for her to speak honestly and personally, necessitated a relationship of trust, which I had with her. Secondly, I could see no logical reason to bring in a director with no proven record in the human rights field to manage such an important piece of filming. Thirdly, there were no leave implications to manage with regard to the filming and production. I was willing to film as required during that summer, take shorter leave around it, and was ready and willing to continue my work as series producer of *Would you Believe* in September. Roisín and Kieran were happy to do the same.

I argued the case, verbally and in writing. I was stung and upset, but also resolute that this would not be allowed to happen. I appealed higher up the organisation, to no avail. In these circumstances, more senior managers feel compelled, almost automatically, to back the line manager. I spoke to Bride Rosney, who was extremely sympathetic to my position. While she could not intervene directly, she said that she would see what she could do.

At this time, my department head and I were in considerable conflict, and he now declared that my contribution to the documentary would not be needed at all. He would be using elements of my treatment, and was revising others. One of the changes he was going to make was to the programme title: it would now be called *There's Something about Mary*. This seemed to be a trivialising and inappropriate title for a serious documentary of international significance, and I said so. I informed Mary Robinson's office of this change, and awaited developments. Later that evening I was informed by Clare Duignan, the Director of Television Programmes, that I would be free to travel as necessary, and that I should recommence my involvement in the planning and development of the programme.

Writers on the psychology of the workplace have said that it is not the work that causes most people their major stress, but the office politics surrounding the work. I can attest to that truth. Now that I was free to throw myself into the creative process of making the programme, things started to become fun again. With Roisín and Kieran, I mapped out the various elements of the shooting schedule.

We began the filming in early July in the old family home in Ballina, where Mary Robinson's father had been the local doctor. We visited the tiny room that had been her bedroom, the sitting room overlooking the River Moy and the Cathedral, where early conversations with her father began her interest in human rights. From there, we went to Kiltimagh to film at an asylum-seekers' centre, where Mary Robinson was greeted with warmth, and listened intently to the individual stories of the people being housed there.

There is a great fragility and shyness to this ostensibly fearless public person. She talked, for instance, about how shaken she was by the hate mail she received when, as a young Senator, she introduced the first Family Planning Bill in 1972. Before we left Mayo, I had to use all my persuasive capacity to convince Mary Robinson to allow us to film her on the beach with her grandchildren. She was very reluctant, and asked me to let her think about it overnight. I knew that it would be a key scene for the film. The next morning, quite early, she rang me to say that she had had a very sleepless night, but was on the way to the local beach as requested. We gathered our camera equipment and were soon shooting a close family scene. Our work in Mayo was done.

A week later we filmed the main interview in her and her husband Nick's apartment in downtown Manhattan. It was a small, relaxed space with pieces of art and details from a life of travel. Bob Dylan was playing as we went in, and Mary Robinson spoke honestly about her life to date. Most importantly, she told of how the United States had worked to deny her a second term as Human Rights Commissioner because of her outspoken criticism of Guantanamo Bay and the use of torture. We filmed her at the United Nations, at her local favourite bookshop, in the park, at a party, on the street, at meetings. It was a whirlwind. We filmed in New York for three days.

After that was over, it was on to Cape Town for Nelson Mandela's birthday. We got unprecedented access to the Elders over our few days there, and it was clear that Mary Robinson had gained enormous respect from Graça Machel, Richard Branson and Kofi Annan. Archbishop Tutu put it most succinctly: 'I love her!' he laughed.

I had asked Kieran to travel out business class with Mary Robinson to film her on the plane. I did not have the budget for all of us to do so, and of course Kieran could be relied upon to get the shots, including some of her asleep on the plane with her shoes kicked off. The next day, at one of the meeting points, someone said to her, 'Have you met Kieran, the cameraman?' 'Of course, we've spent the night together', she quipped.

We arrived home with plenty of material to consider for the edit. A week later I received a positive response from an earlier request to interview former US Vice-President Al Gore in New York. Looking at what was left in the budget, I booked a local cameraman, and Roisín and I went out to do the interview on an overnight turnaround. Gore's work on climate change was dovetailing exactly with Mary Robinson's increased involvement on the issue. He praised her work highly. It was the icing on the cake.

Making documentaries demands the most consistent concentration of all television programme-making. It requires a subject and story of worth, and an interviewee who can deliver in many dimensions. It needs motifs for filming that echo the individual's life interests and beliefs. It needs research and scripting to a high level. Most of all it needs trust, and the integrity of the programme-makers in respecting the essential worth of the person concerned. But with all its complexities, it remains the single most rewarding and engrossing part of our craft in television. I have been fortunate to spend several happy years with some remarkably creative colleagues, making sense of other people's lives for television. Personally, I have learnt countless lessons from the details of how our documentary subjects handled the cards life handed to them, such as the importance of resilience and of community support, and how greatness of character is quietly present all over our small island. I will always be grateful for the chance to experience those diverse and enlightening lessons in documentary programme-making.

10

Garret FitzGerald at Eighty

'Our chaotic health service and our grossly understaffed education system, together with the many serious inadequacies of our social services, reflect very badly upon a political system that has massively maldistributed the huge resources we have created. The harsh truth is that we have allowed far too much of our new wealth to be creamed off by a few influential people, at the expense of the public services our people are entitled to.'

– Garret FitzGerald

Garret FitzGerald's house in Ranelagh was a reflection of himself: comfortable, erratic, self-assured and untidy. The hall was lined with books from floor level: histories of Russia, analyses of the founding days of the European Union, legal tracts on the Rights of Man, theological treatises and biographies of political leaders and writers. I quickly learned not to browse or leaf through them. 'Would you like to take that with you?' was Garret's generous impulse. I decided from then to glance at titles only surreptitiously. His instinct to share ideas was boyish and impulsive.

I first visited Garret at his home in early 2006, when I had been asked to think of a programme series to mark his upcoming eightieth birthday. I would never have felt close to his Fine Gael politics, but I had over the years developed a certain affection for him and his ways. As David Cameron was to remark after his death, Garret was in politics for all the right reasons. I could attest to his legendary courtesy and intellectual rigour. As I mentioned in an earlier chapter, Garret had kindly given me a lift to work after I tried to savage him on a television programme when I was a student. In my early years as a radio producer, he would go out of his way to oblige if I asked him for an interview, even at short notice. As Taoiseach, he had agreed to face a group of angry women on *Women Today* without asking who they were, or what their particular interests might be. He was curious enough to try to engage with them. His press officer was not ecstatic about the encounter.

Contributing to radio and television election programmes, Garret was a major analyst of the PR system. Once the election boxes were opened, he became a neutral, happy to predict accurately where the last seat would go in a five-seater. He would say to me things like: 'What you are overlooking there is those two community candidates who are next to be eliminated; they will help to get X up to a quota!' When I sat with him on the RTÉ Authority, he demonstrated his uncanny knack for figures by excoriating the Head of Finance, who was presenting a seemingly impenetrable document featuring twenty pages of figures. Garret had quickly cut to page 7, column 2, figure 15. The Head of Finance had to admit diffidently that this particular amount was an anomaly. He would come back with further details.

So here I was with a proposal to put to Garret. I had rung to say that I had some ideas for a series connected with his upcoming birthday. 'Come and have tea', he said; 'that sounds very exciting.' In one of the programmes he would later acknowledge having an amount of ego. 'You need vanity in politics', he admitted, so he was tickled and inquisitive to see what I had in mind. We walked through the house, a busy kitchen, which he shared with his daughter Mary and her family, a formal drawing room with a piano and family memorabilia, a cheerful garden with wild birds and a family dog, before we came to sit down in his own sitting room, yellow and bright with comfortable sofas and yet more walls lined with books. An ornamental parrot hung in the window, as if to deprecate the solemn seriousness of most of the political issues we would shortly discuss. This was a happy home, not ostentatious or showy, but extremely restful.

My idea was a straightforward one. Four programmes with four different presenters on various aspects of Garret FitzGerald's life and career. The presenters were essential. It would be their personal estimations of his work that would drive each programme. They would be:

- John Bowman on his family background and early years;
- Vincent Browne on his ministerial career and period as Taoiseach;
- Marian Finucane on the social agenda, and his relationship with his wife, Joan; and
- Martin Mansergh on his Northern Ireland policy.

The series would be filmed quickly over a two-week period, and edited, with archive footage and photographs, over the summer, ready for an autumn transmission around Garret's birthday. When I had outlined this proposal to my then head of department, Kevin Dawson, he objected, considering that Vincent Browne would be too much of a maverick to present one of the programmes. I defended that choice; we needed a hard-hitting interview on the years in power, to avoid the programmes becoming too cosy. Garret would be well capable of fielding difficult questions, but we had to avoid the appearance of hagiography. RTÉ had been justifiably criticised for an earlier four-part series on Des O'Malley, which was entirely uncritical of his political career. Kevin finally agreed. I also proposed the title *FitzGerald at 80* to demonstrate a certain distance from the subject. When I laid out the proposal to Garret, he had no difficulty with Vincent, whom he had known for many years. His only reservation was Martin Mansergh. 'Have you been in touch with Mansergh already?' he asked. I replied that I had sounded him out tentatively. 'Oh well, that's fine in that case.' I realised that he was reluctant about this engagement, but he was not about to make an issue of it. The shape and schedule of the programme was agreed. The idea was that we would film two programmes in the house, as seemed appropriate, with John Bowman and Marian Finucane. Vincent Browne's programme would be filmed in Iveagh House, where Garret had spent happy days as Minister for Foreign Affairs, and the Martin Mansergh programme would be filmed in the library of Newman House, also in St Stephen's Green.

Discussing the line of questioning with each of the presenters, I was struck by how distinct each aspect of FitzGerald's long life was. John Bowman would demonstrate a discerning insight into the forces that had shaped Garret's political development. Vincent Browne intended to dig into the failure to deliver on the Just Society platform, which had been Garret's *raison d'être* in politics. Marian Finucane was to expose the difficulty of dealing with social issues in the fraught period of the anti-abortion amendment in 1983. Martin Mansergh would question him about the policy differences with Fianna Fáil on Northern Ireland. The distinct themes dovetailed well, and the programmes would be a useful archive for future historians. I was aware that the programme was very slimly resourced, consisting of the presenters, camera crew and myself, and we had a six-week window to get the four programmes recorded, viewed, edited and ready for transmission. There was no room for any calamities.

On day one of recording, I am knocking on Garret's door at 8.30 a.m. with the crew. He is already dressed and ready, understanding that we plan to record two programmes during the day. We set up for John's programme in the parlour, a room with many idiosyncratic ornaments and early photographs and pictures. There is a piano, but Garret tells us that he has never played. Every year the whole family go to France for a month, and a piano is rented there to allow the children and grandchildren to practice and play. He is happy to listen. With some difficulty, we manage to overcome a major obstacle: the old electrics in the house keep fusing with our high-wattage lamps. Electrician Kevin O'Toole succeeds in offloading some of the weight to a backup generator, which he has in the van. At eleven o'clock we are ready to record.

John Bowman conducts a revealing interview, full of intimacy and anecdote. John paints a picture of Garret's early life. His Belfast mother, a Presbyterian, a gambler, a suffragette and a socialist-republican, provides one side of his growing up. His father, by contrast, was born in England and took the pro-Treaty side in the Civil War. What they had in common was that they were both in the GPO in 1916 and, for different reasons, both despised de Valera. 'He was never mentioned in the house', Garret relates. His upbringing was genteel and blissful, playing games in the fields around the family home in Bray, County Wicklow. Later, when he went to the Jesuits in Belvedere College, he disputed many things with them, believing that praying for the success of the school football team was wrong. If the prayers led to victory, they were unfair special pleading, and if they did not work, they were a waste of time! He dabbled with the idea of the priesthood, but was too fond of girls to go that route. He was also anxious to have children.

Speaking of Charles Haughey, with whom he had spent time at UCD, he remarks on one of the differences between them. 'He was always with boys. I was always with girls.' He talks about his fixation with the progress of World War II, charting each battle and setback on a large map. He details his fascination as a young man with railway timetables. His regrets, looking back, are all about people. His use of the term 'flawed pedigree' in relation to Charles Haughey is one of his misgivings. This is the context of his visit to Kinsealy to visit Haughey before he died. They didn't talk about politics; it was too late for that. Facing into his eighties, he is stoical about death: 'you keep going till you stop', he tells John. It is one o'clock when the interview finishes.

As we work through lunchtime to set up the second shoot in the airy front sitting room, I am already concerned about the length of the day for our 79-year-old subject. He has given two hours of concentrated interview time with John without flagging. I am wondering if he will have the stamina for a second round with Marian. I am also aware that this is where we confront him on the pledge given to the pro-life amendment campaign. Many people overlook the fact that Garret was the first to give that commitment, and Marian and I have talked about how we will deal with this contentious issue. It is after three o'clock when we get started.

I need not have worried about the exhaustion factor. Garret bounces in, changed and rested, and clearly looking forward to talking to Marian. His relationship with his wife Joan was a key one. He met her while at college at a French Society debate. He would not call it love at first sight, but it was a sustaining relationship. Joan was older than him, and, one gets the impression, more self-possessed in their early years. They had fun in their courtship; she was a swimmer and a hiker. He asked her several times to marry him before she finally agreed. He admits that her judgement was crucial to him in politics. 'You need a critical wife, and critical civil servants to keep you on the right path.' He denies the often-stated rumour that he phoned Joan twenty-eight times a day, but he did come home for lunch almost daily when he was

Taoiseach from 1982 to 1987. He was a hands-on father before that was fashionable. When asked if he could change a nappy, he replies 'of course', with a laugh. When Joan was incapacitated by illness in later life, he nursed her daily, and invited friends around to unconventional dinners around her bed, where she could participate in the debates, as she had always done.

Garret is altogether more uncomfortable when it comes to discussing social policy and, in particular, the early commitment to insert an abortion amendment into the Constitution. Marian quotes Emily O'Reilly, who had written that Garret was 'craven' in giving in to the pro-life amendment campaign. He does not agree, but seems ill at ease about his historic role in the debacle. His early commitment was quickly followed by a similar promise from C. J. Haughey, and the roll towards an inevitable referendum, with all its consequences, was unstoppable. Garret accepts that his initial support for the ambiguous wording of the amendment was rash. He remembers in great detail that first meeting with the anti-abortion lobbyists. The amendment and its attendant misogyny gave him much pause for thought in the 1980s. On a more positive note, he remembers his constitutional crusade and his work to transform Irish society in a more liberal direction. Yet he was clearly outflanked by the traditionalists on the wording for the abortion amendment.

When Peter Sutherland, as Attorney General, warned him about the flaws in the formulation, he says that he tried to involve the Catholic hierarchy in permitting that wording to change. They refused to engage with him on the 'defective and dangerous wording', and he felt forced to put it to the people, with Fianna Fáil pushing the issue as hard as it could. We could feel that this was clearly not Garret's happiest moment in politics. But where the anti-abortion amendment was passed in 1983, his attempt to legalise divorce in 1986 ended in disappointment. He tried to be philosophical about this failure to realise a more compassionate society: 'You do the right thing as often as you can, and occasionally you do the popular thing to get back in. That's what politics is about', he concluded.

Three days later, and we are in Iveagh House with Vincent Browne. The officials and porters there seem genuinely fond of Garret, and are happy to welcome him back. The grand, almost baroque, room looks out on to Iveagh Gardens, a resplendent setting for meetings with foreign dignitaries. The epithet 'Garret the Good', which was originally coined to diminish him, makes many people have a fuzzy, warm attitude to Garret. That feeling does not extend to Vincent, who spent some of his early years in the Just Society wing of Fine Gael as a supporter of the policies of Declan Costello.

We begin the interview, and a tenacious line of questioning on the issue of inequality makes this a promising programme. Vincent's main point is that Garret is not scandalised enough by the scale of inequality in Irish society, and that his periods in office as Taoiseach (from June 1981 to February 1982, and November 1982 to March 1987), saw no diminution of the scale of poverty and inequity. The points are well made, but then become repetitive. The harsh budget of July 1981 is followed by an even more aggressive set of cuts proposed in January 1982. The government fell on this John Bruton budget, when Jim Kemmy refused to vote in favour of taxing children's shoes. FitzGerald's defence is simply that the budgetary restrictions of the time allowed for no other policy. He would have wished to be in power in a different time. As it was, the realities of the economic crisis did not allow for social reform. Vincent, on top form, badgers Garret into admitting that, despite his life's ambition, he had not succeeded in his primary political goal. He then moves on to condemning Fine Gael's failure to disapprove of the sinking of the *Belgrano* during the Argentine war, and the operation of the 'heavy gang' during his earlier period as a minister in Liam Cosgrave's 1973 to 1977 government. This had been a group of detectives who had specialised in beating up suspects, usually republicans, and offering unsafe evidence to the courts on this basis. Nicky Kelly had been the victim of one such interrogation.

When we come to the end of the first tape, I am aware that Garret has been put under extremely fair but repetitive questioning on a number of themes. If I was going to turn this into a programme on his time as Minister for Foreign Affairs, and his two periods as Taoiseach, I realised that he was going to have to be given some space to lay out his own stall, as well as answering Vincent's very entertaining questions. I was also aware that Garret was becoming flushed and flustered under the severe line of interrogation. I called a crew break and spoke to Vincent, making these points. He was, as usual, combative and individualistic. He was not interested in listening to meandering answers where Garret would spell out his career and objectives. I pointed out that in the editing of the programme I would make sure that Garret's own points and the pressure he came under from Vincent's questions would both be underlined, but I needed the high points of his political career, as spelt out by him. With a loud 'harrumph', Vincent agreed to allow a more sanguine line of questioning to follow. When the crew came back in and the tape rolled, he raised his eyes to heaven and said: 'And now this one, for the producer.' I smiled when watching it back in editing.

Technically, it was not an easy programme to put together. Although I had resisted the temptation to have Garret's powder refreshed in the crew break, he looked like a different man on tape two. When the programme was laid out in chronological order, the interview cut between a relaxed affable subject, and one who was red in the face under pressure. I had to use archive footage and photographs to break up the two parts of the interview.

His own family background, with his English-born father and his Belfast-born mother, meant that Garret FitzGerald saw himself as having unique insights into the Northern Irish problem. He was extremely sympathetic to the Unionist perspective, believing that everything possible should be done to alleviate their concerns about 'Rome Rule'. This provided the context for his constitutional crusade. He was also innately hostile to physical-force republicanism. As the 1980s went on, he believed that he could achieve by courtesy and patient explanation what hunger strikes and protest could never merit: an accommodation with Margaret Thatcher.

When Martin Mansergh sat down to interview Garret in Newman House two days later, it was clear that here were two very distinct analyses of the Northern Ireland issue. Mansergh had been Charles Haughey's advisor on Northern Ireland policy during the 1980s. Garret had been Minister for Foreign Affairs during the short-lived Sunningdale Agreement in 1974. This attempt to broker a power-sharing executive was brought down by a power strike led by loyalist paramilitaries. In 1981, in government with Labour at a time of severe tension in Northern Ireland, Garret had departed from his usual charm and courtesy. He held an uncharacteristically hostile meeting with families of the republican hunger-strikers. This was a rather a blind spot for FitzGerald. Instead of listening sympathetically and trying to find some common ground, he lectured the family of prisoner Thomas McElwee, calling for an end to the IRA's military campaign. The gardaí removed the families from the meeting by duress. This did not play well in the nationalist six counties.

Ten years after the Sunningdale agreement, Garret was signing the Anglo-Irish Agreement with Margaret Thatcher (after which she gave her infamous 'Out, Out, Out' press conference). Dubbed 'Sunningdale for slow learners' by Seamus Mallon, it envisaged a role for the Republic in the affairs of Northern Ireland, as well as a power-sharing solution. Fianna Fáil opposed the agreement, and much of the interview between Martin Mansergh and Garret FitzGerald explored their differing analyses of the historical forces of that time. Haughey had of course played the 'green card' for electoral advantage in the 1980s, and it was instructive to find the commonality of nuance between Fianna Fáil and Fine Gael on Northern Ireland. In particular, both men relied on the judgement of the senior civil servants of the day to make progress.

It is a matter for historians to assess the role and legacy of Garret FitzGerald in Irish politics. I met him on many occasions in my years in RTÉ, and found him to be personable, helpful and considerate. I also knew that he had a capacity for harshness when confronted by those he considered to be 'the enemy'. His earnest interest in theology had led him into a room with a number of ultra-Catholic surgeons and lawyers, and to give the first agreement to a constitutional amendment to protect the life of the 'unborn child'. In the harsh economic climate of the 1980s he was frustrated by an inability to move Irish society in a more egalitarian direction. But he had successes too, principally the Anglo-Irish Agreement, which laid the basis for John Hume's inclusive talks and the later Good Friday Agreement.

His famously eccentric wearing of odd socks showed a man little concerned with appearance, but driven by content (in contrast to his arch-rival, C. J. Haughey). His life-long devotion to his wife Joan, who died in 1999, was known and admired by his friends and foes alike. He refused to enter the territory of being reunited with her after death when questioned by John Bowman on the afterlife, but he told us that he still missed her every day – their chats, her insightful judgements on the people they knew. She left him the great gift of a devoted family, with whom he lived in semi-independence until his death in May 2011.

11

The Place of the Arts

To my Mother
And when she was finished they laid her in earth
Flowers growing, butterflies juggling over her....
She, so light, barely pressed the earth down
How much pain it took to make her as light as that!

– Bertolt Brecht[1]

At its simplest, artistic activity gives an insight into the real world, physical and emotional, that transcends other forms of expression. In the words of Cézanne: 'One minute in the life of the world is going by. Paint it as it is.'[2] A true artist refuses to be swayed by the regard of a patron, or the political fallout of a piece of work. He/she attempts to get to the truth about what is represented. And therein lies the attraction.

Walking into the Vangard Gallery in Cork, on 6 December 2005, I am privileged to regard the drawings of John Berger,

---

1   Bertolt Brecht, *Poems 1913-1956*, translated by John Willet (Methuen London Ltd., 1987), p. 49.

2   Cited in Geoff Dyer (ed.) *Selected Essays of John Berger* (Bloomsbury Publishing, 2001), p. 419.

one of the most influential thinkers and writers on matters of art in the twentieth century. His seminal work, *Ways of Seeing*, had captured me at an early age.

> Seeing comes before words. The child looks and recognises before it can speak. But there is also another sense in which seeing comes before words. It is seeing which establishes our place in the surrounding word; we explain that world with words, but words can never undo the fact that we are surrounded by it. The relation between what we see and what we know is never settled.[3]

In that work, Berger argued that the division between men and women in modern society is exemplified by men's position as spectator and women's as gazed upon. In every realm of society, this echoes a universal truth: women worry about how they appear, how they seem. Men take the time to gaze, to judge. In art, they have the temerity to place a mirror in the hand of a naked woman, and entitle it 'Vanity'. The judgement of men, aside from this moralising, gives them power. In Reuben's *Judgement of Paris*, not only do the women parade their nakedness, the most appealing is rewarded with an apple. As John Berger comments, 'Today the Judgement of Paris has become the Beauty Contest.'

Walking through the gallery, I am struck by the simplicity of the work and its perfection. The drawings are the result of a collaboration between Berger and Spanish artist Marisa Camino. They are the result of an artistic conversation by post, without words, in which fragments of drawings are sent from one to the other, and then amended, added to, erased and developed. The process itself becomes an artistic event. It is on show here in Cork for the first time,

---

3   John Berger, *Ways of Seeing* (Penguin Group, 1972), p. 52.

thanks to the intervention and work of artist Jim Savage of the Occasional Press. When John Berger joins us, he is as charismatic and thoughtful as his writings suggest. As a student, I had looked at the reproduction of van Gogh's *Wheatfield with Crows* in *Ways of Seeing*. On turning the page, I saw that the same painting had these words under it: 'This is the last picture that Van Gogh painted before he killed himself.' This context changes irrevocably the meaning of the painting. The image now illustrates the sentence. When I explain the impact of this on me as a young reader, he is charming and effusive in his thanks. We go on to have a great day of filming. Before I leave, he hands me a signed copy of his book, *On Drawing*. It is inscribed: 'To Betty, and the pleasure of working together.'

Working in the arts gave me many opportunities to meet people of superb integrity and talent. It was busy and challenging, but it came with the realisation that it was an inordinate responsibility to show the work of many of these artists. Not all were as comfortable or self-assured as John Berger. They struggled with their own process, to create the best possible piece of work in their chosen genre, and we were there to demonstrate and review it.

The mediator of RTÉ's arts coverage was, and is, John Kelly. John is a kind person. He is warm and funny, sardonic, occasionally melancholic, and with a deep grasp not only of the arts, but of Irish society more widely. RTÉ is lucky to have him, in a field where there is self-importance and lack of self-criticism in abundance. John has an encyclopaedic knowledge of music of course, but in other art forms he brings a truthful set of insights, without ever making the arts seem difficult or inaccessible. Sometimes he needed minding, and is quite self-conscious in meeting the public, but he is always warm in his encounters with people and overcomes his natural reticence. I worked with him over two periods: as series producer of *The View* in 2004 to 2006, and again from

2009 until I departed RTÉ in late 2012. In that last year we developed a new arts programme called *The Works*, which moved away from reviewing and towards an engagement with the making of art. The programme developed into filmed segments with music in the studio. But that was all much later.

When we were working on *The View*, we also made programme specials, called *The View Presents*, and these allowed us to delve more deeply into the lives and work of particular artists. It is quite a striking thing to consider the mind of a person in their creativity, and I will always be grateful to RTÉ for giving me the opportunity to shape programmes around some singularly talented people in Ireland and internationally. I made a *View Presents* programme with the writer Richard Ford, where he spoke about how thin-skinned he was about critics who disparaged him. Peter Carey shared his fascination with the detail of history. Roddy Doyle talked about writing characters, and about his particular captivation with Dublin communities. Christy Moore told us about moving from banking to ballads. Seamus Heaney brought to life his father digging a furrow. Martin Hayes demonstrated his mesmeric technique for us as he rehearsed in Dublin Castle. Julie Feeney moved everyone in the studio with her haunting original compositions. That is to name but a few.

In arts programming, I was joined by a team of creative programme-makers. We all worked incredibly hard, but were united by affection for the themes of the programme. Researcher Paula Shields came from a background in the arts community, and had a depth of connection with the subject matter of the programme. She eschewed saccharine items in favour of content with real depth, and her steady hand contributed enormously to the weekly content. She has a superlative understanding of arts content. Janet Gallagher was a stalwart and beautiful film-maker. She was classically trained in music, and brought real artistry to each of her pieces. She composed and directed a wonderful rendition of James Joyce's *The Dead* for an anniversary programme on Joyce. Her flawless interpretations took a huge toll on her time, but she gave those hours unstintingly. David Whelan was also a film-maker of depth and craft, composing beautiful films about artists like Dorothy Cross, whom he filmed with in her west-of-Ireland home. Marcella Power worked night and day over Christmas 2011 to design a wonderful set for the new programme, *The Works*, giving it a raw, urban, chic look on a very tight budget. Michael McCormack always pushed the boat out in his filming to create special films that were both beautiful and challenging. Barbara Kavanagh brought her flair and enthusiasm to bear on every subject in the programme, and worked tirelessly to improve both its visual appearance and its contents. She also kept everyone's spirits up, and did not suffer fools, either gladly or at all. Alan Byrne, our remarkable studio director, also framed the Julie Feeney programme with splendour and attention to every musical detail. These are just some of the skilled and vigilant team colleagues with whom I worked over my years in arts programming. Each of them treated the programme canvas with the respect and diligence the subjects deserved.

Working with artists was frequently fascinating and enriching. In October 2009 I filmed in the Hugh Lane Gallery for the opening of the Francis Bacon Studio exhibition, for the artist's centenary, and interviewed the Gallery Director, Barbara Dawson. It was intriguing to see at close hand the organised chaos that the studio epitomised: the paint on the walls, the slashed canvases, the preparatory drawings and anatomical cuttings from Victorian journals, each giving an insight into the process by which Bacon researched his finished portraits. The studio was recreated faithfully from Bacon's studio at 7 Reece Mews in South Kensington. The door and window openings were exactly as they were in the original, giving an almost voyeuristic sense of peeking

215

inside the working space. Strewn on the floor were the paint tins, the brushes of various sizes, the walls daubed with streaks of colour. 'I feel at home in this chaos because chaos suggests images to me', said Bacon of the studio. There were seven thousand items in and around the studio, which was bequeathed to the Hugh Lane and the people of Dublin in Bacon's will, and which were handed over by his former partner John Edwards. The items together demonstrate the steps of Bacon's artistic development, and many are now catalogued and archived in boxes chronologically. Barbara Dawson told me, by contrast, that the modest flat where Francis Bacon lived at the height of his success as an artist was a model of tidiness and order. This too was reconstructed at the gallery.

In 2011, I worked with Janet Gallagher on a project close to my heart. It was coming up to the seventieth birthday of folk singer and musician Andy Irvine, and we travelled to his home at Abocurragh, County Fermanagh, to film there. The house is an eco-house, with a circular sitting room filled with the books and varied instruments of a life spent in music. The week before our interview, Janet and I travelled up for a concert Andy gave in a farmyard barn, next door to his home. In the true troubadour tradition of Woody Guthrie, he belted out songs and displayed virtuoso musical technique until the early hours, while the appreciative audience sat on hay bales! John Kelly did a lovely relaxed interview with Andy, about his various musical incarnations, including Sweeney's Men, Planxty, Mozaik and Patrick Street. He spoke about being sent away to school at the age of three, and how that early move upset him for many years. He described how excited he felt when he walked in to O'Donoghue's pub in Merrion Row in the early 1960s. It was like a homecoming, as he discovered and developed his love of Irish folk music. He spoke about the influence on his development of musicians like Joe

Dolan, Johnny Moynihan, Luke Kelly and Ronnie Drew. He travelled to the Balkans in the late 1960s, where he found some of the unusual instruments that he introduced to the Irish music scene. Later he would join musical greats Donal Lunny, Christy Moore and Liam Óg O'Flynn in Planxty, and play in a duo with Paul Brady.

One of Andy's musical mentors was Woody Guthrie, to whom he wrote as a young man. He still sees himself in Woody's footsteps, singing songs of ever more relevance in the new economic recession, songs that echoed the lives of the dispossessed of the US in the 1930s, and of the struggles of the Industrial Workers of the World, led by Joe Hill. Irvine is still able to conjure that righteous anger, with a gentle, sweet and mesmeric voice. He finished his session for us by singing the Guthrie anthem, 'All of you Fascists Bound to Lose'. Janet and I drove home from Enniskillen that night exhilarated, with our ears buzzing after a great day of music and conversation.

The late Seamus Heaney was the subject of another *View Presents*, on the publication of his book *District and Circle*, which was published forty years after *Death of a Naturalist*. Like many of the major artists we had the privilege to talk to, Seamus had a diffident charm, and was perceptive and kind, down to the detail of buying Mars bars for the crew when we had our break from filming. But he also admitted in the programme that poets need some ego in order to give voice to their innermost thoughts. Despite his success as a published poet and lecturer, he said, 'Poetry has to be its own reward ... the gain factor is secondary to the glory factor.' Speaking to John about the pressures he felt he was under as a poet in nationalist Ireland in the years of the Troubles, he put it pithily: 'I think obligation is a human condition ... you're obliged to speak some kind of truth; you're obliged to follow some inner voice of conscience.'

And so he did, as he objected to being included in the *The Penguin Book of Contemporary British Poetry*, he penned an open letter:

> *Don't be surprised if I demur, for, be advised*
> *My passport's green.*
> *No glass of ours was ever raised*
> *To toast* The Queen.

Yet he remained troubled by the disquiet in his home place, and was glad to greet the developments towards peace with the much-quoted phrase from 'The Cure at Troy': '*And hope and history rhyme*'.

But it is the evocation of the personal, his portrait of his father and the rustic world in which he grew up, which resonate the most. *District and Circle* contains a wonderful poem remembering the passing of his sister. It's called 'The Lift', and finishes thus:

> *She took the risk, at last, of certain joys —*
> *Her birdtable and jubilating birds,*
> *The 'fashion' in her wardrobe and her tallboy.*
>
> *Weather, in the end, would say our say.*
> *Reprise of griefs in summer's clearest mornings,*
> *Children's deaths in snowdrops and the may,*
>
> *Whole requiems at the sight of plants and gardens....*
> *They bore her lightly on the bier. Four women,*
> *Four friends — she would have called them girls —*
> *stepped in*
>
> *And claimed the final lift beneath the hawthorn.*[4]

---

4   Seamus Heaney, *District and Circle* (Faber and Faber, 2006), p. 42.

I derived the greatest satisfaction from the six or seven programmes of *The View Presents* that we did each year. But our main bread and butter was turning out the weekly review programme *The View* for thirty-seven weeks of each year. Given that we were a tiny team of five, this was a demanding and seemingly endless assembly line of activity. But we all loved the arts, and the decisions on content, on panellists, on film packages, were constant but energising. Occasionally things went wrong, and then we all felt a huge duty to the artistic community as well as to our viewers.

One such difficulty arose when we decided to review a new production from Calypso Theatre Group in 2005 on the harrowing events in Rwanda in the mid-1990s. Calypso had, since their foundation in the early 1990s, done important work in the field of human rights and development. The play, on this occasion, was called *I have here before me a remarkable document given to me by a young lady from Rwanda*. Written by Sonja Linden, it was directed by one of Irish theatre's most committed and able directors, Bairbre Ní Chaoimh. Based on the story of a young woman Sonja met in a refugee camp, who had written the story of her family's annihilation in the genocide of 1994, it was a stirring and heart-breaking insight into the horror of war, and the grief and healing that must follow for survivors of such distress. When we had discussed a panel to review the play, I had argued for playwright Mannix Flynn, believing that he would have a particular imaginative understanding of the play, and also a political understanding of what had happened in the Hutu-led genocide against their Tutsi compatriots. I did not get what I had hoped for. Naturally, it is in the remit of any reviewer to like or dislike a piece of theatre, but Mannix was particularly harsh. Not only did he express an aversion to the production, but he went further and singled out the young actress who performed the lead role, saying that she had not 'earned the right' to play such a part. My heart sank as I listened to his critique, not least because I had seen and thoroughly enjoyed the production on a preview night. I also felt concerned for the feelings of the young actress.

On the next day, my apprehensions were borne out. Bairbre Ní Chaoimh rang me to say that she now had a major problem. While any critic was entitled to express a strong view, she was faced with an actress who did not feel able to appear on stage that night, so devastated was she by our programme. As for not earning the right to play the part, the actress had herself lost a brother and an uncle in the genocide. I felt a responsibility towards the production company, and also a real sympathy for the actress. I wrote her a long letter, explaining that any critic expresses only their view as an individual, and that the opinion of the other reviewers was very positive. I also told her that I, and other members of *The View* team who had seen the play, had been moved and engaged by her performance. I sympathised with her on her own loss in the war, and urged her not to let herself be defeated by this setback. I knew myself from being married to a playwright and actor what a volatile and difficult world artistic people inhabited. She owed it to herself to go on. The letter was delivered by hand in the late morning. In the afternoon Bairbre rang me back to say that what I had written had proved to be a great comfort to the actress, and that she was now steeling herself for that night's performance. It struck me that reviewers have a great duty to be honest in their evaluation of a piece of work, while needing to temper remarks in the personal domain. I was exhausted, but relieved. A crisis had been averted.

'Art has nothing to do with clarity, does not dabble in the clear and does not make clear', said Samuel Beckett in 1938. In its various genres, artistic endeavour allows us to see deeper into an emotional and metaphysical truth more profound than what normally surrounds us in society. John

Berger, writing about Vincent van Gogh, asked himself why this man became the most popular painter in the world?

> The myth, the films, the prices, the so-called martyrdom, the bright colours have all played their part and amplified the global appeal of his work, but they are not at its origin. He is loved, I said to myself in front of the drawing of olive trees, because for him the act of drawing or painting was a way of discovering and demonstrating why he loved so intensely what he was looking at, and what he looked at during the eight years of his life as a painter (yes, only eight) belonged to everyday life.[5]

It is the tenderness with which van Gogh addresses his subjects, be they people, churches, wilting irises, night skies, walking boots, chairs or sunflowers, which astounds. We each feel enriched by our proximity to his loving intimacy.

At moments, working as a team on *The View* and later on *The Works*, we each had a connection to that sort of intimacy with the found world, but we were also part of the real world, and that meant relentless activity, planning, filming, editing, scheduling, contacting, writing and relating to the wider organisation. For me, as series producer, this meant fighting the biggest battle of all: with scheduling.

Although the Director General, Noel Curran, had pinpointed the arts as worthy of special mention in his 2011 plan for RTÉ, deepening its connection with the audience, in reality we were at the margins. We were minimally staffed, too tightly budgeted, and our transmission time was late in the evening: 11.15 p.m., and sometimes 11.30. Irish people were getting up earlier, and working later, which meant that staying up to watch an arts programme until midnight in the middle

---

5   John Berger, *The Shape of a Pocket* (Bloomsbury, 2002), pp. 87-88.

of the week was a lot to ask for. Audiences for the arts were always a minority by comparison with programmes like *The Late Late Show*, but the scheduling of the programme was making things even more problematic. On my first season, I had managed to increase the audience for the programme from an average of 75,000 to 120,000. I was determined to do battle to get an improved time slot for the programme.

When I look back at notes and memos written during my time on *The View*, and with the development of *The Works*, the most recurrent theme is the lateness of our transmission slot. The first note I sent to then head of department, Kevin Dawson, on taking on the programme in 2004, argued for even a marginal improvement from 11.15 to 10.45 on a Tuesday night. We had constant phone calls and emails from members of the public on this issue, but the Head of Scheduling, Andrew Fitzpatrick, was not for moving.

Andrew had come from a TV3 background, and his instincts, in my opinion, reflected commercial television rather than public service broadcasting. He was bullish and obstreperous, in a charming sort of way. When Steve Carson replaced Clare Duignan as Director of Television Programmes in January 2009, Andrew immediately began the push for scheduling to be placed on an equal footing with programmes in the organisational hierarchy. He achieved a major victory on this in 2012, when he was placed on the editorial board alongside Steve, making him answerable directly to the Managing Director of Television, Glen Killane. Such developments may seem inconsequential to the general public, but in organisational terms it meant placing the person putting together the jigsaw of the schedule on an equal footing with the Director of Television Programmes, who decided on the programme content. In the years from 2004 to when I left in September 2012, I tried every mechanism to convince Andrew to improve our programme time. I sent him notes, sat in his office conversationally, jibed him, went over his head, and offered to change formats. It was all to no avail. Andrew was convinced that the arts were not an audience-winner, and in the competitive game of scheduling this necessitated putting us on air at 11.15 p.m. or even later. It was a source of endless frustration for us as we watched carefully crafted items play to an audience of 80,000 or 90,000 because of the late hour of their broadcast.

Occasionally, we won a small amelioration. When the new arts programme *The Works* came on air in February 2012, after concerted lobbying by me, it was given the slightly improved time slot of 10.45 p.m., but Andrew was quick to point out that this would only be for the first twelve weeks of the programme, until a new series of a bought-in US programme began!

In May 2012, *The Works* was broadcasting the finale of a series of programmes on Ireland's favourite painting. We had filmed some beautiful packages on the paintings and the celebrities promoting them, and had spoken to members of the public and art critics. The programme culminated in an unveiling of the winning painting, and an interview with President Michael D. Higgins about his own relationship with visual art and the National Gallery. The Eurovision Song Contest was to take place that week in Azerbaijan, and Andrew made the extraordinary decision to place a bought-in programme about that country on air after *Prime Time* and ahead of our programme. I was extremely annoyed, on behalf of the President, the programme, our team, the galleries and the public. I was getting chest pains from pure fury and frustration. I sent a note to Andrew, and his boss Glen Killane, and in my exasperation copied it up to the Director General. The note opened:

> If I were a conspiracy theorist, I would definitely believe that the decision to insert the programme below [on Azerbaijan] ahead of next Thursday's *The*

Works was a deliberate attempt to kill the audience
for the programme following.

The note continued in like fashion, sarcasm dripping from
each line. It worked. Whether Andrew was moved by my
rhetoric, or a decision was made higher up the organisation,
The Works Special on Ireland's favourite painting was
transmitted at 10.15 p.m., after *Prime Time*. It achieved an
audience of 250,000.

The artist Robert Ballagh argued in 2004:

> Here, in Ireland ... there has been for a long time
> an inclination to separate art from society ... The
> arts are required to function at arm's length from the
> state. One unfortunate consequence is the mutual
> suspicion that prevails in both camps. Any attempt by
> an artist to import political concerns into the cultural
> sector is viewed as sinister by colleagues, while, on
> the other hand, any involvement in political matters
> by an artist is judged by the political community as
> being not very serious.[6]

He went on to point out that in France there is a word for
an artist who happens to be political: an *artiste engagé*. No
such term exists in the English language. It appears to be a
salient point. It would seem that the artist in a society in crisis
should, in whatever genre, show the world as it truthfully
is. This would mean addressing the conflicts, the hardships,
the emotional hurt at the heart of Irish society today. And
the artist needs to be in a position to do that, without being
in fear of losing whatever paltry grant the State or the
Arts Council has given to them. Over my years of work in

---

6   R. Ballagh, 'Saving Art from Itself – crisis in the visual arts' (*The
     Dubliner*, April 2004).

arts programming, I saw the inventiveness, ingenuity and verve of Irish art practitioners at first hand. In a climate of recession and difficulty they are our best hope of both enrichment and diversion. The State ill serves the public by squeezing artists further while maintaining a bulky arts administration. The artist has a fundamental role in giving us a clearer understanding of our lives and environment, and that contribution needs to be properly respected and resourced. In the time-honoured words of Oscar Wilde: 'We are all in the gutter, but some of us are looking at the stars.' Such a focus seems imperative in the dull and rancid Ireland of today.

12

Pay Cuts

'Almost no large industrial corporation ... has failed or been seriously in danger of insolvency in many years. Where there has been danger, the government has come to the rescue ... The large corporation has been the leader in the retreat from risk.'

— J. K. Galbraith[1]

On the day I left RTÉ, the Director General, Noel Curran, met me to wish me well. After asking me how I felt about the big step of departing the organisation, his next question was characteristic, and it concerned the staff and the difficult period the organisation was going through. He was aware that the strain among the staff was palpable, and that the cuts were being felt most acutely by staff in the lower-paid grades. When he became Director General in February 2011, RTÉs deficit was €30m, and it was going to be a lot higher by year end. The knowledge of the RTÉ financial crisis dominated every decision he was making on a daily basis.

---

1   John Kenneth Galbraith, *The Affluent Society* (Houghton Mifflin Harcourt, 1998), p. 85.

I had been involved in this emergency since it began in 2008, when Cathal Goan was Director General. I had been on the opposite, trade union side and had argued vociferously against the cuts imposed on ordinary staff. It appears to me that when the management, or the government, has a deficit to readdress, it is always easier to cut the meagre salaries of the large number of people on payroll than it is to examine the feather-bedded positions of senior managers and contractors. In the health service, it is less difficult to cut the wages of nurses and porters at the point of payment than to enter into negotiations with consultants and managers, who have, in natural justice, more to give. Similarly, in RTÉ, it is the ordinary staff who were approached to accept and vote for pay cuts. Bonuses to managers and inflated contracts to presenters were addressed later, and only following political pressure to do so.

In 2008, the softening up of the Trade Union Group began. The Chief Financial Officer, Conor Hayes, agreed to share (some) financial information with the unions, to demonstrate what a difficult position the organisation was in. The figures were grim. RTÉ was heading towards a deficit of €80m. The position was unsustainable, and compulsory redundancies were threatened. A series of exit packages were made available to senior staff, and discussions began on a proposal of 'temporary' wage cuts to be put to others.

The difficulty with engaging with the financial details of an organisation is that it inevitably brings the trade unions to a position of arguing the pragmatic, common-sense need for cuts. Organisations that, at their foundation, were to ameliorate the positions of their members, find themselves nowadays arguing alongside the management for cuts in staff wages. It is a bizarre but common ritual now. You pay your trade union subscriptions so that the unions, rather than the management, can tell you just how bad things are, and how best the savings in payroll can be made.

From April to June 2009, there were heated and angry meetings held by the Trade Union Group with different groups of staff around the RTÉ complex. I, along with a number of trade union activist colleagues, Kevin Cummins, Mick Peelo, Emma O'Kelly, Joe Little and Mike Milotte, began to organise in opposition to the cuts. The proposal was couched in terms of saving jobs. There would be cuts of 2.6 per cent to 12.5 per cent, depending on one's salary. There would be no forced redundancies, and the pay cut request was temporary; an effort to get RTÉ through the crisis. Some of us were aware that senior financial management had made the point to the Managers Association that no crisis was worth wasting, and that the cut salaries would become the new norm.

Having worked in RTÉ for thirty years, I had an ardent commitment to the staff and its values. People on the lowest-paid grades worked in repetitive and tiring roles for long years. While those of us in programmes had the buzz of the broadcast to contend with, many staff working shifts and weekends to keep services going were removed from the cut and thrust of programme-making. For all of us, it was a regular thing to postpone family and social commitments to meet programme deadlines. The obligation in the front line in both radio and television was and is arduous. I believe that people are entitled to the salaries and increments that they have worked to achieve.

All these arguments were passionately put in the weeks coming up to the vote, but 'dirty tricks' were also played by the management. Particular groups of staff were taken aside and told of possible job losses if the vote for cuts was not passed. The concert and symphony orchestras, for instance, were told that one of them would be closed down with resultant job losses. Programme and technical personnel, who were on non-permanent contracts, were told that they would be the first affected. Staff, in a collegial sense of honour, did not wish to see anyone lose their jobs. When it was clear that the management's ploys were working, I argued insistently for an end date to the pay cuts. This was resisted by the management. In June 2009, what became a permanent pay cut for staff on average incomes was voted for. The result was 633 Yes to 484 No: or 56.7 per cent to 43.3 per cent.

This was a major victory for Cathal Goan and his management team, but the financial hardship did not end for the organisation. Over the next three years, regular meetings were held with staff to unpick various other pieces of their conditions of service. Increments were suspended, and two and a half days' leave was taken from staff holidays. The same level of output was required of a shrinking staff, because the voluntary leaving packages led to significantly fewer people carrying a similar or increased workload. Although bonuses of senior managers were included in this mix of cuts, the effect of the deficits still fell disproportionately on staff lower down the pay scales. At the end of this process, and with the prospect of further cuts to staff costs, Cathal Goan decided to retire as Director General at the end of 2010. It was a measure of how disillusioned staff were that newsroom Industrial Correspondent Ingrid Miley asked him whether he was leaving on his pre-cut salary. He furiously answered that he had not even looked at his pension entitlements. In fact, Cathal left at the end of January 2011, just in time to avail of a package allowing his pension to be based on his pre-cut Director General's salary. This sum was €320,000, and so his pension on retirement was near to €150,000. This level of entitlement is completely unjustifiable, in my opinion. After all, Barack Obama is paid €293,000 to run the United States, and David Cameron €174,000 to run the UK. The feather-bedding of income at the top of RTÉ, while low-paid staff carry the burden, is a travesty of justice.

It can be argued that these kinds of cuts were happening elsewhere, and were commonplace in the recessionary environment of the late 2000s. I would extend my fellow feeling regarding RTÉ's staff to colleagues in the wider public and private sectors, who are currently living with the most difficult and unsustainable cuts in their living standards. That downward spiral has noticeably affected consumer spending, as well as the prospects for growth of the domestic economy. I believe that management has got to look more deeply into other ways of cost-saving, apart from those obvious and easy clicks of the pen that allow the salaries of the most vulnerable to be reduced.

Parallel to what was happening to its staff, RTÉ was forced by political pressure to deal with the issue of presenter pay. From 2005, a number of Dáil deputies had begun to demand answers on the contracts of RTÉ's top presenters. By 2008 the Houses of the Oireachtas were obsessively focussed on this agenda. In many ways it was a populist stunt, allowing backbenchers to play to their constituents' resentments while at the same time delivering a stinging rebuke to people who often asked them difficult questions on their own pay, expenses and junkets. Having said that, RTÉ was entirely wrong to try to avoid giving out these figures in 2008 on the spurious grounds of contracts being commercially sensitive. It is simply not a sustainable argument to maintain that other broadcasters in Ireland were ignorant of RTÉ presenters' salaries because of the risk that they could attempt to 'poach' the most well-known and popular among them. RTÉ's better argument to hold on to presenters is the range of programmes and audience the organisation has in both radio and television. Similarly, as Pat Kenny is now discovering, the value of having a skilled and experienced team behind you should not be underestimated. As a publicly funded company, the information on presenter pay would have to be furnished eventually, so it would have been better to deliver the fees up front and expeditiously.

The salaries for 2008, when they were published in 2009, soon led to a clamour for cuts. Pat Kenny, the highest RTÉ earner, was seen to earn €950,976 in that year, with Gerry Ryan coming in second on €629,865. These were enormous figures, and they caused an outcry. The following year Pat had decreased to €729,604 and Gerry was on €585,944. Other high earners included Ryan Tubridy on €519,664, Marian Finucane on €513,270 and Joe Duffy on €389,314. Over the next three years, these figures from 2008 were decreased by 30 per cent for the top twenty presenters, leaving them in diminished but still very comfortable circumstances.

For staff, the wrangle about presenter fees in the public press was a double-edged sword. On the one hand, it fed the notion that RTÉ staff overall were highly recompensed, which was not true. Secondly, it damaged the case for an increased licence fee to maintain the balance between public funding and commercial income. As Cathal, and later Noel, struggled to balance RTÉ's books, the screaming issue of presenter pay undermined all attempts to put forward reasonable cost-cutting proposals.

The fundamental fact governing staff issues in RTÉ is the extraordinary nature of the broadcasting enterprise. Most people earn very ordinary salaries, yet have huge responsibilities and stress in terms of delivering programmes. Significant levels of stress are commonplace. Long, unsociable hours are the norm. The camaraderie that sustains this exertion is deep and true. In thirty-three years I can count only three times where a colleague refused to do something necessary for a programme on the basis that they were due to go on lunch or to finish for the day. Most managers are very aware of this monumental and continuing effort. Colleagues try not to stay at home when sick, knowing that the workload of their immediate team will increase in their absence. And because the work is creative, the instinct to strive for excellence is often frustrated by the need to get things finished and on air within a tight budget. The cuts in staff pay, which came in on a temporary basis in 2009, have never been restored, and it is now unlikely that they ever will be.

As in so many things, the attitude of the staff is philosophical. We have all felt lucky to be part of some excellent broadcasting and to strive creatively with colleagues, and that is what allows people to overcome the daily frustrations and pitfalls of a life in broadcasting.

13

What Went Wrong in Current Affairs

'Objectivity, in this sense, means that a person's statements about the world can be trusted if they are submitted to established rules deemed legitimate by a professional community. Facts here are not aspects of the world, but consensually validated statements about it.'

— Michael Schudson[1]

News and current affairs accounts for €39m of the spending of RTÉ One Television. The current affairs office stretches along one side of the new television building, known as stage seven. There are about thirty desks for producers, reporters, researchers and broadcasting support staff. It's a lively place to work, full of bright, argumentative people. As in all workplaces, sometimes people get things wrong, but in the main people are dedicated to the mission of holding to account the powerhouses of society, State, Church and big business. There is no big personal gain to be got from any of this, the hours are long and the issues

---

1   Michael Schudson, *Discovering the News: A Social History of American Newspapers* (Basic Books, 1978), p. 122.

complicated. There is, of course, an amount of ego here, and glory derived from being in the most significant part of television's output, and sometimes people get carried away with the sound of their own voices. Technical facilities would often argue that current affairs sees itself as a kingdom. What they need, they take – it is that vital.

Alongside the open-plan space there are six private offices, and they house the most important people in the department: the editor of current affairs, the executive producers of *Prime Time*, the production manager of the department and the main programme presenters. In the past, senior reporters and producers working on long-term projects also had these offices, but this is no longer the case. The people in the closed rooms deal with the most challenging editorial decisions every day: which stories to pursue, how to shape the output, getting the story right, and managing the legal aspects of programmes. They also develop the long-term programme trajectory, and consider which kinds of stories are to be pursued.

How was it that a department, which many saw as the gold standard of television, could in six short months make two fundamental errors of judgement: the *Mission to Prey* programme, and the *Frontline* presidential election programme? Why did the senior editorial figures in the department fail to call a halt, and why were the most junior members of both programmes made to take the flak, and to carry the public opprobrium alone?

To answer these questions, it is necessary to go back and look at the trends that had begun to emerge in current affairs. Noel Curran, who became Director General in February 2011, had been one of a long line of gifted editors of current affairs, which included Joe Mulholland, Eugene Murray and Peter Feeney. Noel was a particularly successful head of department, presiding over a time when documentaries had uncovered noteworthy wrongdoing in the public sphere.

Cardinal Secrets, Mary Raftery's historic dissection of the Catholic Church's cover-up of child sexual abuse in the Dublin Diocese, led to the establishment of the Murphy Commission of Investigation. It was broadcast under Noel's editorship, as was Mary Raftery's follow-up documentary, *Broken Trust*. When he was promoted to Managing Director of Television in 2003, the team was devastated. I remember Miriam O'Callaghan being close to tears as she spoke of Noel's contribution to the department at his leaving party. Many others felt that a golden period was coming to an end.

His successor, David Nally, who became the editor in 2003, started a change in the tone of programmes. His tenure saw the transmission of the hugely significant *Leas Cross* programme, made by producer Maire Kearney, which led to a government enquiry into the abuse of elderly residents in nursing homes. Nally also began to ask producers and reporters to come up with programme ideas that would be more accessible, involving the 'doorstepping' of reluctant interviewees. He advised staff to 'put the criminals on camera', and he began to drive a more populist agenda, both in the choice of subjects and in the way programmes were made. It is worth noting that during this period the obsessive concentration on audience figures began. Though a seasoned reporter with excellent political judgement, David Nally worried constantly about the failure to attract younger viewers to the programmes. TV3 was beating RTÉ in the under-44 age-group, an audience cohort of specific interest to advertisers.

Five years on, there is evidence that David Nally prepared the ground for Ken O'Shea to take over his role in the months before he resigned as Head of Current Affairs in 2008. Ken had failed to be appointed as a producer-director in a competition held in 2006. Over the next two years Ken O'Shea prospered under David's leadership, becoming first a producer-director in 2007, and then an executive producer of

Prime Time in 2008. He was appointed to this important role one day in June. Nally resigned as Head of Current Affairs on the next day, paving the way for O'Shea to step into his shoes.

When Ed Mulhall, shortly afterwards, decided to appoint Ken O'Shea as editor of current affairs, many people in the separate television programmes area were taken aback. Ken was a likeable colleague, but was seen as lacking the necessary gravitas for the role. I personally felt that he was not keenly interested in hard politics, but would push the department in a more features-oriented direction. His instincts were tabloid. Current affairs was sitting in the main post-news time slot on Tuesdays and Thursdays, and was delivering very respectable audiences, but it was under pressure from the scheduling department to increase the number of young viewers. There were demands to pursue stories with even more mainstream appeal. This is the context in which Ken O'Shea was appointed.

Under O'Shea's stewardship, *Prime Time* and its investigative strand put out programmes that were more sensational. One particular programme, which purported to be an exposé of transport issues in 2010, centred on a black bus driver who was also driving a taxi at night, thus breaching the allowable hours of work. The man quickly lost his job with Dublin Bus. Another person 'exposed' on that same programme was a woman who was driving children from school without enough seatbelts in her car for them. Again, it was an issue to cause an irate rant on radio's *Liveline*, but hardly the stuff of political significance. Another reality-style TV programme broadcast in December 2008 that became an audience winner was a special by Barry O'Kelly on Travellers. O'Kelly spent a significant amount of time with a number of Traveller families, but the focus of the programme was on the bare-knuckle fighting within the community. It was a voyeuristic take on the subject rather than an examination of a social problem that should be overcome. A further *Prime Time Investigates*, aptly entitled *Service with a Snarl*, looked into consumer disappointment with services, and the failure of some businesses to respond competently to complaints. In this period, the emphasis of *Prime Time Investigates* shifted to petty wrongdoers. The major forces of the state, business and the professions remained largely unscathed. As former RTÉ reporter Mike Milotte put it, 'The elite do not lend themselves to secret filming and door-stepping precisely because they are rich and powerful.'[2] Those who choose to hide behind lawyers and PR companies are less likely to be targeted in this scenario. Viewers at home were served up a self-confirming morality tale, which may have been high on entertainment value, but did little to call the government or the State more generally to account. *Prime Time Investigates* was recast in this more accessible guise, again, as Mike Milotte put it, with greater elements of drama where 'The "baddies" got their come-uppance in the end.'[3]

The departure of senior and experienced staff in this period also led to a diminution of the skills and experience available to the current affairs department. One senior former current affairs producer, Michael Heney, reiterated Mike Milotte's point when he spoke at the McGill Summer School in Donegal in 2012. Those who believed that 'ratings chasing' had not made an impact on *Prime Time* were not seeing clearly. Ratings had certainly influenced what *Prime Time* has been choosing to do, and how it has done it. A programme on unseasonal flooding in 2010 saw Miriam O'Callaghan walking through the flood waters wearing a dramatic red coat. Even within RTÉ the next day, the main focus of conversation was on whether Miriam's coat suited her, rather than on what

---

2   Mike Milotte, 'After the libel: How RTÉ investigations must change', *The Irish Times*, 12 May 2012.

3   Ibid.

the government would do for the families affected by the flooding.

Part of the problem was that the current affairs department of RTÉ was beginning to see TV3 as its main competition for audiences, although RTÉ was significantly better resourced. I had warned a senior manager on the day Vincent Browne left RTÉ that it was a mistake to let him go and that he would attract an audience wherever he went. She had dismissed this evaluation. But now, in a time of economic recession, *Tonight with Vincent Browne* on TV3 was frequently garnering audiences of 175,000 viewers. This was still small in comparison with *Prime Time*'s regular 400,000 viewership, but RTÉ was rattled by it, and obsessed about Vincent's popularity with younger viewers and political aficionados. We were never going to be free, as public service broadcasters, to allow presenters to be as opinionated and wilful as Browne was allowed to be. I felt that we should concentrate on doing what we do best, which is making influential programmes that hold society's elites to account. Instead, the relentless conversation continued about how Vincent Browne was doing and how we could counter it. The programmes on which we should have concentrated, on BBC2 and Channel 4, were ignored in this analysis.

Under Ken O'Shea's leadership, from 2008, a number of producers were sought out specifically for their skill at putting together good pictures and flashy graphics rather than for their editorial judgement on political issues. At the same time reporters, who had always been the front-line troops of programme-making, had more and more editorial control over the content of programmes. Executive producers and the current affairs editor took a more background role, even where an issue was legally fraught. By 2011, not one producer-director in the current affairs department had been recruited in the normal way, by public competition. As a committee member of the producer Trade Union Group, I, and other producer representatives, had raised this with the management as a serious concern at numerous meetings. We repeatedly stated that the loss of editorial skills in the current affairs department left the organisation vulnerable to making a serious programme error.

This is the context and background to the problems that later arose with *Mission to Prey*. *Prime Time Investigates* began broadcasting in 2003, and had delivered fifty-six documentaries in its years on air. They were seen as the cutting edge of RTÉ's journalism, and were given the resources and time to produce programmes of quality. In its early years it had produced serious work on issues such as commercial planning, the health service, sweatshops, the destitute Irish in Britain, and the Magdalene Laundries. In Ken O'Shea's period as editor of current affairs, the topics were a little more lowbrow: the illegal cigarette trade, tyres, salesmen, welfare fraud, dodgy cabs and petty crime. Pressure was exerted on producer-directors and reporters to come up with programmes that would be more populist.

In January 2011, reporter Aoife Kavanagh and producer Mark Lappin travelled to Kenya and, after one research trip, believed that they had the elements of a programme on Irish missionaries who had been involved in abuse and inappropriate sexual behaviour. Aoife Kavanagh came under pressure to nail down and deliver a 'new case' (the cases under examination had all been tried in the courts), and she began to centre on the story of Father Kevin Reynolds. Two apparently strong sources, one from within his own Mill Hill Order, claimed that Father Reynolds had fathered a child following a sexual assault on a young woman many years before. He had supported the child and paid the girl's school fees, the source said. The school headmistress appeared to support this version of events. When the mother verified the story, and was happy to give an interview, it seemed like the required new case had been found.

The executive producer of *Prime Time Investigates*, Briain Pairceir, and Ken O'Shea, both agreed that the evidence so far merited a further trip, and Aoife Kavanagh and Mark Lappin returned to Nairobi in April 2011, where they interviewed the alleged mother. According to an internal RTÉ report, the woman demonstrated clarity in her interview, and her apparent recall of details was consistent with other accounts. When they came home from Africa with this key interview, the Managing Director of News, Ed Mulhall, was apprised of the interview, and of other supposedly corroborating details, such as the apparent payment of school fees. He seems to have had some reservations, and raised the possibility of going ahead with the programme on the basis of the sexual assault allegation alone, and removing the issue of paternity. This was the only time that this possibility was raised, and it never resurfaced as a possible strategy. It is clear that, from this time, what was later identified as 'groupthink' came to dominate proceedings. Each and every member of the team was convinced, wrongly as it turned out, that Father Reynolds had indeed fathered this Kenyan child. From this point on, the assumption of the priest's guilt decided the tactics in pursuing the subject.

The producers opted not to approach the priest in the normal way, but to 'doorstep' him outside his church in Ahascragh, County Galway, on 7 May. This was itself a poor instinct. It also contravened both guidelines and usual procedure, in that the television 'doorstep' was used only in the event that an interviewee had refused to participate, but had a serious case to answer. It assumed guilt, and prioritised the tabloid effect of surprise over the need to get answers to very serious allegations. The technique, used most commonly in chasing convicted criminals, makes great footage, but is deeply unfair in a context where Father Reynolds had not even been asked for his side of the story. Alarm bells should have rung when the priest denied the allegation with such conviction, and even more urgently when his Order offered that he would take a paternity test.

In the subsequent intense period, between 7 May and the broadcast on 23 May, the programme team, executive producer, editor of current affairs and Director of News were joined in their deliberations by the RTÉ legal department. The legal department had a full script of the programme from 11 May. A key letter sent by Aoife Kavanagh to Father Reynolds's solicitors on 18 May was written with the assistance and agreement of RTÉ solicitors, and the executive producer and editor of current affairs, but Kavanagh was the only signatory of the letter. This was an unusual way of proceeding. All were aware of Father Reynolds's offer of a paternity test, which was reiterated on 19 May. For some extraordinary reason, all the RTÉ editorial personnel viewed this offer as a delaying tactic rather than as a serious proposition that would illuminate the truth. Even a reference from his bishop stating that Father Reynolds was not a sexual predator was seen as implying guilt.

On Friday, 20 May, the crucial meeting was held to decide whether or not the broadcast should go ahead. It lasted for nearly two hours. The meeting took place in Ken O'Shea's office, and seated around the table were Ed Mulhall, Ken O'Shea, Eamonn Kennedy (Head of Legal Affairs), solicitor Anne McManus, Aoife Kavanagh, Mark Lappin and Briain Pairceir. The legal department warned that the risk was 'considerable', and suggested a re-edit, which would mitigate that hazard. Even as the re-edit commenced, a smaller group of Ken, Ed and Briain decided unanimously that the programme would proceed. Mark and Aoife were informed of this decision on the Friday afternoon. Over the weekend, Ed and Aoife liaised concerning the edits, and a final DVD was sent to Eamonn Kennedy and Anne McManus.

On Monday, the day of broadcast, US president Barack Obama was in town, and most of the newsroom was deployed in covering this significant event. Ed Mulhall was himself down at College Green, involved in the day's live broadcast. Back home in current affairs, two significant emails were received. The first, from Father Reynolds's solicitor, contained the priest's personal offer of a paternity test. This was not seen as changing significantly the similar offer from the priest's Order of the previous week, although Ken and Ed discussed it by phone on the day. Secondly, the Director of Legal Affairs sent an email to Ken O'Shea outlining his continuing concerns. It is always the case that Legal Affairs offers the best advice it can, but can be overruled on editorial grounds by a department editor, or divisional head, as happened in this case. RTÉ's internal report on the programme demonstrates the faultline in the thinking:

> The *Prime Time* team had on several previous occasions been threatened with legal action on the very day of transmission in an effort to prevent a programme going ahead. This led to a general perception that legal threats were largely tactical and considered in that light were scrutinised to see if they were stalling mechanisms or bluff. A judgement call was made in this case that the offer was a bluff.

What is hard to comprehend is why the programme was not postponed until the available paternity test would have confirmed or dispelled the team's view of Father Reynolds's guilt. There is no doubt that when a programme has been made and promoted extensively, as this one was, it would be seen as a considerable climb down to postpone its transmission. Other considerations spoken about at the time were that a delay of a month to carry out the paternity test would have led to lower programme ratings as viewers decline in the summer period. Perhaps 100,000 fewer people would see the programme. The groupthink, identified later by

Anna Carragher in her report for the Broadcasting Authority of Ireland, had indeed become so prevalent that even the consideration of certainty was swept aside in the pursuance of ratings. Another decision could have been made, in view of Father Reynolds's willingness to undergo a paternity test, and that would have been to edit out the eight minutes of the programme dealing with the particular allegation against him. It might have lessened the programme's dramatic impact, but would have allowed transmission only of material that was incontrovertible and unchallengeable. Michael Heney had spoken in an *Irish Times* article about the 'hubris, misguided arrogance and over confidence'[4] of the current affairs department. This certainly offers a portion of the reason why an assumption of guilt became a certainty in the eyes of the team and management. The programme was broadcast in full on 23 May.

Watching the programme at home, I was disturbed by the strength of Father Reynolds's denial. Afterwards, I rang my sister, who worked in the field of global development, to ask her had she ever heard allegations involving the Mill Hill Order in Africa. She said that she had not. My words to her that night were, 'I hope they have got this right'. My concern was both for the interests of natural justice, and the colleagues involved. They had, in fact, got things horrendously wrong.

The errors made in the broadcast programme were exacerbated by the subsequent behaviour of RTÉ personnel. Letters sent by the priest's solicitors in June were ignored. This led Father Reynolds to seek redress in the High Court on 5 July. In August the results of the paternity test became known. Father Reynolds was not the father of the Kenyan child. The programme was undermined fatally, but still there was no effort made by RTÉ to apologise, or make an effort

---

4   E. Edwards, 'RTÉ's decision to broadcast "Mission to Prey" was "a case of hubris"', *The Irish Times*, 27 July 2012.

to undo the damage that had been done. The priest had been removed from his parish duties because of the serious nature of the allegations. He remained suspended, even while RTÉ was aware of the programme's error. His reinstatement to his parish did not happen until October. The paternity test results were revealed in the High Court on 22 September.

Staff on other programmes were in a shocked state about all this. We followed the assertions of certainty from current affairs, the denials and delays, and wondered why so little action was being taken to lance the boil before it would contaminate the reputation of the organisation as a whole. Newsroom staff in particular were concerned that Ed Mulhall could be made to pay for the worsening controversy.

On 5 October, senior RTÉ management finally began to become involved. RTÉ broadcast an apology on the orders of the High Court. It was a lengthy apology to Father Reynolds, which was read out on air. Ken O'Shea supervised the recording of the television apology. The words appeared to be speeded up to the extent that they were barely comprehensible. The Head of Presentation, Isabel Charleton, who had offered to supervise the apology announcement, as would be regular procedure, was unhappy with the form of the apology, and spoke to colleagues of her dissatisfaction. The team of *Morning Ireland*, in radio, took the editorial decision to re-record the correction order, and deliver it at a more normal speed of delivery. The Director General later instructed that the television apology be rebroadcast at a more standard pace. This happened a few weeks later, and the apology was broadcast before *The Late Late Show* on a Friday night, to maximise the audience who would view it. A week later RTÉ appointed Professor John Horgan to carry out an independent review of RTÉ's editorial process arising out of the handling of the case. On 17 November, RTÉ settled the defamation case for approximately €1m in damages and legal fees.

The government was not happy with RTÉ's tardy response over the summer months, or with the interview given by RTÉ's Head of Communications, which contained the memorable line, 'Rolled heads don't learn anything'. It appeared that RTÉ was determined that no one would lose their job over this very significant error. Noel Curran gave an interview in which he forthrightly apologised to Father Reynolds, while underlining that he had no direct involvement with the programme. It seemed like the wagons were circling to protect the most senior people in the organisation. Noel made it very clear that Ed Mulhall had been in Dublin city working on the President Obama visit on the day of the broadcast. He was out of the loop when the final email arrived in current affairs on the day. This email was not, though, the deciding factor. The drift towards broadcast was, at that stage, almost inevitable.

On 22 November 2011, the government ordered an independent inquiry into the circumstances of RTÉ's defamation of Father Reynolds. The inquiry would be carried out by Anna Carragher, a former controller of BBC Northern Ireland, under the auspices of the Broadcasting Authority of Ireland. RTÉ announced that Ed Mulhall and Ken O'Shea would stand aside from their respective positions as Director of News and editor of current affairs for the duration of the inquiry. In addition, reporter Aoife Kavanagh and executive producer Briain Pairceir would not be involved in on-air programming until the inquiry had completed its work.

From September to April, when the BAI report was finally published, RTÉ was placed under severe scrutiny in the public press. Vincent Browne, for example, in his *Irish Times* column of 12 March 2012 pointed to the gross nature of the libel, the 'ambush' of Father Reynolds in the church car park, the pejorative sound effects and the hype prior to the broadcast, as well as the subsequent actions of RTÉ. He was further perturbed by:

... the arrogant treatment of the priest subsequent to
the broadcast; the delay in communicating the result
of the exonerating paternity test; the inaction of the
RTÉ Authority once it was appreciated that what
had been broadcast had been an outrageous libel; the
'rolled heads don't learn anything' initial assertion
of no accountability; and the dismissive tone of the
initial apology broadcast after the court authenticated
settlement of the libel action.[5]

The Authority had indeed been very quiescent in this period,
while staff morale went through the floor. In the spring,
Authority chairman Tom Savage intervened to state, to a social
columnist at the *Sunday Independent*, and before the BAI report
was published, that the final call on broadcasting the programme
had been made by Ed Mulhall. This was true, although Mulhall
did not act alone, but with the full support of his colleagues
Ken O'Shea and Briain Pairceir. By naming Ed in this way, it
was seen that Tom Savage had put the executioner's gun to his
head. He could not come back as Director of News.

Colleagues in the newsroom were devastated. Ed Mulhall
was revered by many of them, who saw him as a dedicated
manager whose journalistic instinct had always been sound.
He had built the prestige of the newsroom with a number of
important stories in his years as director. He had treated his
staff well in industrial relations terms, and in the provision
of facilities to make serious programmes. A number of
respected colleagues welled up with tears as they talked to me
about Ed's now unlikely prospect of survival. The Director
General, Noel Curran, also relied on Ed's friendship and
judgement, and he did all he could in this period to prevent
his apparently inevitable loss.

5   Vincent Browne, 'Gallagher tweet the least of RTÉ's problems', *The Irish Times*, 12 March 2012.

Tom Savage probably made the calculation that the minister, Pat Rabbitte, would need a senior head to roll given the serious nature of the libel. He moved against Ed Mulhall in the hope of preventing further recriminations. Just before the BAI furnished its report to RTÉ on 5 April 2012, Ed faced the inescapable and retired on a voluntary package. This was a difficult finish to a distinguished career, but it caused even more ripples for RTÉ's handling of the crisis. Helen Shaw, of Athena Media, and a former Head of RTÉ Radio, wrote in her blog of May 2012:

> A further and significant question for RTÉ is why they accepted an early retirement package with Mr Mulhall without waiting for the report's findings, and without therefore providing any opportunity to explore what happened and why. The report does not include the transcripts of those involved, but the real absence is an account from the senior manager himself.[6]

It is certainly true that Ed Mulhall's retirement meant that he was no longer accountable to answer questions about the serious error of broadcasting the programme. During that week RTÉ set up a fourth inquiry, under the chairmanship of Dr Maurice Hayes, to look specifically at disciplinary action for the remaining individuals involved in the programme. The final tally of separate reports would be: RTÉ's initial internal inquiry carried out by Acting Director of News Cillian de Paor, the examination of current affairs practice by Professor John Horgan, the government-instituted BAI report by Anna Carragher, and this final internal disciplinary inquiry.

---

6   H. Shaw, 'Good management could have saved RTÉ from bad journalism', *Athena Media* blog, 7 May 2012.

The BAI's report, when it was finally made public in early May, reported 'significant failure of editorial and managerial controls'[7] at RTÉ. A further fine of €200,000 was imposed on the organisation. In its report to the investigating officer, RTÉ had accepted that the defamation of Father Reynolds was one of the most significant errors made in its broadcasting history, and acknowledged that the material relating to Father Reynolds should never have been aired. Although RTÉ's own internal inquiry had found that 'a strong case can be made based on the above that the basic journalism was done and was done well', Anna Carragher now seemed to single out Aoife Kavanagh, referring to poor note-taking and records. Aoife Kavanagh resigned from RTÉ on the day the report was issued, apologising to Father Reynolds, but stating that she had acted in good faith in the making of the programme. She disagreed with many of the findings of the BAI report, particularly its criticism of the way in which she had carried out her work. Seamus Dooley, General Secretary of the NUJ, said that the version of events that pointed to Aoife Kavanagh's signature on the legal letters, when they had been drafted in collaboration with Ken O'Shea, Briain Pairceir and the legal department, 'gave her a degree of executive responsibility that she did not have.'

In the end, Aoife Kavanagh was the only one to resign. Mark Lappin went to London to work for CNN, relatively unscathed by his involvement in the programme. When Maurice Hayes's internal disciplinary report was issued, Ken O'Shea and Briain Pairceir were assigned to other duties in the organisation. Ken went on to become Head of Digital Music for RTÉ Two television, while Briain, who was an admired and respected programme-maker prior to this serious error,

---

7   A. Carragher, *Investigation Persuant to Section 53 of the Broadcasting Act 2009 in Respect of Programme 'Prime Time Investigates – Mission to Prey'*, (Broadcasting Authority of Ireland, 2012).

returned to programmes. Ed Mulhall, as mentioned, took an early retirement package.

The year 2011 was a grim one for current affairs on another front. In October 2011, a *Frontline* programme three days before the presidential election had broadcast a bogus tweet to the effect that election front runner Seán Gallagher had sought funds on behalf of Fianna Fáil from a businessman, and that the latter would be at a press conference hosted by Sinn Féin on the following day. Pat Kenny put the tweet to Seán Gallagher at 10.48 p.m. Gallagher handled the question very badly, and gave people to understand that he was a lot more involved with Fianna Fáil than had been evident hitherto. If he had received the €5,000, it had been in a brown envelope, and he had just collected it, he said. The audience guffawed and jeered at the mention of the brown envelope.

The initial mistake in broadcasting the tweet was understandable. The tweet came from an account named 'McGuinness4Pres'. The official Sinn Féin site was called 'Martin4Prez'. In the pressure of a live programme, this difference could be overlooked. What is harder to fathom is the failure to give Pat Kenny the illuminating tweet from the official Sinn Féin account, which came in to the programme at 11.02, denying any involvement in the earlier message. This came in twenty-six minutes before the programme finished. The *Frontline* viewers remained in the dark about the Sinn Féin clarification, as did Pat Kenny on his radio programme the following day. For some reason a vital piece of information failed to be passed on. *The Irish Times* reported the matter on 15 March: 'a note is made of the tweet and there is awareness of it in the gallery, but it is not passed on to the presenter Pat Kenny.'[8]

---

8   H. McGee, 'Behind the scenes of "The Frontline" – what happened and when', *The Irish Times*, 15 March 2012.

It could be argued that Seán Gallagher's lead in the election campaign was about to evaporate in the final days before polling, as voters wondered how well they knew him. Certainly his own handling of the question based on the tweet appeared unconvincing and evasive, and the further questions on the night about his business dealings left voters concerned. But RTÉ current affairs was once again in the line of fire. Six complaints were made to the BAI compliance committee, and they found that the use of the tweet was unfair to Mr Gallagher. They further found that no effort was made to verify the source and accuracy of the tweet. Later the BAI would comment that 'the production of this programme fell significantly short of the standards expected by the public of Irish broadcasters'[9] and further that the later RTÉ internal report on the matter 'highlight(s) the serious and significant editorial failings that took place during a television debate of utmost public importance and interest.'

Vincent Browne argued in his *Irish Times* column of 12 March 2012:

> The BAI finding was no surprise and no big deal either. No big deal because no unjustifiable damage was done to the campaign of Seán Gallagher. For Gallagher was far more embedded in Fianna Fáil than he had previously talked about. His involvement with Fianna Fáil was such that he was even engaged in the arranging of private meetings of the Taoiseach of the day with rich donors. Yes, it's legal, but it's surely not the kind of thing that Taoisigh should spend their time doing.[10]

9   '"Frontline" a symptom of failings of TV political debates'. *The Irish Times*, 22 November 2012.
10 Vincent Browne, 'Gallagher tweet the least of RTÉ's problems', in *The Irish Times*, 12 March 2012.

RTÉ, still reeling from the fallout of *Mission to Prey*, was now in a parallel controversy, this time involving that most sacred of dimensions: the fair delivery of pre-election broadcasts. An internal set of disciplinary hearings looked into the actions of each member of the programme team in the control room on the night. They were the current affairs editor Ken O'Shea, the *Frontline* executive producer Michael Hughes, and researcher Aoife Kelleher. Michael Hughes was exonerated by the disciplinary hearing, and in fact went on to be promoted to deputy editor of the relaunched *Prime Time* in 2013. Aoife, who gave clear evidence that she had passed on the corrective tweet appropriately, and whose evidence senior management believed, found herself out of contract when *Frontline* was abolished in a current affairs shake-up in late 2012. Ken O'Shea received no further discipline on foot of the errors in the *Frontline* programme.

In November 2012, when the RTÉ internal report was published, David Nally, now back as editor of current affairs, made it clear that he believed that the *Frontline* programme had changed the outcome of the election. He further elaborated: 'There was no mystery about who was in charge. Ken O'Shea had responsibility for the programme, and Ed Mulhall had overall responsibility.'[11]

This was another unhappy episode in the recent history of RTÉ current affairs. Noel Whelan, an incisive commentator and a friend of Seán Gallagher, wrote in November 2012:

> My sense at the time of the broadcast was that Frontline's desire for dramatic and entertaining television, and its boast that the programme could be a 'game changer', caused it to lose perspective and to have almost no focus on the need to be fair to

---

11   R. McGreevy and D. Griffin, 'RTÉ Editor says tweet changed election', *The Irish Times*, 20 November 2012.

all candidates. That appears to be confirmed by this (internal RTÉ) report.[12]

I cannot disagree with this assessment. While no finding of bias was made, it is clear that, once again, the departmental emphasis on drama and entertainment value was demonstrated in an important pre-election programme. By comparison to the libel of Father Reynolds, it was a mistake rather than a catastrophic error. But the *Frontline* debacle added to the sense of siege felt by current affairs personnel.

In conclusion, and to seek lessons for the future, let me try to summarise how the calamity of *Mission to Prey* happened, and why. The reason that RTÉ has a chain of command, with reporters and researchers working to producers and executive producers, is to create a bulwark of defence for the programme team. We have all been in situations where one or two colleagues are convinced of a person's bad behaviour, with sometimes very good reason, and where the judgement of more senior and detached members of the programme team has been to scrutinise all the possibilities. When Father Reynolds offered to take a paternity test, in particular, the executive producer and editor of current affairs should have been severely troubled. It seems that Ed Mulhall and these colleagues made the final call to broadcast the programme, without waiting for the paternity test, which was viewed as a distraction tactic. The final meeting on the Friday before the broadcast saw the legal team advise against the early broadcast, but it is always the case that the programme editor or divisional head may overrule such advice, as happened in this case. There would be no doubt that when a programme has been made and promoted as this one was, it would be quite an important decision to postpone transmission. Yet

---

12 N. Whelan, '"Frontline" report shows RTÉ has still not grasped need for accountability', *The Irish Times*, 24 November 2012.

that clearly is what should have been done. Alternatively, the segment on Father Reynolds and the Kenyan child could have been edited out. Another flaw was that the programme's producer was principally skilled as a director, and seems to have taken little part in the editorial debate before or after transmission. Perhaps also there was a sense of overconfidence in a department that had made so many groundbreaking programmes over the years. There seems to be little doubt that the programme team saw the denial from Father Reynolds as not credible and, more amazingly, that his offer of a paternity test was merely a stalling tactic. This can only be put down to an unsettling amount of arrogance on the part of the department.

In RTÉ's internal report on the programme, its author, Cillian de Paor, suggested that a devil's advocate role be played by a departmental colleague in programmes of importance and controversy. This seems like a worthwhile proposition, and one that might well be considered for current affairs programmes, even at this point. It would challenge the certainty and groupthink that allowed this libel to take place, and would in the future underscore intellectual rigour in programme teams.

While the management team has largely changed in current affairs, and the addition of Kevin Bakhurst from the BBC as overall Director of News seems a welcome appointment, lessons learnt through the *Mission to Prey* debacle need to be put into the oversight procedure for programmes in the future, to ensure that RTÉ can start to regain the trust of its viewing audience. In the end, it will be the broadcasting of well-judged and accurate investigative programmes (such as *Breach of Trust* in May 2013, which concerned deficiencies in Irish crèches, and *Fatal Failures* in January 2014, on the deaths of four babies at the Midlands Regional Hospital) that will help in that rebuilding process.

14

Conclusion

*'We are not afraid to entrust the American people with
unpleasant facts, foreign ideas, alien philosophies, and
competitive values.*

*For a nation that is afraid to let its people judge the truth
and falsehood in an open market is a nation that is afraid of
its people.'*

– John F. Kennedy[1]

When I walked out the door of RTÉ, on 29 September 2012, I was struck by a feeling of immense loneliness. It was understandable at a human level, but there was something more. I would soon immerse myself in a new community of family and friends, but the concerted effort for public service broadcasting would be no more. It had given my life a profound meaning, and provided me with a cohort of like-minded friends for thirty-three years. It was time for new challenges.

---

1   *Remarks on the Twentieth Anniversary of the Voice of America*, 26 February 1962.

The experience of having a strong public broadcaster at the centre of the national conversation has worked well for Ireland. We do not wish to follow the American model where a tiny and starved public service broadcaster competes with commercial, and frequently malevolent, giants such as Fox and Sky News. The mass media in general, and public service broadcasting in particular, has huge responsibilities in our era. Information that is reliable, informed and sustained has a value, regardless of the medium through which it is accessed. The distractions of mass culture, the trivialisation of the celebrity focus and the instant gratification of gossip are the enemies of truth. Increasingly, broadcasters see their role as giving 'the masses' what they want to see and hear, and yet, as Raymond Williams has observed, the masses are always someone else. We do not recognise ourselves as part of the masses, although we stand among them in many different guises.

There are, in my thinking, some fundamentals for a healthy broadcasting future for Ireland:

1. Properly funded national broadcasting, which is public service in its character and remit;
2. Its stations should serve a significant proportion of the national audience, and compete openly and fairly with commercial competition;
3. It should be scrupulously politically independent, and should oppose all forms of censorship;
4. Its staff should be free to pursue journalism, without fear of commercial pressure from powerful individuals; and
5. Programming should feed the imagination of the audience, and should not succumb to dumbing down.

UNESCO defines public service broadcasting rather well as broadcasting made, financed and controlled by the public, for the public:

It is neither commercial nor state-owned, free from political interference, and pressure from commercial forces. Through public service broadcasting, citizens are informed, educated and also entertained. When guaranteed with pluralism, programme diversity and editorial independence, appropriate funding, accountability and transparency, public service broadcasting can serve as a cornerstone of democracy.[2]

This is a grandiose claim, yet it is true in a fundamental sense. The colleagues I worked with in RTÉ, from the most senior to the most junior grades, strived to achieve that excellence and independence. They did not always succeed. The obstacles put in their way went from attempts at government control to direct censorship and financial crisis. At the highest level, the organisation tried to deal diplomatically with the issues that came up without confrontation. At the level of programme-making, the crises manifested themselves in a more direct way, through conflict within programmes, and under-resourced heavy workloads. I have seen the problems at both ends. In the main, I remain a convinced proponent of public service broadcasting as the likeliest purveyor of truth on the airwaves, but of course, as I have detailed in these chapters, there have been important aberrations.

In my earliest days in *Women Today*, the senior management was subject to intense pressure because of the radicalism of our programme. They withstood the onslaught. *Day by Day* developed into a critical and well-resourced vehicle for the questioning of governmental and commercial interests. On *Questions & Answers*, we were allowed a very open dialogue between the public and office-holders in the

---

2   Unesco Website, 'Communication and Information'. (Unesco.org/ci/en/ev).

exercise of democratic accountability. Occasionally, there were pressures and difficulties in pre-election periods, but we found imaginative ways around them as a team. On *The Late Late Show* and *Would You Believe*, we demonstrated universal truths through the medium of human interest stories and hard-fought debates. Interference from on high was rare. The decisions and mistakes we made were entirely our own.

There were major difficulties along the way. The primary one was the acquiescence in the face of State censorship over a period of thirty years. Staff did verbally oppose the restrictions, passed resolutions, had occasional one-day strikes and lobbied politicians on the issue, but there was a reticence about our opposition. Part of it came from a colonial overhang, the deference and politeness of the Irish middle class. Another part came from the fear engendered by the pressure from the Workers' Party members on those of us who were vocal in our opposition. We were all fearful for our jobs and our futures. There can be no excuse for the fact that RTÉ journalists and producers fought less hard than their British counterparts to oppose the poisonous effects of State censorship throughout one of the biggest news stories on this island, the Troubles.

Similarly, RTÉ made a huge mistake, when I was sitting on the Authority, by appealing the *Coughlan* judgment to the Supreme Court. Although this was the result of legal advice, the appearance was of a broadcaster afraid to oppose the political parties, and to allow an ordinary citizen to have his victory on the issue of fair referendum coverage. It was a dismal error, and one against which I fought hard from a minority position on the Authority of 1995–2000. The ultimate outcome was the copper-fastening of the judgment, and RTÉ being forced to limit referendum broadcasts to those for and against the proposition without any special contributions from the political parties. This is how it should always have been, both in logic and in justice.

I have dealt in some detail with the problems surrounding the *Mission to Prey* debacle. I cannot disagree with Anna Carragher's characterisation, in her report for the BAI, of 'groupthink' as a major part of the problem. There were other difficulties. Hubris and overconfidence were certainly issues. So too was a move towards the tabloidisation of the current affairs agenda, with the emphasis placed on presentation over content. The failure to recruit current affairs producers and directors in the normal way by public competition was highlighted by me, and by the producer group, at many meetings with the management. The leadership of the department was also a concern, and a number of poor judgements were certainly made at that level. Furthermore, the disaster of the broadcast was exacerbated by the tardiness of RTÉ's senior management in righting the wrong done to Father Reynolds. But lessons were eventually learnt, and a new management and structure, with an emphasis on dogged journalism, has been placed at the centre of the equation. I still believe that RTÉ's internal report, which called for a devil's advocate on important programmes, has much merit. On a human level, I think that it was unfair that only one person resigned, and that person, reporter Aoife Kavanagh, was made to shoulder the responsibility for significant errors made by five or six people, and the entire editorial structure.

I have, in the course of this work, attempted to address honestly both the highs and lows of RTÉ's broadcasting over the period of my working there. Most of the colleagues I was surrounded by attempted to do their work with a large measure of integrity, and it was a privilege to be a part of that energy.

It would be remiss to fail to identify upcoming dangers in the field of broadcasting. Central to my concerns is the financial squeezing of public service broadcasting, and the concurrent growth of the private sector, which serves a profit-making model.

I have pointed to the financial crisis that threatened RTÉ's survival in 2011, when Noel Curran had just become Director General. He used his considerable powers of persuasion to convince staff to assist him in putting things right. In response to sharp declines in revenue between 2008 and 2012, RTÉ was forced to cut its cost base by €104m euro, or 24 per cent. Many personnel, like myself, took voluntary redundancy deals. Staff numbers have declined by 500 since 2008. Those remaining behind struggled to maintain programme standards with declining staff numbers, and permanently reduced income. It has been a severe price, but the organisation is now run on a sustainable basis, and looks likely to report an operating profit in 2014. It is of the greatest importance, nevertheless, that the paring of staff numbers does not lead to a fundamental erosion of RTÉ's ability to operate as a programme-maker, reducing it to a mere facility house for independent broadcasters. In any company there is a critical mass, below which numbers should not drop. RTÉ, in my opinion, is at that tipping point.

The financial outlook seems more stable. The dual funding of broadcasting fee and commercial income is essential to that solidity. Ireland is too small a society for its national broadcaster to exist on a licence fee, or broadcasting charge, alone. The government will continue to insist on value for public money spent. But the real danger to RTÉ comes not from within, but from without. The next battle will be on two fronts: the growing assertion of media power by commercial operators, and the concomitant pressure on programme-makers to simplify content. RTÉ strives to maintain a television audience share that nears 50 per cent (for the combined audience of RTÉ One and RTÉ Two). In radio, RTÉ's Radio One remains the most listened to single station, with a 23.5 per cent share, while 2FM has 7.3 per cent. This sort of dominance is important, and maintains the conversation in Irish homes and workplaces being principally around RTÉ's programmes. However, the move towards alternative modes of television-watching on the internet through companies like Netflix perhaps shadows the future, and the younger demographic does not share the kind of loyalty to RTÉ of older generations; they need to be courted and won. (The listenership crisis at 2FM does continue, with Today FM now claiming 8.9 per cent of the national share.)[3] The public service remit should allow for these overall targets to occasionally drop, so that programmes of cultural yet minority importance continue to be scheduled. In other words, correct assimilation of the statistics should not become an obsession, nor should audience figures become an excuse for a race to the bottom.

RTÉ, as it goes into the future, needs to cultivate a determined political independence, despite its necessary relationship to the Minister and Department of Communications. A minister who understands the importance of public service broadcasting is welcome, but it is only the scrupulous adherence to a real independence that will guarantee RTÉ a place in audience affections, even in the face of unforeseen problems and errors. For this reason, RTÉ and its staff should vocally oppose any attempts to curtail open debate, whatever their source.

RTÉ was devastated by the defection of Pat Kenny to Newstalk. All the corporate-speak about listeners following time slots and teams was an unsubtle masking of the truth: RTÉ did not expect Pat to go. Perhaps they relied on his age as a conservative influence. Perhaps they believed that he would not break free from his well-resourced team, and the key newsroom backup. But the problem for Kenny lay not in radio, but in television. He had been given the *Frontline* programme as part of a negotiation when he stepped aside from *The Late Late Show*. This was to be his own vehicle, and

---

3   JNLR Results Round-up, 25 April 2013.

it was one that showcased his considerable ease with politics and a live audience. It was a huge success, in both stories and ratings. But *Frontline* got axed in the 2012 shake-up of current affairs, because of the broadcasting of a fake tweet in the final presidential election programme. The failure to pass on the corrective tweet to Pat Kenny left him exposed on air, an issue that was compounded the next day on radio, when he still, extraordinarily, had not been told about the Sinn Féin clarification. The upshot was that *Frontline* was abolished, although Pat Kenny was entirely blameless in the programme fiasco. He was asked to rejoin *Prime Time* as one of three presenters, joining Miriam O'Callaghan and Clare Byrne. Current affairs colleagues told me that, perhaps surprisingly, Miriam and Clare were not the most unhappy members of the team; Pat Kenny clearly took that accolade. While RTÉ's management was shocked by Kenny's decision to go to Newstalk, his colleagues in television current affairs were not at all surprised. They had heard his dismay expressed at a number of programme meetings. A substantial financial offer from Newstalk was clearly part of the reason for his move, but it was not the whole story.

Why is all this relevant to the future of broadcasting in Ireland? For one important reason: Pat Kenny is the first major figure recruited to the commercial radio sector, and carries enough star power to threaten RTÉ's radio audience. Competition is a good thing in broadcasting. Contenders such as Ray Darcy and George Hook have gained a place with listeners, but Pat Kenny is in a different league, and it can be argued that his defection is a direct result of the commercial might of Denis O'Brien in newspapers and radio broadcasting. As well as holding a major shareholding in INM, the Independent Newspaper Group, he also controls 98FM, Today FM, Highland Radio, Spin South, Spin 1038 and Newstalk.

O'Brien's control of various media outlets has become an issue because of the singular nature of his position in

Irish society; apart from his considerable wealth, the Moriarty
Tribunal, established by the Houses of the Oireachtas, and
supervised by the Courts, has made major findings against
him. As Vincent Browne reflected in his column in *The Irish
Times* of 14 August 2013:

> The recent assertion of media power by a person
> found to have paid large sums of money to a
> government minister who improperly assisted him
> to acquire the hugely lucrative second mobile phone
> licence has been largely ignored.[4]

Browne continued by pointing to various examples, which
showed that O'Brien was not content to deal with his media
empire in a hands-off, editorial way:

> His repeated efforts to have Sam Smyth stopped from
> reporting and commenting on the Moriarty Tribunal
> during which time he, Denis O'Brien, was the central
> character, is one instance of that record … What
> the tribunal reveals is sordid. While Denis O'Brien
> has consistently rejected the findings, the weight of
> evidence in the report is persuasive. Denis O'Brien's
> media power demands it be confronted persistently
> by the evidence in the Moriarty Tribunal report,
> threats to sue journalists personally notwithstanding.[5]

O'Brien's response to Browne seemed rather tangential.
He referred to an approach made by Browne to work for
Newstalk back in 2007, while ignoring the substantive
issues raised. No one really believes that Vincent Browne is

4   Vincent Browne, 'O'Brien's record should disbar him from having
    disproportionate hold on media', *The Irish Times*, 14 August 2013.
5   Ibid.

motivated by pique over a career approach six years ago. That has never been his style.

Looking at the issue of editorial interference in the commercial broadcasting market, and the instinct to threaten journalists with the law, the *Village* magazine's editor Michael Smith in August 2013 refers to O'Brien's 'extraordinarily chilling effect on journalism and journalists.'[6] He goes on to refer to a number of approaches he made to journalists to write articles, who felt silenced by legal action emanating from Denis O'Brien.[7]

On the day that the Moriarty Tribunal issued its findings in April 2012, Sam Smyth, who had reported on it fortnightly, had his Today FM Sunday radio show axed. Denis O'Brien claimed that this was because of falling listener figures. Nevertheless, a journalist, who had been a thorn in the side of the station's owner, lost his main income on that day. He survives on sporadic freelance work. All this is relevant to the competitive environment in which RTÉ finds itself. Public service broadcasting should be a bulwark against the journalistic interference that can be possible in a commercial operation. Certainly, RTÉ presenters and producers would not feel undermined in their positions because of a view taken on any particular story. This is where public broadcasting maintains a huge strength.

---

6   M. Smith, 'Profile – Denis O'Brien', *Village*, August 2013.
7   Sam Smyth was one. Eamonn Dunphy's lawyers advised him to withdraw from an interview because O'Brien was suing him. Ted Harding left the *Sunday Business Post* as long ago as 2004, some time after he was forbidden to print material about O'Brien with which his bosses were unhappy. Academic Elaine Byrne received a strongly worded legal threat after a piece she wrote for the *Sunday Independent*. Anne Harris, editor of the *Sunday Independent*, has claimed that seventeen journalists have received legal letters from Denis O'Brien in the last ten years. Information from Michael Smith, *Village*, August 2013.

The other major challenge for broadcasters is the global trend towards the dumbing down of programming. Reality television is matched by 'shock jocks' in radio. Vulgarity and the pretence of revelation leaves no real insight into the human condition. In a well-argued essay, Knight Professor of Constitutional Law at Yale University, Jack Balkin, argues:

> Television tends to emphasise entertainment value. It subjects culture to a Darwinian process. The less entertaining is weeded out, the more entertaining survives to be broadcast.[8]

This is undoubtedly the case, although I will not join the naysayers who have been predicting that television will be the end of civilisation since the 1950s. Rather, our job in this period is to be vigilant against a process of the simplification of content that can erode critical thinking. Thought-provoking programmes are frequently made and broadcast. The injunction is to ensure that commitment and space is allowed for such programmes, in a schedule mix that includes lighter entertaining fare. And that means staff not being so stretched across schedule-filling that they have time to imagine and create such works of excellence, be it in music, history, heritage or art. Even in politics, the way in which we cover issues should allow the substance to be thoroughly examined, not just the form of the contest. Again, to quote Professor Balkin:

> Television encourages coverage that focuses on the personal celebrity of participants, and on the sporting element of political conflict. Over time, television coverage of politics tends to focus less

---

8   J. M. Balkin, 'How mass media simulate political transparency', available online at www.yale.edu (accessed 28.01.14).

on substantive policy issues than on the techniques of securing political advantage and political viability. The question of who's winning, and how they are achieving this victory, tends to dominate political coverage.[9]

Broadcasting looks for a metaphor to represent the often complex forces at play, and to simplify matters to a human dilemma. The move to impeach President Bill Clinton over the Monica Lewinsky affair was a case in point. What was essentially a battle between Democrats and Republicans for control of the political agenda was played out as a character issue: does this man have the appropriate character to lead the United States? The populist agenda of the impeachment process, while engaging and salacious, did not necessarily serve the best interests of American society.

In the end, it comes down to this. A vibrant democracy in the present age needs a critical, functioning national broadcaster. It needs to be properly funded by the public. It needs an engaged staff with the ability and time to create a diverse range of programming. It needs vibrant debate internally, and with the public. It needs to be representative and critical. It needs to be free of censorship and any commercial pressure. It needs to be alert to international trends towards dumbing down, without being po-faced.

My experience of working in RTÉ allowed me to see at first hand the desire to achieve these targets. It also demonstrated how human weakness can lead to cowardice and self-absorption. For me personally, there have been some achievements and steps forward, notably in the legacy of *Women Today*, and the rescission of the contentious Section 31. There have been disappointments too, largely with myself. I didn't shout loudly enough when programmes

---

9   Ibid.

were under pressure from political forces, such as Bertie Ahern and Charles Haughey. Public broadcasting is too important to be left entirely in the hands of the professional broadcasters. It demands the vigilance and critical support of engaged citizens as it faces the challenges of a changing media landscape. Technology is changing fundamentally how we all receive and impart information, and there can be no doubt that RTÉ faces an uncertain future.

In my own life, I see echoes of my instinct towards social campaigning in the activities and interest of my daughters. Katie is writing plays that deal with zero-hours workers' contracts and the sexism of fairy tales. Clara is travelling to Palestine in pursuit of her abiding interest in international human rights. The humanist desire to change things for the better is there, once again. The challenges are monumental, and sometimes overwhelming. We can but focus on making our own small contributions as the wheel of life turns on.

Acknowledgements

There are a number of people who really helped me in getting this book to publication. First, I want to acknowledge the enormous help of my agent Jonathan Williams, who was enthusiastic from day one, and helped me with his erudite wisdom and meticulous attention to detail to shape these chapters. Secondly, I would like to thank New Island Books, and in particular Justin Corfield, who contributed considerably in the final editing of the manuscript. Also, my thanks to Eoin Purcell for agreeing to publish the book, and for his continuing support throughout the process.

A number of friends read early drafts and gave me good advice on improving the text, most significantly Galway Communications lecturer Patsy Murphy, New York film-maker Patrick Farrelly, solicitor Michael Farrell and Griffith College lecturer Niall Meehan.

Other friends stopped me from throwing in the towel when it was all getting too much, and plied me with good lunches and dinners to get me through. Special mention has to go to Marie Redmond, Bernadette O'Sullivan, Hilary Orpen and Sally Shovelin, as well as great RTÉ pals who would probably not benefit from association here. You know who you are! My sister and good friend Mary also read parts of the manuscript, and was hugely helpful in suggesting improvements.

Finally, and most importantly, to my dear girls, Katie O'Kelly and Clara Purcell, who were forever solicitous and supportive, and who made key enhancements to the writing. Clara deserves special mention for making the manuscript presentable for the publishers, and for making sense of all those damn footnotes. This book feels like a therapeutic thing to me; I am finally ready to move on.

To all of you, many thanks.

Index

Index